WHERE THE RIVER RUNS DEEP

WHERE
THE
RIVER
RUNS
DEEP

THE STORY OF A
MISSISSIPPI RIVER PILOT

JOY J. JACKSON

LOUISIANA STATE UNIVERSITY PRESS
Baton Rouge and London

Copyright © 1993 by Louisiana State University Press
All rights reserved
Manufactured in the United States of America
First printing
02 01 00 99 98 97 96 95 94 93   5 4 3 2 1

Designer: Amanda McDonald Key
Typeface: Goudy
Typesetter: G & S Typesetters, Inc.
Printer and binder: Thomson–Shore, Inc.

Library of Congress Cataloging-in-Publication Data
Jackson, Joy J.
    Where the river runs deep : the story of a Mississippi River pilot /
Joy J. Jackson.
        p.   cm.
    Includes bibliographical references and index.
    ISBN 0-8071-1797-8 (cloth : alk. paper)
    1. Mississippi River Valley—Social life and customs.
  2. Mississippi River—Navigation—History—20th century.
  3. Louisiana—Social life and customs.   4. Jackson, Oliver,
  1896–1985.   5. Pilots and pilotage—Mississippi River—Biography.
  I. Title.
  F377.M6J33   1993
  977—dc20   93-7019
                                                              CIP

*This book is dedicated to the memory
of three men whose lifetimes spanned
a century and a half on the Mississippi:
Captain Andy, his son Monroe, and his
grandson Oliver.*

CONTENTS

ILLUSTRATIONS

PREFACE

After his retirement from the river, my father, Oliver Daniel Jackson, loved to entertain neighbors and acquaintances with stories about his experiences as a Mississippi River pilot. His listeners often advised him that a book ought to be written on his life. As his daughter and as a historian, I agreed and began recording his reminiscences on tape. To help me in writing such a book, he collected his notebooks and letters and sorted them according to subject matter. He also wrote down some of his memories of his early life and of his entry into the New Orleans–Baton Rouge Steamship Pilots Association. In addition, he corresponded with relatives whom he felt might be able to reveal something about his family's past. I began a long and complicated genealogical search for his early ancestors in Louisiana and a study of the history of the Mississippi River between Baton Rouge and the Passes in the twentieth century. By the time my father died, I had an outline of the biography and was writing the first chapter. Five years later, shortly after my mother died, the last chapter was completed.

As his story unfolded, it took on several aspects I had not anticipated. The lives of his ancestors who had lived alongside the Mississippi River since the 1720s were fascinating. In the eighteenth century, these ancestors included German immigrants on the first German Coast above New Orleans, a French brickmason from Paris who became proprietor of the King's Plantation on Algiers Point, and two orphan boys whose stepfather was a royal ship's captain. These boys later founded a family that gave its name to one of the last small towns on the Mississippi River before it reaches the Gulf of Mexico. In the nineteenth century some of Oliver's forebears came downriver from Kentucky, Tennessee, and as far away as the upper Ohio River. Some became rice planters or fishermen, one or two were pilots, and others chopped and sold wood as fuel to passing steamboats. For all of them, the Mississippi River was a vital part of their lives, and they, in turn, contributed to the way of life along its banks. My father's story, therefore, is also the story of a network of families handing down traditions from generation to generation, always tied to life and land along the river.

Another unexpectedly fascinating aspect of my study turned out to be the history of the Mississippi River between Baton Rouge and the Gulf, a saga that weaves itself into my father's personal history. During his lifetime, the small maritime communities of Port Eads and Burrwood on the Passes flourished and then disappeared, cotton gave way to petroleum as the major product transported on the lower Mississippi, and steamboats faded away and were replaced by towboats and their long lines of barges. The Standard Oil Company of Louisiana built its mammoth facility at Baton Rouge, one of the first of many plants in the petrochemical industry to rise along the river's banks between New Orleans and Baton Rouge. Natural disasters such as the 1915 hurricane and the great flood of 1927 wreaked havoc along the river, and the early months of World War II brought the menace of German submarines up to the very mouth of the Mississippi. Oliver Jackson lived through it all, working in various capacities as a licensed pilot for forty-six years, from 1918 to 1964.

In documenting and writing his biography, I have had many helpers whom I would like to acknowledge and thank. The late Richard H. Buras, Jr., a longtime family friend, was of tremendous help through his personal reminiscences, his aid in securing information from others, and his skill in unearthing rare, forgotten books. Robert Prinz, as business manager of the New Orleans–Baton Rouge Steamship Pilots Association, and Captain Clifford E. Clayton, as president of that association, were also most helpful in making their records available and in reading portions of the manuscript. Three pilots who worked with my father, Captain Frank Furr, the late Captain Siegfried Sprada, and Captain Joseph Lennox, kindly gave their time to be interviewed or to review chapters in this work. Other pilots I spoke with include Captain Jacques Michell and his father, Captain Albro Michell, of the Associated Branch Pilots, and Captain Gilbert Manson of the Crescent River Port Pilots Association. Captain George S. Vincent, also a Crescent River Port pilot, gave permission for the use of one of his letters. Evans Casso provided information on Captain Tom Spicuzza and his packet boat, *El Rito*. Bailey DeBardeleben furnished materials on the W. G. Coyle Company to Richard Buras. Relatives and genealogists who contributed data on the Jackson family and related families include Ethel Miller, Margie Williams, Dolores Kieff, Estelle Alesich, Irma Clark, Loretta Armshaw, Rita Barlow, James J. Jacobsen, Jessie O'Dell, and Betty Harper. Another relative, who is deceased but who before her death contributed a delightful narrative of the Jackson family's early life on South Pass, was my father's sister Alvaretta Nicholson. My mother, of course, was always ready to assist me with her remarkable memory and sharp intellect. Throughout sixty-two years of marriage, she was the lodestar that guided my father through both calm and stormy waters in their lives.

Others who offered assistance with the book include Ginger Romero, Alice Forsythe, Bertram Groene, Allen R. Saltus, Jr., and Charles "Pie" Dufour, through his book on the Coyle Company.

Thanks are also extended to the staffs of a number of libraries and archives. In Hammond, the first to be recognized for their assistance are the staff of the Linus A. Sims Memorial Library who helped me with newspapers, periodicals, books, and interlibrary loans of materials not available locally. A special thanks is accorded to my own staff in the Southeastern Louisiana University Center for Regional Studies, which administers the university archives. I wish to thank in particular my secretary, Lois G. Wagner, whose assistance in research as well as aid with stylistic problems and the typing of the manuscript was invaluable. Her knowledge of style and her scrupulous proofreading made the manuscript more accurate than it would have been without it. Thanks are also extended to JoAnn Dobbs, a graduate assistant, who helped with the proofreading.

In New Orleans, I wish to thank the staff of the Historic New Orleans Collection; the reference library personnel of the United States Army Corps of Engineers, Prytania Street Headquarters; archivist Wilbur E. Meneray and the librarians of the Louisiana Room, Rare Book Room, and the Special Collections at Howard-Tilton Memorial Library, Tulane University; librarians in the Louisiana Division of the Main Branch of the New Orleans Public Library; the staff of the Louisiana Historical Center, a research center of the Louisiana State Museum located in the Old Mint; and the staff of the Archives and Special Collections of Earl K. Long Memorial Library, University of New Orleans. In Baton Rouge, my thanks are extended to the archival staff of the Louisiana and Lower Mississippi Valley Collections, Louisiana State University Archives in the Hill Memorial Library, and to the staff of Troy H. Middleton Memorial Library at LSU; to the librarians in the Louisiana Division of the State Library of Louisiana; and to the staff of the Louisiana State Archives. One depository that was vital to this study was the Plaquemines Parish clerk of court's office in Pointe a la Hache. The staff's patience with my requests is deeply appreciated.

For financial assistance in travel, copying of materials, and the preparation of my manuscript for publication, I wish to express my gratitude to the Research and Grants Committee of Southeastern Louisiana University for the research grant they awarded me. My final thanks go to the staff of LSU Press, who guided me in an expert but friendly way through the stylistic and artistic changes that had to be made in the manuscript.

Since I began this book with a Prologue and an introductory chapter on my father's family stretching back to the eighteenth and nineteenth centuries, and do not appear in the narrative myself until chapter 8, I decided to write in the third person. My only regret in connection with this work is that neither of my parents lived to see it in print. I can only hope that they would have approved of it, and that its readers get a broader and clearer picture of life and work along the lower Mississippi River during the twentieth century than they had before reading it.

WHERE THE RIVER RUNS DEEP

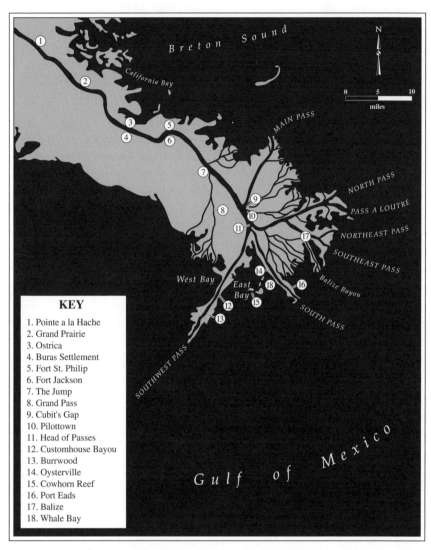

KEY

1. Pointe a la Hache
2. Grand Prairie
3. Ostrica
4. Buras Settlement
5. Fort St. Philip
6. Fort Jackson
7. The Jump
8. Grand Pass
9. Cubit's Gap
10. Pilottown
11. Head of Passes
12. Customhouse Bayou
13. Burrwood
14. Oysterville
15. Cowhorn Reef
16. Port Eads
17. Balize
18. Whale Bay

The Mississippi River from Pointe a la Hache to the Gulf, Early 1900s.

PROLOGUE
Morning Light, August, 1904

A small boy stood looking out of an upstairs window of a rooming house on Canal Street near the New Orleans riverfront. What he saw absorbed his attention completely. He took in the panorama of the broad, dusty thoroughfare with its network of overhead wires, its streetcars, buggies, wagons, and pedestrians, each hurrying to some destination. Everyone seemed to know exactly where he or she was going. The boy was awed by the activity spread out before him.

Although it was still early in the day, the air in the dim bedroom was hot and breath-catching with the high humidity of August. The boy had arrived in New Orleans by L and N train from Biloxi, Mississippi, the previous night with his father, younger brother, and two sisters. The details of the train ride—getting off at the Louisville and Nashville Railroad Depot on Canal Street, walking a few blocks until his father found rented rooms above a place of business—all this would blur in his mind in later life. But he would never forget the brief moment he spent viewing the city in the morning light.

The scene from the window was fascinating; still, he was uneasy. What lay ahead for him in this strange, boisterous city? His name was Oliver Daniel Jackson, and it was just a few days past his eighth birthday, August 5, 1904. He could not comprehend all that had happened within the last two weeks. His mother, Eliza Jackson, had died from tuberculosis on July 31 and was buried in a Biloxi cemetery. Her death was now scattering the family in all directions. Oliver's teenaged sisters, Lillian and Alvaretta, had been taken in by relatives, Lillian in Biloxi, Alvaretta in Destin, Florida (an older sister, Rosaline, was married). Oliver's older brother, Monroe, Jr., would live with their father and had remained in Biloxi. The four youngest children had come to New Orleans with Monroe, Sr. But they would not be together for long.

Although the busy main street below the rooming-house window was dauntingly new to Oliver, he actually had lived for several years in New

Orleans, on the west bank of the river in the section known as Algiers, where his father had operated an oyster shop. Both Monroe Sr., and Eliza had relatives in New Orleans and down the Mississippi River in Plaquemines Parish. The great river's end was their original home: those narrow fingers of land that create passageways such as Pass a Loutre, Southeast Pass, South Pass, and Southwest Pass, with tiny bays and inlets cutting into them as they reach out for the Gulf of Mexico. At the mouth of South Pass lay Port Eads, a remote way station for bar pilots, oyster fishermen, trappers, and government employees engaged in keeping the pass navigable for oceangoing ships. In this serene, water-bound outpost, Monroe and Eliza had met and married. They built their home nearby, set on pilings to protect it from high tide, on an island in Whale Bay, on the west side of South Pass. Oliver was born there. Later, the Jacksons built a larger house on the South Pass bank across from the island. When Oliver was three, they moved to Algiers to make a better life through Monroe's oyster business. But Eliza had grown steadily weaker and they had finally gone to live in Biloxi, hoping that the climate might improve her failing health.

Now she was dead, and her husband was returning to New Orleans on a sad mission. Oliver and his brother Eric, who was six, and their sisters, Sarah, twelve, and Viola, three years old, were to be placed in orphan homes.

Orphans and strangers had come to New Orleans throughout its history seeking haven, a new life, a new beginning after disappointment and family loss. In the eighteenth and nineteenth centuries, it had been a gateway to the heart of North America, and the Mississippi River had been the access path for the venturers. Although Oliver knew nothing about it, his family had connections to New Orleans and the territory along the Mississippi, both above and below the city, reaching back to the beginning of European colonization in Louisiana. Nor was he the first orphan in his family to find shelter in New Orleans.

Through his paternal grandmother, Sarah Celeste Buras, Oliver was descended from several of the earliest French families to migrate to New Orleans and from German families who settled the first "German coast," near Edgard on the west bank of the Mississippi River in the 1720s. Two of these ancestors, like Oliver, had lost one of their parents at an early age. They were Joseph and Jean Pierre Burat, the founders of the Buras family in Louisiana (the spelling had changed by the 1830s). They had come to New Orleans from their birthplace, Mobile, in present-day Alabama, after the death of their father, Jean Guillaume Burat. He had been a corporal in a French regiment stationed at Fort Condé in Mobile. A year after his death their mother, Magdelaine Rouger Burat, remarried. Her second husband was Antoine Negrier, captain of a royal merchant-marine ship stationed at New Orleans.[1]

The Burat brothers came to New Orleans during the last years of Bienville's governorship in Louisiana and grew to manhood just as the Spanish period was about to begin. They had an older brother, Antoine Gentilhomme, who died as a child in Mobile, and a younger sister, Magdelaine, who came with them to New Orleans and was given her stepfather's name. They also had three half sisters, Jeanne, Marguerite, and Catherine, and a half brother, Antoine, from their mother's second marriage. Joseph became a shoemaker, Jean Pierre, a tailor.[2] Joseph married Louise Millet, an orphan living at the new Ursuline Convent, whose father had been proprietor of the King's Plantation on the west bank where Algiers is today.[3] Jean Pierre married Marguerite Frederic, whose father had farmed on the German Coast above the Crescent City before selling that land to move below New Orleans to clear new territory in what is now Plaquemines

1. Baptism of Joseph Guillaume Burat, January 15, 1731, Baptismal Records Book I, 90a; Baptism of Jean Pierre Burat, March 5, 1733, Baptismal Records Book I, 97a; Interment of Jean Guillaume Burat, March 6, 1736, in Funeral Records Book I, 51a; and Act of Marriage, Antoine Negrier to Madeleine Rouger (cited also as Magdelaine Rouger), March 10, 1737, in Marriage Book I, p. 19, Act 3; all in Immaculate Conception Cathedral Archives, Mobile, Ala. Background information on Jean Guillaume Burat, Madeleine Rouger, Antoine Negrier, and the Negrier family appears in William R. Stringfield, *Le Pays des Fleurs Oranges: A Genealogical Study of Eight Creole Families of Plaquemines Parish, Louisiana* (Baltimore, 1989), 25–33; Alice Daly Forsyth to Joy Jackson, August 2, 1978; and Alice Daly Forsyth, "Girault-Giraut-Giraud-Giro and Allied Families," *New Orleans Genesis*, XXIII (January, 1984), 111–12.

2. Joseph Burat is listed as a shoemaker in the 1766 census in Jacqueline K. Voorhies, comp. and trans., *Some Late Eighteenth Century Louisianians: Census Records of the Colony, 1753–1796* (Lafayette, La., 1973), 37. Jean Pierre is described as "a tailor" in Marriage Contract between [Jean] Pierre Burat and Marguerite Frederick [Frederic], November 13, 1762, Doc. 8288, in notarial records of N. Broutin, New Orleans Notarial Archives, New Orleans. An English translation of this document may be found in the WPA translations of the Superior Council Records in the Louisiana Historical Center, Louisiana State Museum, New Orleans.

3. Marriage Contract between Joseph Burat and Louise Millet, September 23, 1758, Doc. 7289, fols. 56882–56886, and Notarized Receipt of Wedding Gift to Louise Millet by Jean Baptiste Claude Bobé Descloseaux, April 13, 1763, *ibid.*, fol. 56887, both in Superior Council Records. René Antoine Millet was listed as proprietor of the King's Plantation when he testified in the trial of a slave accused of murder; see February 10, 1748, Doc. 1146, in Superior Council Records. A translation of this document appears also in *Louisiana Historical Quarterly*, XIX (April, 1936), 471–78.

Parish.[4] In the French census of 1763, Jean Pierre is listed as an associate of his German father-in-law, Sebastian Frederic, and his brother-in-law, Adam Frederic, in farming land on the west bank between English Turn and Pointe a la Hache (English Turn was the historic point on the river where Bienville in 1699 had tricked an English captain into believing that the French had a fort and settlements to the north, causing the captain to turn back downriver and the English to give up their plans for colonizing the area). Joseph Burat and his family followed his brother downriver shortly afterward.[5]

The families of these two brothers survived and multiplied in their new homes. Joseph had eleven children and Jean Pierre nine. Sometime around the 1780s the Burats began moving southward. Some acquired land on the west bank where the small town of Buras is today. Buras Settlement, as it was called in the nineteenth century, was about five to ten miles above and on the opposite side of the river from Fort St. Philip. Joseph Burat died in the early 1790s, and Jean Pierre died around the turn of the century.[6] Although they did not have extensive landholdings to leave their many children, they did instill in them a love of family and an identification with the majestic, but untamed Mississippi flowing past the front of their property, and with the many bays and passes that mixed and

4. Marriage Contract between Pierre Burat and Marguerite Frederick, November 13, 1762, Doc. 8288, in notarial records of N. Broutin, New Orleans Notarial Archives; Act of Marriage, Jean Pierre Burat to Marguerite Frederic, November 15, 1762, in Baptismal Book IV, p. 72, Act 103, St. Louis Cathedral Archives, Archdiocese of New Orleans Archives, New Orleans; Glenn Conrad, ed. and comp., *St. Jean-Baptiste des Allemands: Abstracts of the Civil Records of St. John the Baptist Parish with Genealogy and Index, 1753–1803* (Lafayette, La., 1972), 317–18; and Charles R. Maduell, Jr., ed. and comp., *The Census Tables for the French Colony of Louisiana, from 1699 Through 1723* (Baltimore, 1972), 23.

5. Voorhies, *Some Late Eighteenth Century Louisianians,* 57. See *ibid.,* 133, for Joseph Burat and family in the New Orleans 1763 census. Evidence that Joseph Burat was still in New Orleans as late as 1764 is given in documents agreed upon before the Superior Council in which he took over the tutorship of his wife's brother and agreed to the lease of a house belonging to the Millet (Milhet) family; see translations of the following Superior Council Records: "Release by Joseph Burat to Widow Tourangin concerning rendition of account of her tutorship of the Milhet minors," April 6, 1764, and "Adjudication to Terrière of the lease of a house and lot belonging to the Milhet minors," November 5, 1764, both in *Louisiana Historical Quarterly,* XXV (April, 1942), 564–66. The original records are in the notarial records of Jean (Juan) Garic, in the New Orleans Notarial Archives.

6. The names of the children of the Burat brothers are in Stringfield, *Le Pays des Fleurs Oranges,* 42–43. Joseph Burat was deceased by 1796 when Louise Millet Burat sold land to her daughter Marie Julienne and son-in-law Sebastian Burat (Buras). See two powers of attorney from Joseph Burat, Jr., and Auguste Burat to their mother (Louise) granting her permission to sell land in their deceased father's estate, in Sebastian Buras Succession, Plaquemines Parish Courthouse, Pointe a la Hache, La.

mingled to the back of their land. Traveling on the river and fishing and trapping on the back bayous became second nature to their descendants. It was the same for Americans who migrated after 1803 into the deep delta of Plaquemines Parish and married into French-speaking families like the Burases.

Through his family connections to the lower river, Oliver later found himself drawn back there when he was old enough to leave the orphanage. His ties to Lower Coast families, to oyster fishing, piloting of ships up the passes, and living on the edge of the Gulf came to him mainly through his grandparents Sarah Celeste Buras and Andrew Jackson. Their story and their world form the background to Oliver's life.

I

FROM BURAS TO PORT EADS
The Family Background

Sarah Celeste's grandfather, Sebastian Burat, had been one of the pioneer founders of Buras Settlement. Through special dispensation by the Catholic church in 1795, he married his first cousin Marie Julienne Burat. The following year he purchased his land from his widowed mother-in-law, Louise Burat.[1] During thirty-six years of marriage, Sebastian and Marie Julienne raised ten children on their rice plantation and orange grove. He died in 1831, and two years later his widow and children sold the plantation and divided the money received for it. One of the sons who received $263 as his share of this inheritance was Joseph Raphael Burat or Buras, as his name appeared in his father's succession. His modest inheritance enabled Joseph to embark on matrimony the next year, 1834, with an English-speaking girl from Pennsylvania, Elizabeth Agnes Quoit.[2] They were Sarah Celeste's parents.

By the 1830s, Americans and immigrants from Europe were coming into Louisiana in great numbers. The population of New Orleans rose from 8,000 in 1803 to 49,826 in 1830.[3] Downriver from the Buras Settlement, at the wild, rough Balize—the community at the mouth of the Mississippi

1. Act of Marriage, Sebastian Burat to Marie Julienne Burat, May 16, 1795, Book of Marriages, II, p. 101, Act 443, in St. Louis Cathedral Archives. Sebastian's purchase of the Joseph Burat land is mentioned in Sebastian Buras Succession in the summary of the sale and partition of Sebastian Buras estate, dated February 14, 1833.

2. Sebastian Buras Succession, summary of the sale and partition of Sebastian Buras estate. The date of Elizabeth Quoit's marriage to Joseph Raphael Buras is given on a page from a family Bible (hereinafter cited as Buras-Brown Family Bible), a replica of which page is in the possession of James J. Jacobsen of Poplarville, Miss. In *Seventh Census, 1850: Population*, Plaquemines Parish, 576, Elizabeth is listed as a native of Pennsylvania.

3. Joy Jackson, "When Claiborne Came to New Orleans," *Dixie Roto Magazine*, New Orleans *Times-Picayune*, October 4, 1953, pp. 4–9; Benjamin Moore Norman, *Norman's New Orleans and Environs*, ed. Matthew J. Schott (1845; rpr. Baton Rouge, 1976), 71; Robert Reinders, *End of an Era: New Orleans, 1850–1860* (New Orleans, 1964), 5; Stringfield, *Le Pays des Fleurs Oranges*, 42.

River where river pilots waited to escort ships across the bars and up the river—the pilots were mainly Americans or immigrants from the British Isles. Also, federal land acts that offered for sale government lands along the river at attractive prices lured settlers from other states along the Ohio and Mississippi rivers to travel down to the Louisiana delta.

The coming of the English-speaking settlers from points upriver broke the pattern of almost complete Gallic homogeneity that prevailed along the Lower Coast, the name given to land along the Mississippi below New Orleans. The Spanish, although they had held the Louisiana colony for nearly forty years, had always been a minority. Some Spanish families became prominent and intermarried with the French-speaking natives, but they were never numerous enough to offer a threat to French culture. Now English-speaking settlers became the new minority—a minority which expanded rapidly. Their culture and language became the majority way of life and speech for everyone along the Lower Coast by the mid-twentieth century. In the 1830s and 1840s, however, they were only a small scattered population of newcomers. But they mingled with the na-tives of the Lower Coast through buying and selling land and slaves, and acting as witnesses to legal transactions of their French-speaking neigh-bors. In some cases, cultural differences were bridged by romance and led to marriage, as in the case of Joseph Raphael Buras and Elizabeth Quoit.

Like his brothers, Joseph Raphael farmed rice in the vicinity of Buras Settlement in his early life. It is likely that he lived on his father's plan-tation and helped to work it until it was sold and broken up after Sebas-tian's death. Then he married and set up housekeeping with his new bride. They may have had a small plot of land to work themselves, but Joseph Raphael is listed in the 1850 census as a "laborer," giving the impression that he was working full-time for some neighboring planter. By 1850, Jo-seph Raphael and Elizabeth had four children, ranging in age from six to fifteen. The youngest, born in 1844, was Sarah Celeste. She had two sisters, Mary Julienne and Elizabeth, and one brother, Raphael.[4]

During the childhood of Sarah Celeste and her siblings, their lives re-volved around the everyday chores on their piece of land, occasional hunting and fishing trips when the seasons were right, and Sunday visits to nearby farms of their relatives. In their simple wooden cottage warmed by a clay-chimneyed fireplace, they slept on mattresses stuffed with Span-ish moss and used candles made from wax-myrtle berries. The nearest church was St. Thomas the Apostle Catholic Church at Pointe a la

4. *Seventh Census, 1850: Population,* Plaquemines Parish, 576.

Hache, where Sarah Celeste was baptized.[5] No public school existed yet in the Buras Settlement area, and many of the residents were illiterate. Although steamboats and seagoing sailing vessels passed on their way to and from New Orleans, contact with others outside of their community came to Buras settlers from the Balize. Much of the extra produce they grew, such as corn and beans, the fish they caught, and the migrating fowl they shot in the winter in the marshes behind Buras were sold to the inhabitants of that frontier outpost.

Few settlers lived between Buras Settlement and the Head of Passes in 1850. The land tended to be swampy on both banks. It also grew narrower on the east bank below Fort St. Philip and was crisscrossed by bays and bayous on both sides of the river. But the settlements on the various passes, particularly the American Balize at the head of Balize Bayou where it entered Southeast Pass, were the habitat of river pilots, boatmen, fishermen, and a host of others who supplied the skills for the Balize to flourish. Approximately five hundred persons were living in these settlements by the end of the 1850s, with most of them at the Balize.[6]

The Balize "branch" pilots, as they were called, brought ships across the bar, up Southeast Pass, and into Pass a Loutre to the mainstream of the Mississippi River. Because of the boats and ships that passed this way, there were numerous woodyards in the vicinity of the Balize, stretching upriver to the neighborhood of the Buras Settlement. Steam-powered boats were still fueled by wood on the Mississippi.[7]

Whereas Buras Settlement was a homogeneous community made up mainly of related families, the Balize was probably the most cosmopolitan town of its size on the entire Mississippi. In the 1860 census, branch pilots were listed from such foreign locales as Denmark, Sweden, England, Wales, Ireland, and France. Others came from within the United States—from Maine, Connecticut, Massachusetts, New York, New Jersey, Pennsylvania, Virginia, and of course, Louisiana. A cook at the Balize was from the Philippines, and the schoolmaster was a German from Hannover. There was a lighthouse keeper from Holland, a bookkeeper from Norway, and a gun-shop proprietor from Italy. The three carpenters men-

5. Certificate of Baptism for Celeste Buras, August 4, 1844, Baptismal Register, St. Thomas the Apostle Catholic Church, Pointe a la Hache, La.

6. On the population of the Balize at mid-century, see Rod Lincoln, "The Balize, 1723–1888," Pt. 3, *Deep Delta*, II (May, 1984), 125.

7. See *Seventh Census, 1850: Population*, Plaquemines Parish, for scattered references to woodyards. A humorous description of these facilities and their practices is given in Ray Samuel, Leonard V. Huber, and Warren C. Ogden, *Tales of the Mississippi* (New York, 1955), 169–70.

tioned in the 1860 census were from Louisiana, Illinois, and Holland. Several seamstresses living at the Balize came from New York and Pennsylvania, and there was a Spanish tailor from Florida. Fishermen listed included natives of such diverse places as Turkey, Denmark, England, Scotland, Austria, Ireland, Portugal, and Sicily, as well as Louisiana.[8]

From the earliest French settlement in Louisiana, there had been some sort of Balize at the mouth of the Mississippi. (The name itself is from the French *balise,* meaning "seamark.") The first location of the Balize in the eighteenth century had been an island known as the Isle of Toulouse in the currents of Balize Bayou, a branch of Southeast Pass that entered into the Gulf of Mexico. Only soldiers, slaves, and a few priests inhabited this barren, salt-covered island hugging the bayou's west bank. It was the setting for historic events, however, such as the arrival and welcome to the New World of the Ursuline nuns and the transfer of Louisiana from France to Spain in the 1760s. At that time, the first Spanish governor, Don Antonio de Ulloa, gave orders to move the Balize farther down Balize Bayou. The river had built up land below the French Balize since the 1720s. The new location was to serve as a small station for twenty-four pilots under the military command of Juan Ronquillo, the pilot of the ship that brought Governor Ulloa to Louisiana.

This first Spanish Balize was known as Fuerte Real Católica and was situated below the old French pilot station on Balize Bayou. Balize Bayou, however, was filling up steadily with silt by the late 1760s and was becoming unnavigable. Spanish officials decided to relocate the Balize to the head of Balize Bayou near the entry to Southeast Pass, which was becoming the main pass for ships entering and leaving the Mississippi River. This was to be the most famous Balize and was known as the New Balize, or the Spanish Balize, and finally, in its latter days, the American Balize. In 1800 the aging Ronquillo sold both his right to control pilotage at the Spanish Balize and his land on Balize Bayou to two American entrepreneurs, William Johnson and George Bradish. All three of these men also owned land in the Buras Settlement.

By the time Louisiana became a territory of the United States, Bradish and Johnson were well on their way to accumulating individual fortunes from pilotage fees. They did not pilot ships themselves, but instead attracted sailors, rivermen, and drifters from all over the world to their employ. They paid these adventurers a pittance while keeping the major por-

8. *Eighth Census, 1860: Population,* Plaquemines Parish, 67–78. See also Joyce Hingle Smith, "Census of Balize, 1860," Pts. 1–3, *Deep Delta,* I (November, 1983), 345–47; II (February, 1984), 45–50; and II (May, 1984), 127–31, respectively.

tion of the pilotage fees they collected at New Orleans, the port of entry, for themselves.

Free of government interference, Bradish and Johnson were interested only in profit and did not attempt to regulate the professional or personal behavior of the pilots they attracted to the Balize. No experience in piloting was necessary to work for Bradish and Johnson, and no questions were asked about a prospective pilot's background. As a result, the Balize became synonymous with murder, drunkenness, and debauchery.

In the years immediately following the Louisiana Purchase, the United States government attempted to protect this entrance to the Mississippi Valley by building a diamond-shaped fort, named Fort Wilkinson after General James Wilkinson, at the junction of Southeast Pass and Balize Bayou. In July, 1813, during the War of 1812, before the fort was completed, it was abandoned and its five cannon removed. By December the British occupied it, but they gutted and evacuated it after the Battle of New Orleans. No attempt was ever made to restore it.[9]

The first attempts at reform of the pilotage system came in 1805 and 1806 when the territorial legislature passed several acts that broke Bradish and Johnson's monopoly over pilotage at the Balize. The legislation substituted competition for monopoly. A harbor master and three wardens were created who collected fees and paid pilots for the ships they had piloted. The governor was empowered to create two new branch pilots as often as necessary. These pilots could name deputy pilots to aid them. All pilots and their deputies were subject to rules set down by the harbor master and his wardens, but they were free to compete with other pilots and their deputies for ships. Cutthroat competition developed among these rough rivermen to beat each other to the ships waiting outside the river's passes. It was the toughest and the fastest who got the most ships to pilot—not always the best qualified and most experienced. The first pilot to make voice contact with a ship was considered to have secured its pilotage—this was called "speaking a ship." If two came within calling distance of a ship at the same time, they might engage in a fight over the right to handle it. A pilot, as a rule, would use a whaleboat rowed by a partner or servant to reach ships anchored in the Gulf. But by the 1830s powerful steam-propelled towboats were also available to pull ships across

9. Sources for information in the preceding five paragraphs include Jerome Salomone, "Mississippi River Bar-Pilotage: The Development of an Occupation," *Louisiana Studies*, VI (Spring, 1967), 39–52; R. Christopher Goodwin *et al.*, *Evaluation of the National Register Eligibility of Burrwood, Plaquemines Parish, Louisiana* (New Orleans, 1985), 44–73; and Lincoln, "The Balize," Pts. 1–3, *Deep Delta*, I (November, 1983), 331–38; II (February, 1984), 38–42; and II (May, 1984), 124–26, respectively. See also Samuel, Huber, and Ogden, *Tales of the Mississippi*, 17–18.

the silted bars of Southeast and Southwest passes and, indeed, all the way to New Orleans.[10]

Although the monopolistic aspects of pilotage had been addressed by the 1805–1806 acts, the professional qualifications and character of deputy pilots were outside of government supervision until 1837. In that year the Louisiana legislature investigated the state of affairs at the Balize and passed legislation to initiate reform. The system of deputy pilots was abolished. A board of three pilot examiners was created. They interviewed and recommended suitable applicants for pilot's licenses to the harbor master and wardens of the port of New Orleans, who in turn considered the candidates. Those they approved were then recommended to the governor, who retained the final power of appointment. Appointees had to be citizens of the United States and residents of Louisiana for two years. These reforms encouraged pilots of good character with wives and families to replace the loners and drifters who had inhabited the Balize in the early nineteenth century. The result was a transformation in life-style.[11]

It took a number of years, however, to accomplish this metamorphosis. In 1839 the professional manner of pilots at the Balize was still buccaneer, as Gustav Dresel, a passenger aboard a ship bound upriver, later recalled in his *Houston Journal*:

> I took sail . . . in Galveston for New Orleans aboard the little schooner *Kosciuszko*, and we made this voyage along the coast in four days. At the mouth of the Mississippi a pilot came aboard from the Balise, stationhouse of the pilots, and asked the captain how many feet of water his vessel was displacing. When the latter declared four, the pilot did not seem to believe him and steered the schooner across a very shallow and dangerous spot. When we had safely passed it, he declared that if the captain had told him a lie, we should have stuck fast and that this was his (the pilot's) intention. Pilots are paid according to the draught of the boat, and many captains deceive these good people by false statements. Instead of a keel our schooner had a centerboard that can be pulled up into the hold of the vessel and thus passes over very shallow places.[12]

By mid-century, the Balize was a quiet little maritime village with women and children in over half of the households. It boasted a light-

10. Salomone, "Mississippi River Bar-Pilotage," 44–48; Lincoln, "The Balize," Pt. 3, 124–26. See an 1835 letter from an unidentified person in the New Orleans *Morning Star*, December 30, 1905, p. 13, for a description of a steam-powered boat pulling ships across the bar and up the river to New Orleans.

11. Salomone, "Mississippi River Bar-Pilotage," 45–48; Lincoln, "The Balize," Pt. 3, 125–26.

12. Max Freund, ed. and trans., *Gustav Dresel's Houston Journal: Adventures in North America and Texas, 1837–1841* (Austin, 1954), 42.

house, three groceries, a tavern, a dry goods store, a public meeting hall, and a church. Shells were used to create a finely powdered roadway along the levee for carts, carriages, and men on horses.[13] From the river, the town presented a graceful appearance, with two-story as well as single-story dwellings. A telegraph station connected the village to New Orleans. The Balize was easily the most populous and busiest town in Plaquemines Parish.

The vitality of the Balize reflected the incredible expansion of the population and commerce of Louisiana, and particularly of New Orleans and its outlying territory, in the 1840s and early 1850s. Immigrants from abroad poured into the Crescent City along with arrivals from the East Coast and the Midwest to bring the population of New Orleans from 49,826 in 1830 to 119,460 in 1850.[14] This rapid growth brought about sanitary problems and intensified the havoc of infectious diseases in the city's humid climate. Epidemics of epic proportions in the 1850s were the result—yellow fever claimed thousands of lives within the city and spread into the countryside, affecting Plaquemines Parish with striking severity.[15]

Infectious disease may have accounted for the death of both or at least one of the Burases. Joseph Raphael Buras died on January 25, 1857 at fifty-one years of age, and his wife, Elizabeth, forty-six, died on August 24, 1858. Their three eldest children were of age, but the youngest, Sarah Celeste, was only fourteen when her mother passed away. Friends who were also neighbors of the family were appointed by the court as her guardians. They were a widow, Mary Clay of Indiana, and Marshal Lorry, a lifelong resident of Plaquemines Parish. Both were in their thirties.[16]

The year her father died, Sarah Celeste found employment as a housemaid with the married daughter of a rice planter, Jean Pierre Cosse. The daughter, Amelia, had married a young man who worked for several years as a helper on her father's plantation. He was Andrew Jackson, whose family came from Kentucky. Born in May, 1825, the year after the Tennessee judge and general Andrew Jackson had first run (unsuccessfully) for president, he had been named for this national hero.[17]

13. Lincoln, "The Balize," Pt. 3, 126.

14. Schott, ed., *Norman's New Orleans*, 71; James Calhoun, ed., *Louisiana Almanac, 1984–85* (Gretna, La., 1984), 134–35.

15. John Duffy, ed., *The Rudolph Matas History of Medicine in Louisiana* (Baton Rouge, 1962), II, 135.

16. The Brown-Buras Family Bible contains dates of deaths of Joseph Raphael and Elizabeth Buras. Sarah Celeste's guardians are identified in a Permission to Marry Statement filed in the Plaquemines Parish Courthouse. This permission was dated "Buras Settlement, April 18, 1859."

17. In *Twelfth Census, 1900: Population*, Plaquemines Parish, 12B, the date of Andrew Jackson's birth is given as May, 1825. In *Seventh Census, 1850: Population*, Plaquemines

According to one family tradition, Andrew had come to Louisiana as a boy with his mother to join his father. Upon her arrival in Louisiana, Mrs. Jackson discovered that her husband was dead. She later remarried, to an English immigrant named John Clark. Andrew had a half brother, Adolph Clark. In an obituary in 1902 recalling Andrew's life, it was reported that he was born on Southwest Pass in 1814. That appears to be inaccurate. In every census between 1850 and 1900, Andrew Jackson listed himself as born in the mid-1820s. In 1850 he gave Kentucky as his birthplace. The place mentioned in the obituary, however, is significant. There was a Thomas Jackson who got a branch pilot's license in 1828. He purchased a house at the mouth of Southwest Pass on Holden Island in 1833 and had a whaleboat built in New Orleans to use in boarding ships. He died in 1834. It is highly possible that he was Andrew's father. Andrew did spend his childhood on Southwest Pass, and there were a number of individuals named Clark living at the mouth of the river in the early nineteenth century. Andrew's mother may have met her second husband when she came down to Southwest Pass searching for Andrew's father.[18]

Both Andrew and Adolph were on their own by 1850. Andrew worked for Jean Pierre Cosse and lived on his plantation. Adolph was living on the plantation of François Ragas, for whom he worked.[19] In 1851 Andrew purchased from Robert Johnson two arpents of land facing the river by forty arpents in depth at Ostrica on the east bank of the Mississippi for three hundred dollars (the arpent was a French measure approximately the same as an acre).[20]

It was probably around this time that Andrew built a small house at Ostrica and married Amelia Cosse. They were definitely married by 1853,

---

Parish, 565, Kentucky is listed as his place of origin. Despite this, Indiana is listed in *Eighth Census, 1860: Population*, Plaquemines Parish, 52, as his place of origin, and Louisiana is listed as such in the subsequent census reports through 1900. His son Monroe always stated that his father was born in Kentucky. It is possible that he was born in Kentucky and lived in Indiana for a brief period before coming to Louisiana. No definite proof of place of birth has been found for him.

18. The tradition of coming from Kentucky to Louisiana was told to the author by Irma Clark, a descendant of Andrew's half brother Adolph Clark. The obituary on Andrew Jackson stating he was born on Southwest Pass is in New Orleans *Daily Picayune*, January 24, 1902, p. 3. See Thomas Jackson Succession in Plaquemines Parish Courthouse for information on Thomas Jackson.

19. For records on places of residence of Andrew Jackson and Adolph Clark, see *Seventh Census, 1850: Population*, Plaquemines Parish, 565, 571. See also Hewitt L. Forsyth, comp., "Census, Parish of Plaquemines, Louisiana, August 1, 1850," *New Orleans Genesis*, XXII (October, 1983), 461–62, for Andrew Jackson on Cosse plantation, and *ibid.*, XXIII (January, 1984), 14, for Adolph Clark living on Ragas plantation.

20. Sale of land, Robert Johnson to Andrew Jackson, Notarial Book 5, No. 863, p. 354, Plaquemines Parish Courthouse.

since they sold other land that year to one Francisco Lacosta.[21] When Sarah Celeste came to work for the Jacksons in 1857, Amelia was expecting a child. She confided to her young housegirl a premonition that she would not survive the pregnancy. Since Mrs. Jackson was a young woman, this seemed to Sarah Celeste to be only a groundless fantasy. But it proved to be accurate. In January, 1858, Amelia Cosse Jackson died in childbirth and left two daughters, Amelia Adeline, three years old, and Euphanie Virginie, the infant, who survived. It was a sad and confused time for the young widower. Honoring the entreaties of his in-laws, Andrew agreed to place his two small daughters with his wife's family. The grandparents took the youngest, Virginie, and Adeline was sent to other relatives. In August of that same year, Sarah Celeste had further reason to mourn, when her mother passed away.[22]

After months of sorrowing, Andrew turned to the young girl who had been his wife's confidante and domestic helper. In April of 1859, he asked Sarah Celeste Buras to marry him, and she accepted the proposal. He was thirty-four, and she was not quite sixteen. But they were both lonely people who had lost beloved family members—and this bond led to a deep love that would last a lifetime. After getting the written permission of her guardians, Sarah Celeste married Andrew Jackson on April 30, 1859, at Buras Settlement. Justice of the Peace Baptiste Breny performed the ceremony, and Sarah Celeste's two brothers-in-law, John Brown and Frank Morgan, served as witnesses.[23]

Sarah Celeste, from descriptions of her in later years, was a small, energetic girl with brown hair and light blue eyes. She had robust health all of her life, and a knack for storytelling that her children later remembered and emulated. She could converse equally well in French or English, hav-

21. Sale of land, Amelia C. Jackson to Francisco J. Lacosta, Conveyance Book (hereinafter cited as COB) 7, No. 1129, p. 329, Plaquemines Parish Courthouse.

22. The story of Amelia's premonition of her death was told by Sarah Celeste to her son, Thomas Jackson, whose granddaughter Margie Williams is the source for this anecdote. Andrew's daughter Euphanie (Euphemia) Virginie appears in the 1860 and 1870 censuses in the household of her maternal grandfather, Jean Pierre Cosse. In 1877 she married Jean François Breny and was living at Nairn in 1900; see Stringfield, Le Pays des Fleurs Oranges, 244. Adeline's place of residence during childhood has not been determined. She married John Labash on March 2, 1876, in New Orleans and after living briefly at Port Eads, moved permanently to Biloxi, Mississippi; see Nicholas Russell Murray, ed. and comp., Computerized Indexed Marriage Records, Orleans Parish, Louisiana, 1830–1900, Gust B to Juzan (Hammond, La., n.d.), 924, for Adeline's marriage.

23. See Permission to Marry Statement granted by Sarah Celeste's guardians on April 18, 1859, at Buras Settlement, and Marriage Certificate for Andrew Jackson and Celeste Buras, April 30, 1859, both in Plaquemines Parish Courthouse.

ing grown up in a household that included both. But English was the language spoken by the Jacksons and later by their children. Andrew was a tall, fair, rawboned man with a broad Kentucky accent who had tremendous endurance and a natural talent for boats, navigation, and fishing, to which he turned as a profession after marrying Sarah Celeste. He loved the outdoors and knew intimately the many bayous and gulfward passes behind and below his land. Neither Andrew nor Sarah Celeste had any formal education. Along the Lower Coast there were few schools. The children of modest homesteaders had to learn the skills of everyday living. Reading and writing were not required to plant rice, catch redfish, harvest an oyster bed, trap muskrats, or guide a sailboat across the river.

In 1860, Sarah Celeste had her first child, Andrew Jackson, Jr. If this was a time of happy domesticity for the young couple, however, it was short-lived. The Civil War broke upon the nation the following spring, and Andrew senior soon found that his knowledge of the waterways at the mouth of the river was of value to the Confederacy in helping to run the blockade the Union navy had set up in the Gulf. He acted as a pilot for small craft carrying cargo between the river and the Gulf ports of Mississippi and Alabama. This furtive occupation continued until April, 1862, when the Union fleet ascended the Mississippi with the intention of taking New Orleans. Then Andrew may have entered a Louisiana militia unit to help defend the forts that were so near his home; brief service as a Confederate soldier is mentioned later in his obituary, although no formal enrollment of his name in a Confederate regiment has been verified.

The invading Union forces coming up the river had to run the gauntlet of cannon crossfiring at them from Fort Jackson, on the west bank and Fort St. Philip, somewhat farther up the river on the east bank. Stymied by a chain-and-hulk barricade strung across the river, the Union fleet anchored for over a week firing on Fort Jackson. They finally forced their way through the barricade on April 24 and ran past the forts. Sarah Celeste later described that terrible night to her second child, Monroe Jackson. She had been five months pregnant with him at the time of the Union invasion. Fort St. Philip was only a few miles below the Jackson's house at Ostrica. The sounds and repercussions from the shelling of the forts shook the little cabin. Sarah Celeste remembered the terror of the night, with the sky constantly lighting up from the bombardment. The very bed she tried to sleep in shuddered and shook along with the house.

The Jacksons had almost a front-row seat to the end of the conflict since they lived near the Quarantine Station. It was here that the Union fleet rendezvoused before proceeding upriver to New Orleans, the Confederate ships having fled or been disabled. United States Navy flag officer

David Farragut also left some gunboats at the station to aid the troops under command of General Benjamin Butler, whose mission was to seize Fort St. Philip.[24]

Not quite four months after the enemy takeover of southern Louisiana, Sarah Celeste gave birth to her second son, Monroe, on August 17, 1862. A third son, Thomas, was born on February 27, 1864.[25] Like most of the rest of the population living under Federal occupation in Louisiana, the Jacksons resented the invaders and tried to keep their lives as free as possible from Union army interference. Andrew continued occasionally to aid boats smuggling goods and cotton out of Louisiana to the beleaguered Confederate states to the east. He became well known to the natives of the Lower Coast as one of the "moonlighters" who helped captains sneak small craft through back bayous to the open Gulf to make a run for the Mississippi state shoreline.

After the war Andrew followed the occupation of professional oyster fisherman. His and Sarah Celeste's family grew. In addition to Andrew, Jr., Monroe, and Thomas, they had Joseph Penrose (known as Penny) in 1867; Isabella (called Ella) in 1869; two daughters who died in childhood (Mary Elizabeth in 1870 and Mary in 1872); Angeline in 1874; Agnes in 1875; John Walter in 1882; and Pearl in 1885.[26] At about the time Agnes was born, the Jacksons left the familiar home at Ostrica and moved, if not to the end of the earth, at least to the end of the land, where the brown waters of the great river rolled into the turquoise of the Gulf and a settlement was burgeoning that had not existed a year before.

The family was hardly unique in its exodus. Like the sandbars in the Mississippi, the population of the Lower Coast shifted dramatically in the last half of the nineteenth century. The prosperity of the Balize as a center for river pilots waned after the Civil War. Many pilots and their associates moved to Pilot Bayou on Southwest Pass as that inlet to the Gulf deepened its entrance, making it a better channel for ships than Southeast

24. For detailed accounts of the battle to pass Fort Jackson and Fort St. Philip, see John Dimitry, *Confederate Military History: Louisiana* (New York, 1962), 5–48, Vol. X of Clement A. Evans, ed., *Confederate Military History*; Charles Dufour, *The Night the War Was Lost* (Garden City, N.Y., 1960), 219–85; and *The War of the Rebellion: A Compilation of the Official Records of the Union and Confederate Armies* (1880–1901; rpr. Ann Arbor, 1985), Ser. I, Vol. VI, pp. 503–52.

25. For Monroe's birthday, see his obituary in the New Orleans *Times-Picayune*, January 18, 1944, Sec. 1, p. 2; for Thomas' birthday, see his baptismal record in Our Lady of Good Harbor Catholic Church, Buras, Louisiana.

26. Baptismal records for the eight Jackson children following Thomas are in Our Lady of Good Harbor Catholic Church records.

Pass, or to Pilottown on the east bank above Head of Passes. Two hurricanes in 1860 had devastated the houses at the Balize. Seven years later, a third hurricane broke the levee and poured river water and silt all over the hapless town. Most of the remaining population moved away, leaving only hunters and trappers. Even these solitary residents abandoned the site after yellow fever struck in the late 1880s. By the end of the century, the Balize was a ghost town fast disappearing into the sand and water that surrounded it. [27]

As the Balize declined, the increasing size and draft of oceangoing vessels made it difficult for them to enter not only Southeast Pass but all of the Mississippi River passes. The United States Army Corps of Engineers undertook a study of the problem, with the possibility of a canal in mind. But the Corps got as bogged down in red tape and controversy as the ships were doing in sandbars. A dynamic, self-educated hydraulic engineer, James B. Eads of St. Louis, came up with the solution in the 1870s. He made an offer to Congress, which was studying the navigation difficulties on the Mississippi, to construct jetties at the mouth of one of the passes. The jetties would force the river current into a narrower passageway to the sea. This, in turn, would increase the speed and pressure of the current and thus deepen the entrance to the river as the rushing waters cut a path to the Gulf. Eads promised that the jetties would create a ship channel twenty-eight feet deep. His price tag for this accomplishment was ten million dollars. If he failed, he would receive nothing.

This was an offer that Congress could not refuse. They made one change in Eads's proposal, however: they stipulated that the jetties were to be built on South Pass, which was not as wide or deep as Southwest Pass, the one Eads had suggested. Although disappointed at the substitution, he accepted the contract. Work began on the jetties in June, 1875. [28]

When James Eads set up operations on South Pass, Andrew Jackson and his family moved down this pass. They could find work for about a year on the jetties and a ready-made market for their oysters in the community created by the project. One of the Jacksons' sons, Monroe, went to work as a messboy helping the cook prepare meals for the construction crew. It was an exciting adventure for the thirteen-year-old. He had the

27. Lincoln, "The Balize," Pt. 3, 124–26.

28. For early discussions of a canal and Eads's plan, see "Historical Summary Giving Scope of Previous Projects for Improvement of Rivers and Harbors in the New Orleans (La.) District," in Department of War, *Annual Report of the Chief of Engineers, U.S. Army, 1915* (Washington, D.C., 1916), II, 1847–50, and Samuel, Huber, and Ogden, *Tales of the Mississippi,* 56–57.

pleasure of watching a small village come to life at the lower limits of South Pass. First known as Eadsport, it was eventually called Port Eads. A wood-frame hotel became the local landmark and the living quarters for many of the crew who had been brought in from other localities. This was where Monroe labored in the kitchen.

Over the four years that it took to construct the jetties and dredge the channel of the pass to thirty feet—two below the depth Eads had promised—Port Eads acquired about twenty buildings. They were all built on pilings up over the marsh with wooden sidewalks to connect them to one another and to the river levee. By the end of the century, the village included homes for workers, a store, a school, and a lighthouse. All of the buildings were constructed of wood with the exception of the lighthouse, built in 1881, which was brick with a metal structure surrounding and buttressing it on the outside. Replacing an old wooden lighthouse built in 1848, it served as a refuge for the inhabitants of Port Eads in time of hurricanes.

Port Eads grew up mainly on the east bank, but the lighthouse and a few other houses and storage buildings were on the west bank. At the lower end of the pass, the branch or bar pilots also had a station on the west bank with several buildings. It was, in effect, a community on both sides of the river.[29]

In later years Monroe had a story that he liked to tell about his experience as a messboy. An alligator had been killed by some of the crew clearing brush and cutting willow trees along the riverbank. The carcass was deposited on the dock at Port Eads. When the cook saw the alligator, he got Monroe to help him drag the dead reptile back to the hotel, where he proceeded to skin it and cut away chunks of meat. "Have you ever eaten alligator meat?" he asked. Monroe's reply was a quick "No, sir!" "Well, tonight you will have your chance," the cook chuckled. "I am going to serve him for supper." The man cautioned Monroe not to say anything about the alligator to the crew. He wanted their alligator meal to be a surprise—although some residents of southwest Louisiana ate it, alligator meat was far from being routinely served for human consumption elsewhere in the state.

29. Reminiscences of Monroe Jackson and Oliver Jackson. Monroe Jackson in conversation with Joy Jackson, spring, 1940, New Orleans; Oliver's recollections are in Oliver Daniel Jackson Interviews conducted by Joy Jackson, 1978–1982, Hammond, La.: thirteen interviews on tape and in transcript, in possession of the author and hereinafter cited as Jackson Transcripts. See Jackson Transcripts, No. 1, June 20, 1980, pp. 1–18 and No. 3, July 2, 1980, pp. 10–16. On the lighthouse, see Goodwin et al., Evaluation of the National Register Eligibility of Burrwood, 75.

Since alligator tastes somewhat like chicken and can be quite tender, the men who were served it did not realize what they were eating. After they finished, the cook asked if they had enjoyed the meal. Several replied in the affirmative and noted that the meat was tasty. Then the cook revealed with great hilarity that they had just eaten alligator. The dining room turned into an uproar with shouting, cursing men who tried to rush the mischievous cook. He danced around the room relishing the practical joke he had played on them. Monroe used to end this story by noting that rivermen like to call themselves "half horse and half alligator," and this was one time when they were half right.[30]

During 1875 and 1876 the primary stage of the jetties' construction, the laying of willow "mattresses" between double rows of pilings on each side of the channel, was completed. The willow branches for the mattresses came from trees cut upriver near the Jump, an outlet from the Mississippi into several passes to the Gulf, on the west bank near Buras. The branches were transported by barge to Port Eads where they were assembled into mattresses about 100 feet long, 35 feet wide, and 2 feet thick. These were taken to the construction area and sunk between the pilings; each mattress was weighed down with a layer of loose stones called "riprap." Between 1876 and 1878 a series of 150-foot wing dams were built at right angles from the jetties into the channel they had created. This narrowing of the river accelerated its flow, thus scouring and deepening the channel.

At one point the government stopped funds to the project as it investigated charges that Eads's plan was faulty. He had to ask his crew to work without pay until funds were restored. Then yellow fever killed eleven of the seventy-four men still employed on the project. Despite these setbacks, by December, 1878, concrete slabs were finally placed atop the jetties, bringing the construction work to a close. The river itself had to do the rest—cut a deeper channel through the narrow two-mile passage extending between the jetties into the Gulf. By July of 1879, the channel reached a depth of thirty feet at average flood tide.[31] Eads's project was a success. Port Eads became a thriving little village, a center for fishermen, bar pilots, and the government workers who maintained the jetties.

It was here that Monroe Jackson met his future wife. Although isolated at the mouth of South Pass, Port Eads residents were not without their diversions. They got together frequently for dances accompanied by a

30. Monroe Jackson in conversation with Joy Jackson, spring, 1940.
31. Richard A. Weinstein, *Cultural Resources Survey of the Proposed South Pass Bulk Terminal, Plaquemines Parish, Louisiana* (Baton Rouge, 1984), 25–27; Samuel, Huber, and Ogden, *Tales of the Mississippi*, 57–60.

fiddler. They went sailing and fishing, and swam along the sandy beaches on the Gulf sides of their peninsula. They gossiped in the dry goods store and on the pier while waiting for the mail boat or the supplies packet. They visited over hot, strong coffee in their houses or fishing camps near Port Eads. Somewhere between dancing, fishing, and visiting, Monroe fell in love with a tall, statuesque girl named Eliza Jane Loar, who had masses of dark hair, a fair complexion, and deep blue eyes. She was spirited and quick in movement. Monroe was shy, gentle, and easygoing. Eliza had a temper that was legendary, Monroe never raised his voice. They seemed an unlikely couple to attract each other, but they were married early in 1884. Monroe was twenty-three. Eliza was a precocious sixteen.

Eliza probably came to Port Eads as a young child in the 1870s when Eads was constructing the jetties. Her parents were Thomas Loar, born in Indiana, and Mary Louisa Boyce, a native of Tennessee. Thomas Loar, like Andrew Jackson, was attracted to South Pass by the prospect of work during the construction period and the hope of other livelihood in the new settlement at Port Eads. He moved his family down from Cubit's Gap, just above the Balize, where he had been a woodchopper and supplier of kindling to passing boats. Eliza had six brothers and two sisters (two of the brothers were from her mother's first marriage, to Firmin Denesse, who had died). She was the youngest of the nine children.[32]

The Loar family had been in Plaquemines Parish since the early 1830s. The patriarch of the family was old John Loar, born in 1784, probably in western Pennsylvania. As a young man, he lived in what is today Brooke County in the panhandle of West Virginia (it was part of Ohio County, Virginia, at that time). Nestled on the banks of the upper Ohio River between Pennsylvania and Ohio, this region was the center for much Indian fighting in the Revolutionary era and for a number of years afterward. Land titles were also bitterly disputed. Whether these reasons influenced his family to head westward is uncertain, but John Loar did move into Ohio as a youth. His first wife was Mary Williams. Several children were born to them in Ohio and others in Indiana as they followed the Ohio River southwestward. In the early 1830s the entire family—John Loar, his wife, at least seven children, and the spouses and children of some of them—came down the Mississippi to investigate the new lands opening

---

32. For family of Thomas and Mary Loar, see *Seventh Census, 1850: Population*, Plaquemines Parish, 576; *Eighth Census, 1860: Population*, Plaquemines Parish, 66; *Ninth Census, 1870: Population*, Plaquemines Parish, 247. For Eliza's birth date see Monroe Jackson family in *Twelfth Census, 1900: Population*, Plaquemines Parish, 12B.

up in Louisiana. In 1835 and 1836 the Loars acquired land on the east bank below Pointe a la Hache in the area known as Grand Prairie.[33]

When Mary died, John married an Irish immigrant widow, Eliza Bride Boyle, who had one son of her own. John and Eliza had two children in the 1840s, naming them Robert and Eliza. Later Thomas Loar named his two youngest children after these two.[34]

Even in the marshlands of Louisiana, the Loars retained the clannish, forceful, individualistic spirit of frontiersmen that John Loar had bequeathed them. Nobody fooled with a Loar if he did not want a quick retaliation from the entire clan. But they could be generous as well. John Loar took in a nephew by marriage after the boy's mother died, leaving only a renegade husband from whom she had separated. Loar also donated land for the Episcopal Church of the Good Shepherd in Grand Prairie when it was being built. He lived to be eighty-three.[35] When he died in 1867, he had outlived most of the family members who accompanied him on the odyssey down the Mississippi River to a new home in Grand Prairie. He was outstanding in one respect: he had migrated almost the entire length of the Ohio and Mississippi rivers in his lifetime, spanning the period from the end of the Revolutionary War to the Reconstruction days following the Civil War.

When Monroe married Eliza Jane Loar in 1884, his brother Andrew was already married to a Loar—Mary, Eliza's orphaned cousin. Monroe's other brothers and sisters married between the 1880s and early 1900s.[36] Since Eliza was the youngest in her family, most of her brothers and sisters were also married, and several of them lived nearby. Eliza's sister Louise was married to Richard "Dick" Williams, a river pilot and professional

33. For John Loar's connection to Brooke County, West Virginia, see COB 7, No. 1055, pp. 69–72, Plaquemines Parish Courthouse. His name is misspelled "Logue" here. The land he bought in this transaction in 1850 from Eli Broughton was adjacent to the land of his daughter, Mary Loar Hingle. For the name and death date of John Loar's first wife, Mary Williams, see Declaration of Death, dated November 28, 1845. She actually died on November 11, 1840. Loar children born in Ohio included John, Jr., Mary, Charlotte, Lucinda, and probably Elizabeth Ann. Those born in Indiana were Thomas and Peter. Morgan Loar, born in Louisiana, may have been a son or grandson of John Loar. For information on the panhandle of West Virginia in the eighteenth century, see Otis K. Rice, *The Allegheny Frontier: West Virginia Beginnings, 1730–1830* (Lexington, Ky., 1970), 118–49.

34. For John Loar's second wife and their children, see *Seventh Census, 1850: Population,* Plaquemines Parish, 538.

35. Obituary of John Loar in Gladys Stovall Armstrong, ed. and comp., *Plaquemines Parish Obituary Notices, 1865–1898* (Buras, La., 1983), 5. This obituary was extracted from the Pointe a la Hache (La.) *Empire Parish.*

36. See Appendix A for a listing of the Andrew Jackson family and their spouses.

fisherman at Port Eads. Maggie, Eliza's other sister, was married to a government employee at Port Eads, Duncan Douglass. Her brother Thomas was married to Josephine Bailey, the daughter of Irish immigrants; the couple lived on a waterway that bore the name Tom Loar's Pass.[37]

Like his brothers who had set up their households along the banks of South Pass, Monroe found a suitable place. It was a stretch of west-bank land bordering on Whale Bay. This site was about seven miles from the Gulf and about five miles above Port Eads. He acquired a lease from the state of Louisiana to seed the bay with oyster beds. Wild oysters grew in abundance on the east side of South Pass. Oystermen would go over to that side and gather clusters of small seed oysters from the oyster reefs to reestablish in their own beds on the west side. Monroe, with the help of his father and brothers, built a camp on an island in the bay. The island had sparse vegetation, with only a few trees near the water's edge. The lumber for the camp was salvaged from a discarded coal barge brought downriver to supply government boats. It was cheaper to demolish the barges than to haul them back upriver, and many structures on the lower river were built from such remnants.

Most of Monroe and Eliza's children were born in the island cabin, including Rosaline, Lillian, Alvaretta, Monroe junior, Sarah, and Oliver Daniel. A seventh child, Eric John, was born after a larger house had been built on the mainland at Whale Bay across from the island. An eighth, Viola, was born after the family moved to Algiers in 1901. The ninth and last, Charles Vincent, was born in Biloxi, Mississippi.[38]

One of the children, Alvaretta, recalled many years later what life was like when she was eight years old (in 1896, the year her brother Oliver was born):

> When I, Retta, lived on the island in the bay, about a mile from us lived an Italian family named Spongia. They had twelve children. Mr. Spongia owned some oyster beds. So did my Dad in the bay. My Dad had a boat in the bay and one in the river. At first he used Mr. Spongia's wharves. Then he built one of his own. Every Tuesday and Friday, he would go down to Port Eads. First he would go through Port Eads to the [pilot station of the] bar pilots, and they would always have a nice breakfast fixed for him. Then they would buy oysters from him. He would open the oysters—as many as they wanted. Then

37. Louise Loar Williams and her husband are mentioned in *Ninth Census, 1870: Population,* Plaquemines Parish, 247. Margaret "Maggie" Loar Douglass and her husband, Duncan Douglass, are in *Twelfth Census, 1900: Population,* Plaquemines Parish, 13A. Thomas William Loar and his family are mentioned in *Twelfth Census, 1900: Population,* Plaquemines Parish, 21B.

38. See Appendix B for a listing of the Monroe Jackson family and their spouses.

he would go back to Port Eads and sit in this boat, and people would come with their little buckets, pitchers, and bowls. He would open as many as they wanted. Then he would go back home.

On Wednesdays and Saturdays, he would take the oyster shells and put them on another reef to make more oysters. While we lived there, we drank rain water. We had a gutter that ran along the house to catch water which ran off the roof into a barrel at the corner of the house. When it would not rain for a long time, we had no water. We would put a barrel in the boat and pull over to the river bank. We would carry river water from the river to the bayside. When the barrel got full (which was a good many trips) we would pull back home and put water in another barrel. Put alum in the water to settle [mud and sediment] down. Later Dad built him a wharf from the bay to the river. At the river wharf was a great big weeping willow tree that hung down to the water. In the summer time a great big black alligator would lay under the tree where it was shady and cool.[39]

Although the great hurricane of 1893 had killed hundreds of inhabitants of the Lower Coast and destroyed much property, the Jackson families were fortunate and all of them had survived. Captain Andy, as the elder Andrew Jackson was called, was slowing down, but he continued to fish and take an active interest in his children, grandchildren, and the bar pilots and sportsmen who visited him to enjoy his genial conversation and a cup of strong coffee. Captain Andy had a knack for preparing oysters. One of his special recipes for pickled oysters won him a gold medal and a blue ribbon in a contest between Louisiana oystermen and Boston oystermen for the best oyster dish.

All of the skills that he had learned in a lifetime, he passed on to his sons. Thomas was gifted as a carpenter—he could take a cypress log and make a dugout pirogue that was a work of art. In addition to boatbuilding and house carpentry, he did finer woodwork, such as a remarkable delicate little model of the lighthouse at Port Eads. Monroe developed great expertise at weaving cast nets for trawling and in tending oyster beds. John acquired his father's skill at navigation and became a pilot, first at Port Eads for the government and later upriver between Pilottown and New Orleans.

In 1900, Captain Andy lost his eyesight. That year, his granddaughter Rosaline, Monroe's eldest child, was married from her home on Whale Bay to Hugh Kelley. It was a June wedding with one of the neighboring

39. Alvaretta Jackson Nicholson, "My First Memory of My Family," a handwritten manuscript composed in the 1970s, exact date unknown. This manuscript was read into Jackson Transcripts, No. 1, pp. 12, 13, 14, 19. The original manuscript is in possession of the author.

Spongia girls serving as a bridesmaid. This was probably one of the last times that Captain Andy, his children, and his grandchildren all gathered together for a family occasion. In 1901 Monroe and his family moved up to Algiers to open an oyster shop. Captain Andy went to visit them once, and to consult a doctor about his eyes. Unfortunately, the doctor could do nothing. Glaucoma had caused permanent damage. Monroe's young daughter Alvaretta accompanied her grandfather back to Port Eads. They took the train down to Boothville and from there went by boat.

In the last months of his life, Captain Andy and his wife were both ill, and his youngest daughter, Pearl, came home from a convent school in New Orleans to care for them. Captain Andy died on January 10, 1902. He had seventy-four descendants, including thirteen children, forty-eight grandchildren, and thirteen great-grandchildren. Fifty-nine of them survived him. In his last years at Port Eads, he had become a sage and a grandfather figure to the entire community. His death and burial were stirringly chronicled by an unknown reporter in the New Orleans *Daily Picayune* on January 24, 1902:

> The death and burial of Andrew Jackson, better known as Captain Andy, oldest fisherman at the passes, was an unusually sad event, and a source of profound grief to the sportsmen who were visitors to his camp. Captain Andy was known far and wide, and his genial manner and open-hearted hospitality won him friends who were true. All his life was spent on the delta of the great Mississippi, and he regarded it with a veneration that was sublime. . . .
>
> Captain Andy's camp was a rendezvous most delightful to those who had the entree, and he was not at all exclusive. The latch string was always on the outside, and no matter who came along, he was sure of a hearty welcome, and a savory meal. To the pilots he was of great service, and they all loved him. In going to and from the open Gulf, they often stopped at his camp to chat and enjoy a cup of coffee. And his coffee was nectar. He could brew it as few even of the old Creole cooks could, and it is no wonder that the hardy men of the sea liked to linger over its delicious aroma. But it was not only as a host that Captain Andy served them. Having lived all his life in that vicinity he knew it as no others did. The depths and shoals beneath the water were as plain to him as the letters of the alphabet, and he watched and followed the changes in the channel as a mother watches her babe. He knew it every inch, and loved it as he loved his life. In times of storm he was always ready to respond to a call for help, and many times his prompt action saved precious lives.
>
> When the Civil War broke out he cast his lot with the Confederacy, and served as a soldier and pilot, and many successful piece[s] of blockade running were due to his unfailing knowledge of that vicinity.
>
> Two years ago he became blind, and the affliction was a sore trial to the hardy old fisherman who fretted under the restraint which it imposed. But he

lived on in the freedom of majestic nature, and in a way continued to ply his vocation, with his venerable wife at his side.

One by one his children married and scattered to the four corners of the globe, all but Pearl—Pearl of the Passes, as she is lovingly called. Even she, seeking knowledge and culture, went to a convent, but the moment the old folks needed her, she returned to her duty and never once relaxed her care. The mother and father were both ill, and the young woman, with the fortitude and devotion of the Roman matron of old, sustained the burden of the household, and remained beside her dying father until Captain Andy's boat sailed into the waters of the great beyond.

Captain Andy's funeral was in keeping with his life. He died on Friday Jan. 10, and on Sunday he was laid to rest under the shade of a lone cypress tree, rising out of prairie waste, 10 feet from the water's edge, near the head of the passes. When he knew that death was near he expressed a last wish to lie under this tree so that even in death, as in life, he could watch the great ships as they went to and fro. The pilot-boat *Jenny Wilson*, bearing the officials from the quarantine station, and the pilots and residents from Port Eads went down to the fisherman's home, and there took charge of the body. It was brought up to the head of the passes, and there deposited in the sand soil, with the blue dome of heaven for a sepulcher, and the music of the wind and the murmuring of the great river to sing a never-ceasing requiem. There were no carriages, no preachers, no flowers. In impressive silence, with grand simplicity, the rude coffin was lowered into mother earth and nothing was heard but the pent-up sobs of sorrowing friends, and ever and anon the thud of a clod of earth, as it struck the coffin, until at last a little mound arose in the place of the yawning hole and at its head was placed a wooden cross. There sleeps Captain Andy, and in death, as in life, he will keep his vigil, with the waters of the great river purling and murmuring at his feet, and the fresh breezes of the gulf forever cooling his brow under the shade of the old and lone cypress tree.[40]

40. New Orleans *Daily Picayune,* January 24, 1902, p. 3.

2

THE BOY FROM RIVER'S END
Early Years

When Captain Andy died in 1902, Oliver Daniel Jackson, one of his thirty-seven surviving grandchildren, was five and a half years old. His memories of his grandfather would be only fragmentary in future years. But he remembered a little about the oyster fisherman's camp where he had lived as a child. Born on August 5, 1896, in the house Monroe and Eliza Jackson had built on the island in Whale Bay, he later lived in the larger house they constructed on the mainland.[1] This roomy dwelling, set on pilings high above the ground, was the first home he could recall. The family remained there until 1901, when they moved to Algiers, on the west bank of New Orleans.

Oliver was named for his two godparents—Olivia Clark, a grandchild of Captain Andy's half brother, Adolph Clark, and Daniel Douglass, Oliver's cousin. Daniel was the son of Maggie (Margaret Loar) Douglass, Eliza Jackson's sister. Both of these young sponsors were fourteen years old at the time of Oliver's baptism by a visiting Methodist minister, the Reverend C. T. Munholland, who was preacher at a church in Daisy, Louisiana, upriver from Buras. Munholland came down to Port Eads on occasional mission visits. There were no regular services by any one denomination in Port Eads. Protestant ministers and Catholic priests from elsewhere took turns traveling down to minister to the spiritual needs of the river village. Although Monroe was raised Catholic and Eliza was Presbyterian, it was not unusual for parents to have their baby baptized by whatever clergyman happened to visit on the Sunday they decided to christen the child. Oliver was a little more than six months old when he was baptized on February 27, 1897.[2] He wore a special long christening dress and was later photographed in this finery with his bare feet protruding from under the lacy hem.

---

1. Oliver's birth date is given in an insurance policy (No. 1692023) taken out on him by Aunt Nan Lawrence on June 11, 1906, with the Life Insurance Company of Virginia.
2. Certificate of Baptism for Oliver Daniel Jackson, signed by C. T. Munholland of the Methodist Church, February 27, 1897, in Oliver D. Jackson Papers.

Like his sister Alvaretta, Oliver remembered well his father's activities as an oyster fisherman:

> Dad had a lot of ambition and he worked really hard. He would get up at four or four thirty in the morning and would be out in the bay by five o'clock fishing oysters. After loading his boat down or full, he had to sit down and cull them—that means clean them. When you fish oysters you have to break them apart as they come in clumps of from three to five or six oysters or more. You have a small, little culling hatchet in your boat, and you break them apart until you have only one or two. The rest, which would be very small oysters and shells, he would throw back into the water in a special place he had for that. In those days, a sack of oysters consisted of fourteen dozen oysters, and they were fifty cents a sack. Then after he had fished the oysters, culled them, and packed them in the sacks, he would ship some to New Orleans.[3]

The oysters Monroe Jackson shipped to New Orleans were loaded aboard a packet boat operated between the city and points along the Lower Coast all the way down to Port Eads. In addition to shipping oysters upriver, Monroe sold them at Port Eads (as Alvaretta described) and even rowed upstream to the Head of Passes and down Southwest Pass, where he sold some to the inhabitants. Sometimes he came home from Southwest Pass by using a bayou, probably Customhouse Bayou, that led him into East Bay, which opened onto Whale Bay. Other times he might be towed back upriver to Head of Passes by a passing boat.[4]

When Monroe reseeded his oyster beds, he chose shallow grassy areas in which to throw oyster shells with the small seed oysters. Such spots might be no more than two to three feet deep on the average and no more than three to four feet at high tide. The oysters were placed among grass and reeds growing in the bay to hide them from drumfish, which loved to crack open the small oysters with their powerful jaws and eat them before they reached maturity. When the oysters reached a "certain size," Oliver later related, his father would move them to a slightly deeper water—but it was never more than four feet deep. The plump, salty oysters from Whale Bay were delicious and became one of the first distinct memories of food that Oliver acquired as a small boy.[5] Other memories he had of his earliest years on Whale Bay were of playing on the wooden walkways his father had built to connect the house to the bay and to the wharf on the river side of the mainland, and of sailing with his father along the edge of the bay with the salt spray tickling his nose on windy days. Nights were

3. Jackson Transcripts, No. 1, p. 10.
4. *Ibid.*, 9.
5. *Ibid.*, 8–10.

spent in a large bed shared with his siblings. They huddled together under a net called a mosquito baire (or bar) with the sound of the distant surf along the bay lulling them to sleep.

The Jacksons moved to Algiers partly because of the encouragement of a boat captain friend, William Heuer. He was captain of a tugboat used to haul barges of coal and a collier down to the bar pilots for their vessels, the *Jenny Wilson* and the *Underwriter*. According to Oliver's memory, Heuer and his crew would

> throw the coal ashore and then when they'd go back up to New Orleans with the collier and the barge, they'd sometimes just let the barge go, turn it loose out in the Gulf and it would go around . . . and beach itself. When they got through putting the coal off, on their way back upriver they'd stop at my father's place and buy oysters from him. One time—once or twice—they left a barge there because they wouldn't tow a barge back upriver—lumber was plentiful and they could build all the barges they wanted. It was cheaper to sell them or give them away or turn them loose and let them go out to sea . . . they'd wash up on the beach or on a reef. One time they gave my Daddy one [barge] and my Daddy used that to build the wharf [on the river].[6]

Captain Heuer urged Monroe to come up to Algiers and open an oyster shop, telling him he felt certain the delicious oysters from the Whale Bay area would be very popular in the city. When Monroe finally did make the move, he found a place for his shop only about a block from the river, near W. G. Coyle's tugboat yard—this was the company for which Captain Heuer worked and one that Oliver would know very well in later years. The location on Whale Bay where Monroe Jackson had his oyster beds and habitation was taken over by several investors who opened up an oyster-packing plant there. The spot became known as Oysterville.

Algiers was a dramatic change for the Jackson family from their secluded fishing camp. Oliver had considered Port Eads to be an adventure to visit when he first was allowed to take an occasional ride in his father's small boat. But the voyage upriver on the packet boat to Buras, the journey on the New Orleans, Fort Jackson, and Grand Isle Railroad—known to regulars who used its services as the Orange Blossom Route—and the entry into Algiers from the railroad's terminal on the riverfront was awesome to the children from the Lower Coast. The depot sat precariously close to the Mississippi (indeed, a portion of it had fallen into the river in 1894), and was graced by a well-kept flower bed and cinder walkways. Its roundhouse and machine shops were located farther upriver. The line offered between two and four round trips each day.[7] Its name, however,

6. *Ibid.*, 17.
7. William H. Seymour, *The Story of Algiers, 1718–1896* (Gretna, La., 1971), 60, 63.

expressed as much dream as reality: when the Jacksons came to Algiers, the line had progressed no farther than Fort Jackson. (By coincidence, Captain Andy, Oliver's grandfather, who owned land up and down the Lower Coast during his lifetime, had sold a piece on the west bank near Buras to the railroad line for its tracks.)[8]

The trip on the Grand Isle line was just the beginning of a new life for the Jacksons. Algiers, with a population of about eighteen thousand, was more like a small river town than a suburb of a big city. Natives knew one another and kept abreast of local happenings over the back fence, through gossip on their front stoops, or at the market. They had their own court-house and a local newspaper. The river was a vital part of the life of the community. Numerous dry docks and boatbuilding yards were located in Algiers. Tugboat companies such as Coyle's had their headquarters there. The United States Naval Station occupied 215 acres of the suburb's terri-tory.[9] When natives of the Lower Coast came up to New Orleans to live, Algiers was usually the spot they chose. Its dependence on the river and the Grand Isle railroad kept them in touch with Plaquemines Parish. The headquarters of the Southern Pacific Railroad at Algiers also connected the Mississippi to western traffic by rail. Algiers was thus a true terminus in those days, a hub from which one could go downriver by boat or rail, westward by train, or eastward by ferry to greater New Orleans.

Oliver's sister Alvaretta remembered their house in Algiers quite well:

> There was a double house for rent in Algiers. Dad rented one side for us to live in and the front room on the other side he rented for an oyster shop, and a family rented the back part of that house. This house had a big cistern in the back. There were two fences on one side and one on the other side for the other folks. Across on the other corner George Hahn had a barber shop. On a third corner, a Mr. Hince ran a barroom and on the fourth corner was a big white fence. Father got his oysters from down on the coast. He had somebody bring them up. They were big and he soon had all the oyster shops around buying sacks from him. He got an old man and the man's son to meet the train in order to get the oysters and to deliver them for him. They had an old horse and wagon.[10]

8. *Ibid.* The sale of land by Andrew Jackson to the New Orleans, Fort Jackson, and Grand Isle Railroad is in COB 28, No. 6436, p. 539, Plaquemines Parish Courthouse. The location of this property can be found on Chart No. 81 of the map series *Survey of the Mississippi River* (N.p., 1893).

9. *New Orleans City Guide,* written and compiled by the Federal Writers' Project of the Works Progress Administration for the City of New Orleans (1938; rpr. St. Claire Shores, Mich., 1974), 93, 358–60

10. Nicholson, "My First Memory of My Family," in Jackson Transcripts, No. 1, p. 19.

The house in which the Jacksons lived and ran the oyster shop was 241 Slidell Street. In addition to opening oysters and selling them either on the half shell or by the dozen in buckets, pitchers, or cans, the Jacksons fried oysters and made hot sandwiches of them on French bread. An in-law, Charles "Monk" DeSeamus, who was married to Eliza's niece Lena Loar, would take a basket of sandwiches to the barroom across the street and to others in the vicinity where patrons played cards.[11] He got a commission on every sandwich he sold for Monroe and Eliza. After a while the Jacksons added fruit to the wares they offered. Their little business prospered.

Knowledge of their financial well-being and the large amount of cash that Monroe carried to make change for his customers got around the neighborhood. Unfortunately, the easy, casual life they had lived at the mouth of the river, where the windows and doors could be left open day and night without loss, did not apply in the city. One night little Oliver woke up. He was with two other Jackson children in a big bed, and there was a large armoire against the wall across from the foot of the bed:

> All of a sudden, I don't know what time in the morning or after midnight it was—everything was dark—I woke up and I saw this Negro ransacking the armoire amongst the clothes we had there. Oh, I got scared, and I pulled the cover over my head and I must have fallen off to sleep. . . . The next morning my Daddy went to look for his pants and his pants weren't there at all. He'd laid his pants on a chair by the bed in the next room where my Daddy and my Mother slept. . . . He always carried his money in his pocket. He had a lot of money to make change in selling stuff. So he looked for his pants and there his pants were hanging on the [clothes] line out in the yard where the thief had taken the money out of the pants and just thrown the pants on the line. He had slipped in through the back door where they had a great big hook. They used to hook the door. He must have put a knife through [the crack in the door] and raised the hook up and got in.[12]

Although the small boy in Oliver had naturally stuck his head under the pillow to escape the presence of the intruder, he was basically a lively, boisterous, devil-may-care child. In appearance he was a cherub in scruffy trousers and suspenders—tousled light brown hair, piercing deep blue eyes, a sculpted nose and chin, and a wiry, catlike way of running, jumping, and moving about that got him in and out of endless trouble just ahead of an avenging mother or sister. In physical appearance and person-

11. *Soards' New Orleans City Directory, 1902* (New Orleans, 1902), 466; Jackson Transcripts, No. 1, p. 21.
12. Jackson Transcripts, No. 1, p. 21.

ality, Oliver was his mother's child. He had Eliza's proud bearing, her bold derring-do and her warm personal charm. Unfortunately, he also had her temper. Where his older brother Monroe had the gentle, easygoing disposition of their father, Oliver had the restless, fiery nature of his mother.

Oliver, five years old when his family moved to Algiers, was fascinated by the neighborhood of his new home. Houses stood close together, usually separated only by narrow passageways with a wooden fence along the property line; at the front of the lots, wooden doors or iron gates led into these narrow "alleys," as they were called. Those families whose homes bordered on empty lots might keep a cow or two grazing there. Sometimes a goat was tethered in the backyard. The closeness of neighbors meant numerous children to play with, along with countless pet dogs and cats. The wide, deep gutters, often partially filled with rainwater, that ran down almost every street for drainage purposes hardly constituted obstacles to a boy born on an island. Wooden bridges spanned the gutters at intervals, but when he was in a hurry, Oliver simply made the running jump across.

Oliver quickly learned to follow the bigger boys in street games. One game he learned to his sorrow was "jumping the horsecars" (actually, sturdy mules pulled the streetcars that ran along nearby Brooklyn Street). The boys in the neighborhood taught him how to jump on the back of the car as it stopped to take on passengers. The stowaways could usually ride a few blocks before the motorman noticed them and chased them off. One day as the motorman approached the back of the streetcar with a whip in his hand, Oliver was the last to jump off. He landed disastrously on the median strip—the "neutral ground," as New Orleanians call it—cutting his foot badly on a broken bottle. "I laid there and cried and cried," he recalled, "and somebody told my Daddy about it and he came and picked me up. He took me down the street to Stumpf's Drug Store."[13] The druggist washed and sterilized the cut and bandaged it. Monroe kissed and petted Oliver until he stopped crying. But when they got home, Eliza gave him a spanking and made him go to bed early as punishment for horsecar jumping. He never played that particular game again.

Oliver was a great favorite of old Mr. Vatter, who drove the wagon to the train station to pick up Monroe's sacks of oysters. After dropping off at the shop what Monroe would need for his own business, Vatter delivered orders Monroe had sold to other shops and barrooms. When his work was over and he returned to the Jacksons', he sometimes told Oliver stories. One game Oliver liked was being bounced up and down astride Mr. Vatter's leg while the old man sang "Oh Where, Oh Where Has My Little

13. *Ibid.*, 20.

Dog Gone?" Oliver would laugh and sing along in great delight. At five, he never seemed to tire of that song.[14]

Both Monroe and Eliza had relatives living in New Orleans. Monroe's brother Penrose—"Penny"—sometimes stayed temporarily in New Orleans while working at the Custom House, although his permanent residence was at Port Eads. Eliza's brother Thomas, almost nineteen years older than she, had two daughters living in the city and had come up to New Orleans about the same time that the Jacksons did.[15] It was his daughter Lena's husband, Monk DeSeamus, who worked for Monroe as a sandwich man. Another daughter, Alice, was married to a Joseph Salon.[16] She was a warmhearted, friendly young woman who took a special interest in her aunt Eliza, who was only nine years older than she was.

Alvaretta, who was thirteen in 1901, remembered the years 1901 to 1903 as a busy time. After she returned to Algiers from the trip downriver with her grandfather, Captain Andy, and visited briefly with her married sister Rosaline Kelley, her cousin Alice helped her to get her first job. As Alvaretta recalled: "Cousin Alice Salon was working in a clothes factory in New Orleans. She got me a job there. She talked Mother into renting a place by the factory and cooking lunches for the factory hands. Then she talked to the workers and factory hands about Mother serving hot lunches."[17] Eliza did well in her lunchroom business, but within a year her health began to deteriorate.

At the time Eliza abandoned the serving of lunch at the factory in 1903, she was pregnant with her ninth child. She already had one married daughter living down the river, a baby daughter, Viola, a little over one year old, and six other children at home ranging in age up to seventeen. Her husband Monroe had contracted malaria and was in the hospital recovering. Eliza's own main health problem was tuberculosis, a disease that afflicted other members of the Loar family. Her brother Tom and his son Walter also had it, and Tom's daughter Lena DeSeamus had died from

14. *Ibid.*, 22.

15. *Soards' New Orleans City Directory*, 1902, pp. 440, 527.

16. Lena Loar DeSeamus was christened Angeline Agnes Loar and her sister Alice Loar Salon was listed as Alice Caroline Loar in the baptismal records of Our Lady of Good Harbor Catholic Church at Buras, Louisiana (Lena was born in 1874 and Alice in 1877, both were christened in 1886). Alice Loar married Joseph Salon in New Orleans on October 4, 1894; Vital Statistics of New Orleans, Marriage Records, 1894, in Main Branch, New Orleans Public Library (microfilm). Lena's husband, C. (Charles) A. DeSeamus, is mentioned both on her Death Certificate, issued June 3, 1902, by Board of Health, Parish of Orleans, copy in possession of the author, and in her obituary, New Orleans *Daily Picayune*, June 3, 1902, p. 4.

17. Nicholson, "My First Memory of My Family," in Jackson Transcripts, No. 1, p. 19.

tuberculosis in Charity Hospital in 1902.[18] Tuberculosis was a common malady in Louisiana in the early twentieth century. There were no miracle drugs to stop its insidious destruction of the lungs of its victims. Bed rest and fresh air were usually prescribed. Sometimes, if begun early, this regimen was enough. But tuberculosis was one of the biggest killers of native Louisianians, and Eliza's chances of recuperating were lessened by her responsibilities to her family and her pregnancy.

When Monroe was released from the hospital, the couple decided to give up their business and move to Biloxi, Mississippi, on the Gulf. They hoped the fresh air might be more healthful for Eliza than the Crescent City atmosphere. Eliza's brother Tom had moved to Biloxi in 1902, and his son Walter joined him in May, 1903, probably about the time the Jacksons made their move. But Walter succumbed to tuberculosis a month later. Monroe's half sister Adeline Jackson Labash also lived in Biloxi. Monroe rented a house about a block from Adeline and settled his family in their new home. Lillian, as the oldest girl living at home, was in charge of the household and the cooking. Monroe junior and Alvaretta went to work in a local packing plant. They opened and bottled oysters in the winter and canned fruit in the summer. Monroe senior got a job on a fishing boat operated by a local seafood plant. He would go out with the rest of the crew on a lugger to fish along Horn Island and Ship Island. They remained on these islands for about a week, camping on the islands at night, then returned with their catch.

Eliza gave birth to her ninth and last child, Charles Vincent, on July 22, 1903, shortly after the family came to Biloxi. Her ill health doomed the infant. Puny and sickly, he died on September 11, not yet two months old. This was a severe blow to the Jackson family. All of the other children of Eliza and Monroe had been born healthy and had survived. Eliza never regained her strength and energy. Sorrow over the loss of her baby and the ravages of tuberculosis drained her physically and emotionally.

As Eliza gradually became an invalid and Monroe's job took him away from home for long periods, Lillian assumed the burden of disciplining her brothers and sisters in addition to her household duties. While Eliza lay in bed or sat listlessly in a chair, the smaller children, Oliver, Eric, and Viola played in the backyard oblivious to their mother's worsening condition.

18. Eliza's niece Lena Loar DeSeamus died in Charity Hospital in New Orleans on June 2, 1902. Eliza's nephew Walter Loar died in Biloxi in 1903. Her brother Thomas (their father) died in Biloxi in October, 1904. All succumbed to tuberculosis. Sources for deaths include Lena DeSeamus' Death Certificate, June 3, 1902; New Orleans *Daily Picayune*, June 3, 1902, p. 4; and Interment Ledger, Biloxi Cemetery, 220 (Walter Loar) and 251 (Thomas Loar), copy on microfilm in Biloxi Public Library, Biloxi, Miss.

Sometimes they ran around the corner to Adeline's house to visit. They called Adeline "Aunt Sis."[19] Lillian had a struggle keeping up with her brother Oliver. She chased him with a piece of kindling when he misbehaved. But he always outran her, and she would fling the chunk of wood after him in frustration.

Tom Loar's daughter Alice Salon came to visit him several times during 1903 and 1904 and would drop in on Eliza as well. There was no encouraging news to take back to relatives in New Orleans. Each time Alice came, she found her father and her aunt growing gaunter and sicker.

One day in early July, 1904, Lillian was working in the kitchen when she looked out of the window and saw a large white bird land on the backyard fence. "Look at that bird, how large and white it is," she said to several women who were visiting. They came to the window, but after staring silently for a moment, they asked Lillian where the bird was. "It's right there on the fence in front of us," Lillian answered in amazement. But they still did not see it. As Lillian continued to stare at the bird in surprise, it slowly flew off toward the Gulf. Since she did have occasional premonitions (which she considered to be of a psychic nature), Lillian was convinced that the white bird was an omen of her mother's approaching death.[20]

Eliza died on July 31, 1904.[21] She had talked with her husband and with Alice Salon, making them promise to place the youngest children, Sarah, Oliver, Eric, and Viola, in an orphanage rather than parcel them out among relatives. She told Alice that she worried about how they might be treated by a stepmother if Monroe decided to remarry. She also wanted her children to have an education. She herself could read and write, but Monroe was illiterate. She did not want her children to suffer that fate. Alice and Monroe promised to abide by her wishes.[22]

Eliza was buried in the Biloxi Cemetery on August 1, 1904.[23] Her brother Tom would join her in this cemetery within three months: he died in October. Her sister, Louise Loar Williams, who had long lived in Florida by this time, came to Eliza's funeral. Louise agreed to take Alvaretta back to Destin to live with her. There were no maternal grandparents to share the burden. Old Tom Loar and Mary Louisa Boyce Loar, having left

19. Jackson Transcripts, No. 2, June 20, 1980, pp. 2–3.
20. *Ibid.*, 7.
21. *Ibid.*, 9.
22. *Ibid.*, 6.
23. Interment Ledger, Biloxi Cemetery, 245. Eliza's age is incorrect in this ledger. But her name is given as "Mrs. Lizzie Jackson," and her date of burial is recorded as August 1, 1904.

Louisiana in the late 1880s to move to Florida near Louise, had both died in 1895.[24] Lillian stayed in Biloxi with Aunt Sis. Monroe junior was going to remain with his father, who would return to Louisiana after closing the house in Biloxi. Alice Salon accompanied Monroe and the younger children to New Orleans on the L and N train. She also promised that she or one of her sisters would go with him to the orphanages where the children would be placed.[25]

Oliver was subdued for the first time in his young life. The death of his mother was an overwhelming catastrophe. The ride on the train and the trek to find rooms for the night wore him out, and he slept deep all night. The next morning he stood looking out of the window at bustling Canal Street below him. Where was he going in all this confusion? What would happen to him?

Over the next few days, arrangements were made to place the children in orphanages. Viola went to St. Vincent de Paul Home for Infants. Sarah was put in an orphanage for a short time but soon taken out to live with her aunt Maggie Douglass in Port Eads.[26] Oliver and Eric were kept together. Monroe felt that they would make out better if they were not separated. They entered St. Mary's Orphan Home for Boys at 4111 Chartres Street, located in the Ninth Ward below the Vieux Carré, on August 12, 1904.

St. Mary's was located one block from the river in a neighborhood of double houses. Interspersed among them were two-story houses, camelback buildings, or one-story shotgun dwellings. The orphanage occupied an entire block, shut off from the structures that surrounded it by high brick buildings and brick fence along the sidewalk. The square was bounded by Chartres, Royal, Mazant, and France streets. This was a working-class neighborhood of largely white Creole or German extraction. Street corners were occupied by small groceries and saloons. The streets were mainly unpaved and rut-ridden. Stray cats lived in a world of their own under the houses and in the alleyways. Housewives liked to spend their idle moments sitting on their stoops to catch a cool breeze and the latest gossip, while children played on the brick banquettes (sidewalks).

Inside the St. Mary compound, the sights and sounds of the neighborhood disappeared. Only the moans of boat whistles from the river penetrated the brick walls. Three-story brick buildings formed a portion of the

24. Thomas and Mary Loar are buried in Mary Esther Cemetery in Mary Esther, Florida.

25. Nicholson, "My First Memory of My Family," in Jackson Transcripts, No. 1, p. 19; Jackson Transcripts, No. 2, pp. 3–4, 6–7.

26. Statement of Rita Barlow, daughter of Maggie Douglass, to Oliver Jackson and the author, 1977.

surround, and a jewel of an old plantation house sat in the center of the courtyard. Here the youngest boys, including Oliver and Eric, were housed. The house had been the original orphanage; the other buildings were added later. Built in 1820 by Daniel Olivier, a wealthy planter, it conformed to Louisiana plantation architecture. Although it was shabby and showing the ravages of time by 1904, the Olivier mansion remained distinctive with its steeply pitched roof, galleries all around the second floor, doric columns, and dormer windows.[27]

In 1838 a schoolmaster by the name of Louis Cabocha, who had acquired the Olivier mansion, used it for a young gentlemen's school. In 1840 the mansion was purchased from Cabocha's creditors by the Catholic Orphans Association and turned into an orphanage. The orphanage came under the direction of the Brothers of St. Joseph, later known as Brothers of Holy Cross. In 1871 older boys were moved to a vocational and agricultural school at another location. (The Brothers of Holy Cross later set up a secondary school at that location, which eventually became Holy Cross College.) The younger orphans remained at St. Mary's under the Sisters Marionite of the Holy Cross.[28]

Presiding over the orphanage was "La Mère du Désert," Mother Mary of the Desert, the venerable and vivacious mother superior who had come from France in the middle of the nineteenth century to dedicate her life to the care of homeless children. Mother Mary was quite elderly by the time Oliver and Eric came to St. Mary's and was held in awe by downtown Catholics who knew the extent of her charitable deeds, which extended back into the legendary past of the city. She had been a nun for fifty-seven years, most of them spent in New Orleans within the sheltered walls of St. Mary's. But through her young charges she had known much heartache and deprivation. She had seen boys come to the orphanage after their parents were struck down by yellow fever or cholera. She had taken in defiant delinquents and troubled abused boys. She had lived through the Civil War, the uneasy times of Reconstruction, and the satisfaction of constructing a new chapel for the orphanage in 1891.[29]

27. For a description of the Olivier Mansion, see Roulhac Toledano, Sally Kittredge Evans, and Mary Louise Christovich, eds. and comps., *The Creole Faubourgs* (1974; 2d pr. Gretna, La., 1984), 22–23, Vol. IV of *New Orleans Architecture*, text by Samuel Wilson, Jr., *et al.*, ed. and comp. Christovich *et al.*; *New Orleans City Guide*, 283.

28. New Orleans *Times-Picayune–New Orleans States*, combined Sunday edition, December 19, 1948, Sec. 2, p. 2; New Orleans *Times-Picayune*, May 1, 1949, Sec. 2, p. 6; New Orleans *Item*, April 30, 1949, Sec. 1, p. 6.

29. On "La Mère du Désert," see *Marionite Centennial Book* (New Orleans, 1907) and New Orleans *Times-Picayune–New Orleans States*, combined Sunday edition, December 19, 1948, Sec. 2, p. 2.

St. Mary's seemed to be a safe haven for Oliver and Eric. But the Jackson boys were not prepared for the shock and homesickness that followed their father's departure. Although Monroe promised to visit them and there were about three hundred boys housed in the orphanage, Oliver and Eric felt alone and lost. Later they remembered crying every night. Each time Monroe or one of their aunts came to visit, they pleaded to be taken out. Oliver also recalled that some of the boys were rough and bullied the smaller inmates. He and Eric lived in terror of such boys. One day in the courtyard during recess one of the orphans got in an argument with a nun. The boy cursed her, then pushed her against the brick fence and began pelting her with punches to her stomach. She couldn't break loose. The other children cried out in dismay, and someone ran to get one of the Holy Cross brothers, who came running out to pull the boy off.[30] The nun was more distressed than injured, but the smaller boys like Oliver were frightened.

Sometimes Oliver thought back over his brief life and the mother he had lost and the father, sisters, and brother he had been separated from. At those times he took comfort in Eric's companionship. Eric looked to Oliver for protection from bigger boys. Having a big brother was a consolation to him, and Oliver did all he could. But at night, after Eric fell asleep and Oliver was really all alone, the "big" brother was afraid. Flashes of traumatic moments from his brief past surfaced as he lay wakeful in the dark. Finally he discovered a trick that helped him to dispel the phantoms: he repeated to himself, over and over, the little song that Mr. Vatter used to sing. Almost always, the music-box melody and nursery-rhyme lyrics lulled him to sleep at last.[31]

30. Jackson Transcripts, No. 2, pp. 7–8.
31. The incidents from Oliver's early childhood that haunted him in the orphanage stayed in his mind for the rest of his life, and he recalled them and his difficult time at St. Mary's in conversations with the author on a number of occasions.

3

THE IRISH CHANNEL ORPHANAGE
1906 – 1910

Oliver swung at the baseball left-handed and made contact with a re-
sounding smack. As Sister Hyacinth and his teammates cheered, the ball
sailed high over their heads onto the roof of the three-story building across
the courtyard. Home run! For once, Oliver was the center of attention
without negative overtones. So often it was for talking after lights-out, or
drawing when he should be doing homework or worst of all, fighting with
some other boy. But now he was filled with quiet satisfaction. Oliver listened with pleasure while Sister Hyacinth complimented him on a good
hit and assured him that the ball could be retrieved by a yardman.[1]

This was Oliver's new home, St. Joseph Orphan Asylum, and he felt
at ease with his surroundings, a part of the routine. He and Eric had stayed
in St. Mary's for fifteen months, a harrowing period of trauma and adjust-
ment to life without their family. At last, on November 16, 1905, their
father removed them. His sister, Mrs. Angeline Lawrence, whom they
called "Aunt Nan," took them in for about two months while they waited
to be admitted to St. Joseph, which was near her residence in the Irish
Channel section of the lower Garden District in uptown New Orleans.
Since Aunt Nan was separated from her husband and had a small daughter
to support, she had neither the time nor the resources to rear two boys
herself. But she was a warm, gentle woman who had been deeply distressed
by their alienation in St. Mary's. At least with them in St. Joseph, she
could visit more often and keep an eye on their progress. They were admitted to St. Joseph on January 12, 1906, and remained there for the next
four years.[2] Monroe, who had returned to Port Eads to work for the Customs Service as a boatman, agreed to pay six dollars a month per boy for
their room and board.

The Irish Channel acquired its name from the droves of Irish immigrants who settled in that part of New Orleans in the early nineteenth

1. Jackson Transcripts, No. 3, p. 6.
2. *Ibid.*, No. 2, p. 11.

century.[3] St. Joseph stood on the edge of the original Irish Channel, which lay between the Mississippi River and Magazine Street with Felicity Street as its lower boundary and Jackson Avenue as its upper boundary. Today, as a result of the movement of original Irish Channel residents into adjoining neighborhoods, the Channel's boundaries might be said to stretch from St. Joseph Street all the way uptown to Louisiana Avenue. This entire district above Canal Street was developed out of several separate plantations that were subdivided as the city's population increased and spread upriver. The Channel itself had begun as the small, separate town of Lafayette, which the larger community soon engulfed.[4]

St. Joseph Orphan Asylum was part of an enclave of buildings and churches owned and maintained by the Redemptorist Fathers. The Redemptorists, who were of German origin, first came to the area in 1842 and by the next year had constructed a simple wooden church on Josephine Street for German-speaking Catholic immigrants. By 1858, they were able to replace this first church with a beautiful edifice in the German baroque style, St. Mary's Assumption Church, with bells imported from France and stained glass from Bavaria. Earlier, in 1855, for English-speaking residents of the area, artisan lay brothers of the Redemptorists had built St. Alphonsus on Constance Street, around the corner from the site of the German-oriented church.

St. Joseph Orphan Asylum was built on a separate block from the two churches and opened its doors in 1854 to children orphaned by the terrible yellow fever epidemic of 1853. Built in the same baroque style as St. Mary's Assumption and St. Alphonsus, St. Joseph was a flourishing institution by the time of the Civil War. Many Germans migrated into the upper Irish Channel in the 1840s and 1850s, and St. Mary's Assumption

3. Good sources for information on the Irish Channel include Lyle Saxon, Robert Tallant, and Edward Dreyer, comps., *Gumbo Ya-Ya: A Collection of Louisiana Folk Tales* (Boston, 1945), 50–74 and *New Orleans City Guide*, 345–57.

4. The original limits of the Irish Channel in the short-lived Lafayette—not to be confused with the present-day south Louisiana city of that name—are discussed in Saxon, Tallant, and Dreyer, comps., *Gumbo Ya-Ya*, 50–51. The district's larger boundaries are given in *New Orleans City Guide*, 345. Earl F. Niehaus, in *The Irish in New Orleans, 1800–1860* (Baton Rouge, 1965), 27–28, points out that the name "Irish Channel" should not be construed to mean that Irish immigrants segregated themselves and dwelt only in this part of town. There were several communities of Irish in the Second Municipality and some in the French Quarter as well. The plantations above Canal Street that developed into faubourgs or suburbs in the early nineteenth century are graphically depicted in Mary Louise Christovich, Roulhac Toledano, and Betsy Swanson, eds. and comps., *The Lower Garden District* (1971; 4th pr. Gretna, La., 1979), 3–33, Vol. I of *New Orleans Architecture*, text by Samuel Wilson, Jr., *et al.*, ed. and comp. Christovich *et al.*

Church, its parochial school, and St. Joseph Orphan Asylum retained their Germanic ethnicity into the early twentieth century. The German language was used in the church, and many of the sisters who were called to service in the orphan asylum were of German descent and spoke the language. They belonged to the Sisters of Notre Dame, whose mother house was in Milwaukee. The order had come to New Orleans in 1856 by invitation of the Redemptorists to teach in St. Alphonsus' and St. Mary's schools. When the newly opened St. Joseph Orphan Asylum encountered difficulties, the Notre Dame sisters agreed to take over its administration. In 1860, after helping informally for several years, they received legal control of the orphanage. They were still in charge of it in 1906, when Oliver and Eric arrived.[5]

Oliver never learned German, although the sisters tried to teach its rudiments to their charges. But he did learn some things that served him far better in his adult life. He acquired pride in and dedication to hard work—doing a job as well as it was possible to do it and taking a deep satisfaction in physical labor as a worthwhile activity. He also learned lifelong habits of cleanliness and good grooming, of keeping his surroundings neat and tidy, and of staying busy at all times.

The Irish Channel in the nineteenth century had been a frontier of ethnic aspirations and conflict, with occasional violence from warring street gangs. St. Mary's Market was the stomping grounds of a notorious gang of street ruffians. Despite its name, the Irish Channel had also been home to numerous German immigrants and Americans from its earliest beginnings. Some free black residents were living in mixed racial areas in the late antebellum period, and freedmen after the Civil War resided there as well. In the early twentieth century, the newest group of immigrants, Sicilians, began to move into the section. It was, therefore, a multiethnic and mainly working-class area, with warehouses and businesses connected with river trade crowding the riverfront streets. Workingmen's cottages, built side-by-side, dominated the district in shotgun and camelback conformation. But there were occasional faded genteel residences from an earlier age, built in the 1830s and 1840s by merchants and planters.[6]

Beyond Constance Street toward St. Charles Avenue lay the true Garden District with the elegant homes of the rich and elite. The typical Garden District residence had leaded-glass front doors, white columns, Greek Revival wooden decoration, and iron fences protecting a

5. *New Orleans City Guide*, 348–49; Christovich, Toledano, and Swanson, eds. and comps., *Lower Garden District*, 33.

6. *New Orleans City Guide*, 345–47.

garden lush with orange and fig trees flourishing alongside oleanders and magnolias.[7]

St. Joseph Orphan Asylum and the rest of the Redemptorist community was located at the crossroads of the two worlds—Garden District and Irish Channel. Some of its patrons and sponsors might come from the venerable houses in the Garden District to sit in the orphanage parlor and take tea with the mother superior or attend one of the numerous festivals and benefits put on in the orphanage to raise funds. But its juvenile inhabitants were children of the working class. Most came from the Irish Channel.

St. Joseph occupied over half of the block—or "square," as New Orleanians put it—bounded by Josephine, Laurel, St. Andrew, and Annunciation streets. Built of brick similar to that of St. Mary's Assumption Church, the three-story main building of the asylum bordered Josephine and Laurel. The asylum chapel abutted Josephine. The residential portion ran along Laurel. The residence contained dining rooms and the nuns' parlor on the first floor, with the children's dormitory rooms on the second and third floors. There were both boys and girls in St. Joseph, but they were strictly segregated. An average of 150 children lived here, about evenly divided by sex. The study halls were located in a wing extending into the middle of the courtyard from the main building. The nuns' house faced Annunciation Street. Where there were no buildings to provide a barrier, an eight-foot brick wall separated the property of St. Joseph from the streets and the dwellings outside. To keep out intruders, broken glass studded the top of the wall. Within the courtyard were a greenhouse with a garden of vegetables and flowers, a shoe shop, a furniture shop where chairs were caned, a two-story school building, the laundry, chicken yards with henhouses, and stables where wood was stored for the fireplaces and where the orphanage horses and cows were housed. By the time the Jackson brothers entered St. Joseph, the orphanage had such utilities as hot and cold running water, natural gas, and electricity.[8]

All of the units of the orphanage community ran smoothly because of the superb organization of the nuns. Furnishings were plain and sparse, but they were kept spotlessly clean and shining—as were the windows,

7. For examples of such residences, see Italo William Ricciuti, *New Orleans and Its Environs: The Domestic Architecture, 1727–1870* (New York, 1938), plates 23–33, and Christovich, Toledano, and Swanson, eds. and comps., *Lower Garden District,* 57–112.

8. Jackson Transcripts, No. 2, pp. 8, 11–14. For the layout of St. Joseph, see *Sanborn Insurance Map of New Orleans, Louisiana, 1909* (7 vols.; New York, 1909), IV, 355 (on microfilm in the Linus A. Sims Memorial Library, Southeastern Louisiana University, Hammond).

floors, and walls. Everyone from the mother superior to the youngest juvenile resident shared in the work. Their days were carefully arranged around a schedule that varied little.

The boys' dormitory rooms housed about fifteen orphans each and had a curtained off-area at one end where one of the sisters slept as a monitor. At five o'clock in the morning, she would awaken the children in her care, see that they got dressed, and march them downstairs and out into the yard, where each boy washed his face and hands in the cold water from a yard faucet. There were tin tubs that could be set up inside for warm-water baths, but this was done at night before bed. Morning ablutions were spartan and guaranteed to wake up even the most obstinate sleepyhead.[9]

After washcloths and towels had been put away and the beds made, the boys marched downstairs to the chapel for mass. Next, breakfast was served in two large dining rooms. Before the children sat down to eat, grace was said. A hardy meal followed, consisting of blackstrap molasses, bread, eggs, and grits. Sometimes there was ham, sausage, milk, or cheese. The meal ended with a prayer of thanks.[10] At the beginning of the spring or fall, epsom salts would be served as the opening fare at breakfast; the sisters felt that a seasonal purgative was good for their charges.

After breakfast, the orphans proceeded to the two-story school building for morning classes. There were at least four or five class levels, with one nun teaching each. In a typical classroom, the desks were attached to the benches on which the students sat. Two students shared a desk. Boys sat on one side of the room, girls on the other. In addition to reading, writing, and arithmetic, the nuns taught German, religion, and drawing. Among the teachers Oliver remembered fondly were Sister Hyacinth, Sister Veronica, Sister Dimitri, and Sister St. Philip, whom he particularly recalled as a talented artist.

On the second floor of the school building a broad gallery faced the front, overlooking a patio with a large circular fishpond where goldfish swam in and out of little ceramic castles and under bridges carefully placed among aquatic plants and rocks. The pond was a spot especially favored by Oliver. He liked to slip away to watch the fish when he had a brief moment to himself—perhaps after lunch before the bell rang for the afternoon session, or at the end of the play period in the evening.[11]

The children got a lunch break at noon and returned to school at one

9. Jackson Transcripts, No. 2, p. 19.
10. *Ibid.*, 13, 16.
11. *Ibid.*, 16.

o'clock. Around two-thirty a half-hour recess was called, during which they were given a snack—usually an apple, orange, or banana. Then classes resumed until four o'clock. From four to five was playtime.[12] Children might go off into a corner of the yard in small groups to play jacks or hide-and-seek, or organize larger groups for baseball. The girls, once again, were kept in a separate part of the yard and not allowed to play with the boys. On very cold or rainy days, the study halls were open for the play period.

In addition to their regular schoolwork, the orphan boys were taught how to repair shoes by a hired man in the orphanage shoe shop, and how to cane chairs in the furniture shop. They were also expected to help with the daily tasks of the institution. They might be assigned to work for a few hours cleaning the stables, milking cows, collecting eggs, raking leaves, or watering plants in the greenhouse. They would fit these tasks into their recess and playtime, or get off a little early from school to do the work. Oliver's assignments included sweeping out the stables, painting the walls in several rooms, cleaning windows by rubbing them vigorously with newspaper, and trying to milk the cows. When he proved a failure at the latter—he was too afraid of the creatures to get the hang of it—he was assigned the chore of chopping wood.[13]

St. Joseph received donations of loads of large pilings from lumber companies in New Orleans. Four boys, two on each end of a big crosscut saw, cut the pilings into sections. Oliver's job was to split these smaller pieces into kindling for the kitchen stove and the fireplaces. Once the ax caught on an overhead clothesline, bounced back, and hit him on the cheekbone, cutting his cheek and causing his eye to swell up. Fortunately, it was the heel edge of the ax and not the blade that struck him. His eye was not damaged, but he did have a slight scar from the accident for the rest of his life.

Sometimes chores could be enjoyable. When Oliver had kitchen duty, he and the other boys who washed and wiped dishes would make a game of it, trying to see who could hold the most plates in his hands at one time, or who could wash or dry the most dishes.[14] Obviously, such shenanigans went on only when a sister was not directing the operations in person. Another chore Oliver liked was an outside assignment: at least once a week during his last two years at St. Joseph, usually on Saturday, he was sent to the home of a widow a few blocks from the orphanage to

12. Ibid., 17.
13. Ibid., 11–14, 16.
14. Ibid., 14.

scrub her front stoop and steps with soap powder and ground brick. This left the steps a clean white and earned a quarter for Oliver. Of course, he had to bring the quarter back to the sisters, but he did enjoy getting outside and walking in the neighborhood near St. Joseph.

The favorite chore of all was going to markets and bakeries. Usually on Fridays or Saturdays, two boys would be selected to accompany two nuns and their hired man in the orphanage wagon to make the rounds of neighborhood markets. Oliver was chosen quite frequently. "Two of us boys would . . . hold a big basket on each side and two of the sisters would go with us. And I remember we'd go up to the butcher and we'd say 'Good morning, sir.' He'd turn around and look and say, 'Oh, good morning boys,' and he'd reach over and grab a big hunk of meat and roll it up in paper and put it in our basket. 'Thank you, sir.' I remember saying that, and the sisters would thank him too. They'd say, 'Thank you and God bless you.'"[15]

In addition to his market forays, Oliver was often chosen as one of two boys to go on their own to local bakeries to collect donations of bread, rolls, cakes, and cookies for the orphanage:

> We'd take the basket and I remember in the next block from the home, we'd pass by a couple of women sitting out on the steps on the banquette, and they'd stop us and talk with us. . . . We wouldn't stay long because we had to get away to the bakeries. They used to say oh, what nice boys we were—all dressed up in starched and ironed shirts and all. . . . Anyhow, we'd go to different bakeries and they'd give us loaves of bread. Another would give us rolls and give us doughnuts. They'd give us cream puffs and . . . we'd be going down the street with a basketful of stuff and we'd be eating the cream puffs and wine cakes. I used to like those wine cakes.[16]

When school and chores were over in the afternoons, just before supper, the children would be called together in the schoolyard for the saying of the rosary. Supper was served at five o'clock. There was always a prayer before and after every meal, as well as the rosary. Following supper, the children did their homework in the study halls and used what free time was left to play. A long evening prayer ended the day. Lights-out and bedtime came at eight o'clock.[17]

On Sundays, after attending mass in their own chapel, the children of St. Joseph marched two by two from the orphanage to the next block, where they attended Sunday services at St. Mary's Assumption Church.

15. Ibid., 20.
16. Ibid.
17. Ibid., 18–19.

This beautiful church had taken two years to build in the 1850s. Its masonry work is some of the most accomplished in the city, and on sunny days its stained-glass windows give a rich glow of color to the interior. Oliver was always awed by the intricate decoration of the interior columns and complicated carvings on the pews, by the soaring high altar with its stately graceful statues, and by the rose window above it. The altar was hand-carved in Munich and installed in 1874. Its cost at that time was $8,500. Buried inside the church was Father Francis X. Seelos, a Redemptorist priest who had been stationed at St. Mary's Assumption in the middle of the nineteenth century and had died during the yellow fever epidemic of 1867. He had been renowned for acts of healing, and many persons came to St. Mary's Assumption after his death to pray for his intercession.[18]

Going into St. Mary's Assumption was an emotional experience for Oliver, who had never seen anything like it before he came to St. Joseph. It remained an awesome and mysterious place to him for as long as he went there.

Oliver and Eric were baptized in the orphanage chapel on St. Joseph Day, March 19, 1909. The one thing Oliver remembered about this occasion later was that the two boys got the entire day off in honor of their baptism—no chores or classes. They had to choose saints' names to use when baptized. Oliver chose the name of one of his favorite nuns, Hyacinth, and the name Sebastian, perhaps a suggestion of his aunt's in memory of their ancestor Sebastian Burat. Although both are listed on his baptismal certificate—Hyacinth Sebastian Jackson—he never used either of them again. They remained a bittersweet reminder of his time at St. Joseph and the Sunday mornings at St. Mary's Assumption. Oliver was confirmed in the Catholic faith on May 8, 1910, in St. Mary's Assumption Church, and his aunt took him to a neighborhood photographer to record the momentous occasion.[19] Oliver's confirmation picture, like that of many Catholic children of the day, shows him standing next to a table in the photographer's studio in his one dress suit and straw hat, holding a communion candle.

18. *Ibid.*, No. 3, p. 4; *New Orleans City Guide*, 349; "Silent Nights at St. Mary's," *Dixie Roto Magazine*, New Orleans *Times-Picayune*, December 20, 1970; *St. Mary's Assumption Church*, (N.p., n.d.) a pamphlet printed by the Redemptorists.

19. St. Mary's Assumption Church Baptismal Records No. 48D for "Hyacinth" (Oliver) and No. 49D for "Joseph" (Eric), dated March 19, 1909, show that the boys were baptized in the chapel at St. Joseph Orphan Asylum. Oliver's record, No. 48D, has a note at the bottom recording that he was confirmed May 8, 1910, in St. Mary's Assumption Church. Oliver briefly mentions his baptism and confirmation in Jackson Transcripts, No. 3, pp. 3, 7–8.

The daily routine at St. Joseph was interrupted by fund-raising festivals in the spring, summer, and fall. In outdoor booths decorated with colored paper lanterns volunteers dispensed refreshments, staged white elephant sales, or enticed fairgoers with wooden tenpins that could be knocked down for prizes, along with other games of fortune. German singing societies and marching bands provided musical entertainment. Another break in routine was the annual St. Joseph picnic when the children went to one of the city parks for an all-day outing. Box lunches with lemonade were spread out on wooden picnic tables. The children were kept busy all day in such games as baseball, chasing a greased pig for a prize, climbing a greased pole, hopping in a potato-sack race, and playing on the swings, seesaws, and shoot-the-shoots. Also once a year, the boys of St. Joseph would compete with other orphan homes in drill-team contests. They were trained by a German immigrant of military background. He came to the home several times a week to instruct the boys in marching and in handling single-barreled shotguns, which were always kept unloaded. The drill team wore blue uniforms with caps and leggings and white belts. They had a drummer to set the pace, and a standard bearer. Several boys who acted as officers were allowed to carry swords. During the years that Oliver participated, the St. Joseph team won several awards—once even first place.[20]

Chopping wood at St. Joseph helped Oliver to develop his physique. By 1909, when he was going on thirteen, he was agile and muscular. As the champion of his younger brother and as a cocky youngster quick to accept a challenge to fight, he got into a lot of scraps with other boys at the orphanage. In stand-up, bareknuckle fisticuffs, he could beat every boy in the home except one. That one was Pal Moran, a spunky fellow who went on to become a professional lightweight boxer.[21]

Fighting came easy to the youngsters at St. Joseph. Their Irish Channel background was filled with legends of the marathon fights in waterfront bars such as the Bucket of Blood, or in the notorious St. Mary's Market. The idol of most of them was the world-famous pugilist John L. Sullivan, who had lost his title to James Corbett in New Orleans in 1892 but had continued to fight exhibition bouts and popularize boxing. Oliver had

---

20. Jackson Transcripts, No. 3, pp. 6–7. "Pictures out of Our Past," in *Dixie Roto Magazine*, New Orleans *Times-Picayune*, July 26, 1964, includes a photograph of boys in the uniforms of the St. Joseph Orphan Asylum *ca.* 1898. It is probable that the uniforms had not changed much by the time Oliver was there.

21. Jackson Transcripts, No. 3, pp. 1–2. Art Burke, "Pal Moran: 'Virgets Gave Me Worst Whipping,'" New Orleans *States*, January 24, 1959, Sec. 1, p. 12, gives a description of the career of this well-known New Orleans boxer.

cards with pictures of Sullivan and other great fighters, as well as of base-ball players. A friend of his father's, Johnny Fitzgerald, slipped them to him during monthly visits. The boys were not supposed to have these cards, since the nuns considered sports heroes a bad influence. But Fitzgerald couldn't see any harm. He got the cards in packs of cigarettes. Oliver hid the forbidden cards under his mattress. When the nuns were not around, he took them out and studied the stances of the fighters in the pictures. Sometimes if his teacher left the room briefly, he would draw a quick sketch of the great John L. on the board. When she returned, she would be furious and demand in vain to know who had drawn the offending cartoon. Oliver's love of fighting must have given the sister a suspicion that he was the culprit, but she had to catch him in the act.

One day the teacher did catch Oliver drawing in his notebook when he was supposed to be reading a lesson. She picked up the ruler from her desk and moved swiftly down the aisle to rap him across the knuckles. His desk partner, a boy whose first name was Rosalius, desperately hit his arm to warn him. As Oliver looked up, the sister was bearing down on him. He swiftly pushed Rosalius onto the floor in the opposite direction from the avenging nun, leaped over the sprawling boy, ran to the girls' side of the room, and sat down at an empty desk. When the nun recovered from her surprise and outrage, she came after him. This time Oliver headed for the long French windows opening onto the front gallery. He ran through the open window and across the gallery to the posts that held up the structure. Without heeding the nun's cries to stop, he swung himself over the gallery porch, grabbed a post, and slid down to the yard below. Since it was almost noon, he remained in the yard until it was time to go in to lunch. There was a buzzing and whispering in the dining hall when he came in to take his place at the table. The other boys stole curious glances at him. But the nuns pretended not to notice.

After lunch he returned to class. There the authority of the orphanage caught up with him. His teacher entered the room with the mother superior. That formidable lady called Oliver forward and demanded that he apologize to the teacher and the class for his recent behavior. By this time Oliver was feeling guilty and foolish. He couldn't run away again. In almost an inaudible voice, he apologized. [22]

That night the mother superior summoned Oliver to her office. She told him that she was going to write to his father to tell him that St. Joseph could not keep his son Oliver any longer. "You are too difficult to control," she said, "We cannot handle you anymore." She instructed him

22. Jackson Transcripts, No. 2, pp. 20–22, and No. 3, pp. 1–2.

to write to his father also. Deep inside, Oliver felt relief. He was happy to be getting out of the orphan home. The house painter Johnny Fitzgerald and Aunt Nan were the only visitors he and Eric ever had at St. Joseph, and the boys had never received one card or letter during their stay at either orphanage. But Oliver sensed that it would not be proper to appear pleased; he kept a long face and tried to look sad. Monroe was informed that he could leave Eric, who was well behaved, but the "big one" must go. His reply was to release both boys. He did not want to separate them.[23]

Johnny Fitzgerald came to the asylum on July 14, 1910, and picked up the brothers and their scanty bag of belongings.[24] Monroe had instructed him to put them on a boat for Port Eads. Fitzgerald had booked them on the *El Rito*, a packet boat that carried supplies and passengers to Lower Coast communities, with Port Eads as its last port of call. The *El Rito* was a relatively new riverboat, built locally in 1909. It was eighty-nine feet in length and twenty-two feet in breadth, with a draft of five and a half feet. Typical of the boats that traveled to remote communities above and below New Orleans, it was a double-decker with a trim railing around its upper level, where passengers could lounge. Owned by the Spicuzza Brothers Transportation Company, its captain was Tom Spicuzza, president of his family's business. A gasoline-powered vessel, it had a crew of eight.[25]

Oliver and Eric boarded the *El Rito* at midday at the Governor Nicholls Street Wharf near the French Market. This was the boys' first trip on the river since their early childhood. Neither could remember those days. Now they glided past the lower quarters of the city and could look down at the roofs of wharves and houses, past the Chalmette battlefield site, past sugar plantations and English Turn, past Pointe a la Hache, and on into the darkness as night fell.

The moon came out and made a sparking path on the churning river. As farms and fences became fewer, willow trees lined the banks like sen-

23. *Ibid.*, No. 3, pp. 2–3.

24. Date of release is in Jackson Notebook No. 6, p. 1 of unnumbered pages. This information was obtained by Oliver Jackson in 1943 from the original St. Joseph Orphan Asylum records for 1910; Jackson Transcripts, No. 3, p. 8.

25. On Thomas Spicuzza, see *Soards' New Orleans City Directory, 1907* (New Orleans, 1907), 1077, and Louisiana Scrapbook 28, p. 96 (Port), "Funeral of Boat Operator Today," clipping from the Centennial Edition, New Orleans *Times-Picayune*, January 25, 1937, Sec. 1, p. 6, in Louisiana Division, Howard-Tilton Memorial Library, Tulane University, New Orleans. See Department of Commerce and Labor, Bureau of Navigation, *Forty-Second Annual List of Vessels of the U.S.: Lists of Vessels Belonging to the U.S. Government for the Year Ending June 30, 1910* (Washington, D.C., 1910), 179, for statistics on the *El Rito*; although this publication lists mainly government vessels, it does contain a list of privately owned vessels, in which the Spicuzza packet appears.

tinels guarding every bend and turn. Behind the boat lay a flat world lost in darkness. Oliver and Eric had watched the passing scenery with rapt attention ever since leaving New Orleans. At first they had talked about the things they saw. But after darkness came, they grew silent. Eric fell asleep. Then Oliver looked forward and saw a remarkable sight—the Head of Passes. Here before the *El Rito* were several water passages outlined by beacon lights from their banks. Which one would they take? The boat moved slowly but unerringly into South Pass. Oliver's journey was almost over. He was passing his grandfather's grave, although he was not aware of it, as he gazed in wonder at the beauty of the Passes at night. In another hour the *El Rito* reached Port Eads. Oliver and Eric had come home.

4

PORT EADS: THE HALCYON DAYS
1910–1911

The first few days Oliver and Eric spent in Port Eads seemed like a dream to them. The night they arrived, their father emerged out of the darkness on the wharf and hurried them to the small one-room dwelling assigned to him by his employers, the United States Customs Service. He worked as a boatman rowing the customs officer and the quarantine doctor out to incoming ships. For several years he had roomed with his sister and brother-in-law, Aggie and Louis Castell.[1] But when he received word that the boys were coming out of the orphanage to join him, he secured the use of the one-room house. It measured about twenty by twenty-five feet and had a wooden table and several chairs, a cupboard, and against one wall a single bed and two bunk beds. Several nails in the wall served as clothes hangers. An iron wood stove with a stovepipe through the ceiling completed the furnishings. Rainwater was caught in a cistern for drinking, for washing dishes and clothes, and for bathing. The dishpan was a wooden tub that was kept on a hook on the outside of the house. A kerosene lamp lighted the quarters at night.[2] An outhouse stood behind the dwelling. After sleeping in a room with fifteen boys, the brothers found these quarters spacious and private.

In the light of the next morning, Port Eads was a revelation to Oliver and Eric. The small community of wooden houses set on pilings high above the prairie grass was far removed in atmosphere from the close, sheltered world of the two orphanages where the boys had spent almost half their lives. Used to the regimen and discipline of the St. Joseph orphanage with its brick walls enclosing their activities, the Jackson boys were intoxicated by the freedom of their new surroundings. The landscape was flat and sparse in vegetation: willow trees might grow at the Head of Passes and on South Pass at the entrance to Grand Pass, but down at Port

---

1. Jackson Transcripts, No. 3, pp. 10–11. Monroe is listed in the Castell household in *Thirteenth Census, 1910: Population*, Plaquemines Parish, 23A.
2. Jackson Transcripts, No. 3, pp. 11–12.

Eads only canebrakes and marsh grasses thrived—the canes on patches of uncleared high ground, the marsh grasses carpeting the rest of the flat, boggy fingers of land stretching to the Gulf. The Mississippi cut the village into two parts set on opposite banks. A few blocks back from the houses on both sides the salt water of the bays opened toward the Gulf. Looking in any direction, one's eyes followed flat land and water to the horizon.

Gulls and pelicans sunned themselves on the posts sunk in the lower pass to hold the willow mattresses that made up the jetties. Long-legged egrets and terns waded in the shallow waters along the sand beaches on the saltwater sides of South Pass. Sometimes there was the rare sight of a frigate bird majestically soaring overhead.[3] Always there was a breeze bringing the bracing fresh salt smell of the sea. At night the surf on the bay sides of the two fingers of land that made up South Pass sang a soothing lullaby. Years after he had left the lower river, Oliver would remember that sound and imagine that he heard it as he was falling asleep. Sunrise and sunset were spectacular as the sky became a beautiful dome of changing colors and intensities. At night the stars were pristine and bright. But storms could be awesome, churning the river into angry whitecaps and making it dangerous to try to cross it or to set out to sea.[4] Everything turned gray as the clouds lowered. When it was over, the smell of fresh vegetation drying in the sun was pungent and refreshing.

Including its segments on both banks, Port Eads consisted of about thirty-two houses and other buildings.[5] These were simple wooden structures, some freshly painted, others weatherworn, all built on pilings about six to eight feet off the ground. They were strung out in a long row facing the river and were linked together by wooden walkways. The South Pass lighthouse on the west bank rose high above the other buildings, offering a beacon to ships at sea and a place of refuge to Port Eads inhabitants in times of storm. A family lived in the lighthouse and tended the light. A steel-reinforced tower surrounded the body of the building, giving it an indomitable appearance. Near the lighthouse was an observation tower from which a watchman could scan the sea for incoming vessels.

The quarters of the customs officer, Captain Harry E. Gilmore, were also on the west bank. He was a jovial old gentleman of seventy, a native

3. Harry Hansen, ed., *Louisiana: A Guide to the State*, (1941; rpr. New York, 1971), 408.

4. Jackson Transcripts, No. 3, p. 19.

5. *Ibid.*, 13. For the exact number and location of buildings at Port Eads in 1910, see "Chart of a Part of South Pass, Mississippi River," surveyed and plotted under the direction of Col. Lansing H. Beach, Corps of Engineers, U.S. Army, in Department of War, *Annual Report of the Chief of Engineers, U.S. Army, 1910* (Washington, D.C., 1910), n.p.

of Ireland. His wife, Noelie, a Frenchwoman much younger than her husband, took a motherly interest in the two Jackson boys. She would bake cakes and pies and bring them over to share with the Jacksons, who lived nearby.[6]

On the east bank were the yards where coal was stored for use by United States Army Corps of Engineers boats, and below these yards a large wharf and the hotel that had originally held the men employed in building the jetties.[7] Rooms in the hotel were now rented to men, some with families, involved in maintaining the jetties and dredging the pass. Monroe Jackson's youngest brother, John Walter Jackson, and his new wife, the former Mary Buras, lived there in 1910. John Jackson was the captain of the *General Reese,* a boat used by the Corps of Engineers to tow barges and do survey work.[8]

The east bank also featured a general store selling groceries and hardware. Maggie Douglass, the sister of Oliver's late mother, lived next to it. Her husband, Duncan Douglass, was an engineer on a Corps of Engineers steamboat. Five of the couple's six surviving children, ranging in age from seven to twenty-one, were living with them. Another member of the household was Sarah Jackson, Oliver's sister.[9] She had spent a short time in an orphanage in New Orleans before Maggie asked Monroe's permission to take the girl to live with her. Now Sarah was seventeen, a beautiful young woman with large expressive eyes and a kindly nature that made for easy friendship with her young brothers. Although the grown-up Sarah seemed almost a stranger to Oliver, he was overjoyed to see her again and quickly resumed the close feeling he had for her when he was a small child.

Actually, one of the amazing things about South Pass to Oliver was the many family ties he seemed to have to its inhabitants. Living above Port Eads and engaged in oyster-reef fishing was Oliver's uncle Tommy Jackson, Sr., whose eight children, ranging in age from four to twenty, were still at home. Tommy, Jr. was sixteen, just two years older than his cousin Oliver.[10] The pair quickly became close friends. At the request of Oliver's father, Uncle Tommy, an accomplished carpenter and boatbuilder, made Oliver a sailboat he could use to cross the river. It was square on both

6. *Thirteenth Census, 1910: Population,* Plaquemines Parish, 24A.

7. See "Chart of a Part of South Pass, Mississippi River," in *Annual Report of the Chief of Engineers, U.S. Army, 1910,* for location on east bank of coal bins and the large wharf in front of the hotel.

8. Jackson Transcripts, No. 3, pp. 15–16. The *General Reese* is mentioned in Department of War, Cornelius Donovan, "Sub-Report to Appendix S" of the *Annual Report of the Chief of Engineers, U.S. Army, 1904* (Washington, D.C., 1904), 1444.

9. Jackson Transcripts, No. 3, p. 19; *Thirteenth Census, 1910: Population,* Plaquemines Parish, 23B.

10. *Thirteenth Census, 1910: Population,* Plaquemines Parish, 22B.

ends, and the mast could be lowered and the sail folded into the boat when Oliver tied it up to a wharf. Monroe and Oliver made the sail themselves. Among the other boats Uncle Tommy and young Tommy built were cypress pirogues carved out of logs they found washed up on the riverbank. "He'd make a pirogue so nice and light that one man could pick it up and put it on his shoulder and carry it from the river to the bay," Oliver recalled years later.[11]

Other Jacksons living on South Pass or at Port Eads were all Oliver's uncles and aunts—Uncle Penrose "Penny" Jackson, who worked as a boatman for the engineers; Uncle Andrew, an oyster fisherman; and Aunt Pearl Jackson Ronquillo and Aunt Aggie Jackson Castell, both married to men who worked for the Corps of Engineers.[12] Each of them had families numbering from three to eight children, giving Oliver and Eric more cousins than they could keep straight in their heads. In addition to Maggie Douglass, there were several other families related to Oliver through his mother. His uncle Robert Loar lived at Port Eads with a wife and four children.[13] After being half an orphan for years, it was bewildering, but satisfying, to have so many relatives all at once.

At the lower end of South Pass, the Associated Branch Pilots (or "bar pilots" as they were called) had their camp, which consisted of several buildings on the west bank. This was the headquarters for pilots waiting for ships that wished to enter South Pass.[14] When the watchman informed them a ship was coming in, a pilot boarded their boat and headed out into the Gulf to meet it. He transferred to a yawl that was lowered from the pilot boat and used to row him to the inbound vessel. He boarded by climbing a rope ladder, and then guided the ship safely across the treacherous shifting sandbars and up South Pass past Port Eads, past the Head of Passes, to Pilottown, on the east bank of the river. There he left the ship. Another pilot from a different association, the Crescent River Port Pilots, would guide it up to New Orleans. One of the bar pilots' boats would return the first man to the mouth of South Pass again, or he might remain at Pilottown to await ships sailing downstream. When ships were coming downriver, the procedure was reversed. Pilots usually spent two weeks on and two weeks off duty at the mouth of the river.[15]

11. Jackson Transcripts, No. 3, p. 17.

12. *Thirteenth Census, 1910: Population,* Plaquemines Parish, 22A, 22B, 23A, 24B.

13. *Ibid.,* 23B, 24A.

14. For the camp's location, see "Chart of a Part of South Pass, Mississippi River," in *Annual Report of the Chief of Engineers, 1910.* A contemporary description of the camp appears in Weinstein, *Cultural Resources Survey of the Proposed South Pass Bulk Terminal,* 56–59.

15. Description of bar pilots boarding ships was recounted to the author by Oliver D. Jackson informally in 1970s.

Although most of the pilots from both associations made their permanent homes in New Orleans, there were some who had houses or camps on the lower river, mainly at Pilottown. One bar pilot had a large camp with cattle on South Pass between Port Eads and the bar pilots' camp; Penny Jackson cared for this miniranch when the owner was not in residence.[16] The cattleman-pilot and all other settlers along South Pass, however, were dwelling there through the consent of the federal government, which had purchased all of the land along the Pass in 1903.[17]

From the 1870s to 1903, the Eads family had owned this land, and from 1881 to 1901 they had held a twenty-year contract to maintain the channel, jetties, and auxiliary works at South Pass. The contract had expired on January 18, 1901, after which the federal office of the secretary of war took charge of maintaining South Pass and the jetties.[18] The Corps of Engineers became the major proprietor and employer at Port Eads. By 1904 the Corps had a local work force of sixteen in addition to its own men, and it maintained a floating plant that included one tug, one steam launch, one pile driver, one derrick boat, eight barges, and five skiffs.[19] In addition to the operations of the Corps of Engineers in keeping a channel of between twenty-six and thirty-one feet in depth in South Pass, the Customs Service and the Quarantine Service had representatives at Port Eads to check on incoming crews and passengers.

The function of Port Eads as an outpost at the Mississippi's mouth to keep South Pass a safe passage for incoming and outgoing vessels was always apparent. Almost every two or three days a ship passed the little village going up or down the river. During daylight hours, the passengers or sailors waved to Port Eads inhabitants. At night, large, ghostlike ships glided by as the lighthouse sent out a beam to sea and, in overcast weather, the foghorn sounded.

Oliver and other boys at Port Eads would climb the lookout tower and watch for ships at sea that might be approaching South Pass. Shortly after he arrived, Oliver got a job working as a helper in Frank Marshal's general store, on the east bank. With some of the money he earned, he bought a spyglass from an itinerant merchant who came occasionally to Port Eads aboard the *El Rito* to sell sundry items to the inhabitants. The little telescope made Oliver a hero to the other young people, for with it he could

16. Jackson Transcripts, No. 3, p. 18.

17. "Improvement of Rivers and Harbors in the New Orleans, Louisiana District," in *Annual Report of the Chief of Engineers, 1910*, p. 493.

18. *Ibid.*, 492–93.

19. Donovan, "Sub-Report to Appendix S," *Annual Report of the Chief of Engineers, 1904*, p. 1444.

spot the most desirable ships long before anyone else. These were the sleek fruit ships, painted white to repel the heat of the sun. The banana boats of the United Fruit Company were particularly popular with Port Eads residents. In those days the boats had no refrigeration, and any ripe bananas, or even those about to ripen, were thrown overboard to eager youngsters who came out in skiffs. The bananas were jettisoned in "hands"—large bunches—which the lucky recipient hung with a rope from a hook in the ceiling on his front porch. (The Jackson's simple one-room cabin did not have a porch, so Oliver hung them inside.) To assure that they would get choice bananas, Oliver, Eric, and their cousin Tommy sometimes took the prettiest girl they could cajole into joining them on these fruit-scavenging adventures.[20]

In 1911, a total of 240 vessels drawing twenty-five feet or more passed through South Pass, 77 bound upriver from the Gulf, 163 outward bound. Two of those coming downriver drew twenty-nine feet, only two feet short of touching the bottom of the deepest point in the river's channel.[21]

The tugs and dredges of the Corps of Engineers were constantly in evidence up and down South Pass, repairing the jetties, dredging the channel, and unloading coal into the coal bins. Workers on land built wharves, drove pilings, repaired houses and plank walks, unloaded ballast from ships, and cut back the ever-encroaching grass and canes on both banks of the village. They also closed small bayous leading from South Pass or the lower river into the adjacent bays. This was done to increase the volume and pressure of the water flowing through South Pass.[22]

Ships found to have diseased persons aboard were ordered to stop at the Quarantine Station upriver, above Cubit's Gap on the east bank. Often ships were required to go through fumigation to kill any disease-carrying or otherwise harmful insects that might be aboard.[23] Since the break-

20. Jackson Transcripts, No. 3, pp. 16–17.

21. Department of War, Major H. Burgess, "Appendix S" to *Annual Report of the Chief of Engineers, U.S. Army, 1911* (Washington, D.C., 1911), 1741.

22. Maintenance and improvement of the South Pass channel is discussed in *Annual Report of the Chief of Engineers, U.S. Army, 1910*, pp. 492–96, and in *Annual Report of the Chief of Engineers, U.S. Army, 1911*, pp. 1741–46.

23. The Quarantine Station that the Union forces occupied during the Civil War was located just above Ostrica on the east bank and had been opened in the 1850s. In the 1890s, a station operated farther downriver on the east bank above Cubit's Gap and remained there until about 1920, when the new Quarantine Station at the lower end of Algiers was put into operation. See Goodwin et al., *Evaluation of the National Register Eligibility of Burrwood*, 62, 65. The background to the Quarantine Station and its work can be found in Joy J. Jackson, *New Orleans in the Gilded Age: Politics and Urban Progress, 1880–1896* (Baton Rouge, 1969), 170–78. See also Virginia Parsons, "A Study of the Activities of the Louisiana Board of

through discovery of the connection between mosquitoes and yellow fever, though, there was far less to fear from incoming vessels, and the quarantine doctor's duties were largely routine and uneventful. Those duties were carried out in style, however: Oliver's father and the other oarsman, Frank Morgan, who rowed the customs and quarantine officers out to ships wore uniforms reminiscent of the British navy.

Oliver's job kept him busy for at least half the day. He helped out in sweeping up the store, waiting on customers, and delivering groceries to housewives. His little sailboat came in handy to reach his place of employment. But Oliver did not know how to swim, and his foolhardy confidence in sailing on rough days set the Port Eads wives to shaking their heads in alarm. "You better be careful boy," Mrs. Henry Clark, the mother of his godmother Olivia, warned him. "You're going to drown if you aren't more careful." If one incident he described was typical, such concern was not entirely groundless:

> They had a big wharf there [on the east bank]—the hotel wharf—and I used to sail over and I'd tie my boat up on the inside, in behind the pilings . . . The wharf was built out a little and . . . I'd put my boat in and take the mast down, lay it down. Nobody would bother it. Tie it up on the inside, and go walk on up to the store. One time I was coming across there and the sheet rope that held the sail got jammed on the cleat and I was heading right in for the dock! I went head on into the pilings! Split all the bow and I got mad and I pulled the cleat out and took my mast down [and] my sail. . . . It took a little water, but not much. It was cracked [but] the flat boat would sit up. Wherever you sat, the other end would go up out of the water.[24]

Oliver enjoyed working in Marshal's store. It gave him a chance to meet and talk with most of the residents of the small community who wandered in and out. He was getting old enough now to welcome the company of the opposite sex. Although he had been carefully segregated from girls in St. Joseph, he found that he had a talent for getting along with them. Sometimes when a pretty girl came into the store to make a purchase, Oliver would give her free of charge a few of the hard, round candies known as "jawbreakers" that Mr. Marshal kept in a glass bowl on the counter. The New Orleans custom of giving something extra as "lagniappe" was one Oliver himself had enjoyed when visiting bakeries and other stores for the nuns of St. Joseph. However, it was a custom that had

---

Health From 1855 to 1898 in Reference to Quarantine" (M.A. thesis, Tulane University, 1932).

24. Jackson Transcripts, No. 3, pp. 18–19.

not reached Port Eads, and Mr. Marshal put an end to it when he discovered his helper giving away the profits one day.[25]

The Marshal store carried mainly groceries and hardware brought downriver from New Orleans on the *El Rito*. Other types of merchandise, such as needles and thread, dress materials, ready-made clothes, shoes, and jewelry, were brought down occasionally by itinerant merchants. Oliver later remembered two men of foreign origin, probably Lebanese, who came to Port Eads. One sold jewelry that he brought in cases, and the other sold clothes and shoes he carried in big bundles. They went from house to house to hawk their wares. If they did not have the desired item or size, they would take an order and bring it down on the next trip. Oliver had purchased his spyglass from the jewelry salesman. He also bought a ring for his godmother Olivia.[26]

Although Oliver had been baptized a Catholic in St. Joseph, his original baptism by a Methodist preacher took on a special importance for him when he returned to Port Eads. His godparents in the Methodist ceremony were both living there, and he saw them every day. They were grown-ups now. Daniel Douglass had a wife and several small children. Olivia Clark was married to Frank Richmond, captain of a Corps of Engineers tugboat, and had three children. Oliver became particularly fond of Olivia. Having lost his mother at eight years of age, he now reached out to the friendship of his godmother. She was both touched and amused at the affection Oliver held for her. Her husband was a jovial man who loved to tease. Sometimes when Oliver was talking to him, Richmond would suddenly reach over and pull the young man's shirt out of his pants and laugh. If Oliver got mad, he laughed all the harder.[27]

The warmth of the Richmond family and the good-natured pranks they played on him taught Oliver to relax and enjoy life. This was a much-needed change from the constant and spartan discipline of St. Joseph, which had made him a good worker and an achiever but had also created a tension and nervous energy in him. In the orphanage, this tension had come out in fits of rebellion and fighting. Oliver still had a few fights. One involved a boy Eric complained had hit him; Oliver fought him on the hotel wharf. Another was with a local youth who was older and much bigger than Oliver. The two got into an argument on the porch of the Marshal store. When the other boy wouldn't go down onto the plank walk and fight, Oliver grabbed him by the pants leg and pulled him off the

25. *Ibid.*, 19.
26. *Ibid.*, 14–15.
27. *Ibid.*, 15.

porch. Several men who were nearby stopped the scuffle. By the end of his first six months in Port Eads, he did begin to adjust, and there were no more fisticuffs in his relations with others.[28]

In addition to working as an oarsman, Oliver's father did some trapping in the marshes up South Pass. Raccoons and muskrats were the main target. Otters and minks could also be found around the Head of Passes. Monroe showed Oliver and Eric how to set traps, but Oliver disliked trapping altogether. He hated to go back and find an animal caught in a trap. (Once the Jacksons found the remains of a bloody foot; a raccoon caught in the trap had chewed off its own foot to escape.) Monroe would club the hapless animals to death and take the carcasses back to the house, where he skinned them and put the pelts on a frame to dry. Oliver never could bring himself to kill any of the trapped creatures and finally stopped setting traps for his father.[29]

Fishing and crabbing came more naturally and allowed Oliver to row out into East Bay: "We had a skiff in the bay and we'd go out there and set trotlines and catch crabs. . . . You could catch all the crabs you wanted. Plenty out there because it was all a big oyster bay out there and wherever there's oysters, there's lots of crabs. You [could] take a cast net and . . . catch a lot of shrimp and mullet, small fish and . . . drums."[30] Fish were plentiful and always available. Sometimes schools of redfish were so dense and came so close to land that persons on the beach could see a reddish reflection shimmering on the top of the water. Game was just as plentiful. Hunting in the fall and winter drew not only the natives of South Pass, but also influential sportsmen from New Orleans or sometimes from other states, even politicians from Washington, D.C.[31] They were often guests at the bar pilots' camp. Ducks would literally darken the sky in their migratory flights. No hunter went away disappointed. It was a hunter's paradise.

On Saturday evenings in the summer, families from Port Eads would row out to reefs along the end of South Pass or to Cow Horn Reef in East Bay. Some of them would stay all night, Oliver recalled, on a kind of island campout-cookout, frying fish and shrimp and boiling crabs. Others would row skiffs in the shallow water along the beaches of East Bay, where flounder lay in the sand at night. The fishermen would attach a pipe to the front of the skiff and hang a wire crab basket on it with burning pine

28. *Ibid.*, 19.
29. *Ibid.*, No. 3, p. 20, No. 4, July 2, 1980, p. 1.
30. *Ibid.*, No. 4, p. 1.
31. *Ibid.*, No. 3, pp. 17–18.

branches to light the water. When they saw a flounder they would spear it and pull it into the skiff.[32]

Other amusements the folks of Port Eads pursued included occasional dances and baseball games. The musical accompaniment for the dancing was supplied by two men, one of whom played an accordion and the other a violin. The violinist was a member of the Buras family. He was a jovial old man, short and stout, who patted his foot as he fiddled. As for baseball, although the population was small and there was just enough dry, open ground for a small diamond, two teams did exist and played in good-natured competition throughout the long summer days.[33]

Monroe Jackson liked to cook a seafood supper and invite several of his friends to play cards and drink red wine. On these occasions, Oliver and Eric heard many a tall tale told by the supper guests. The stories ranged from disasters at sea to funny incidents in work along the river to the antics of some marsh or sea creature the narrator had encountered.

Somewhere among all these activities, Oliver passed what was in those days a major milestone in a boy's life: he acquired his first pair of long pants. He purchased them from one of the itinerant merchants. Now that he was out of school, working and earning money, he felt he was entitled to dress and be treated as a grown-up. (Neither he nor Eric attended the small school at Port Eads. They were satisfied with the basic knowledge of reading, writing, and arithmetic that the sisters had drilled into them.)

Another rite of passage was less gratifying. One weekend not long after getting his new pants, Oliver decided to ride the mail boat up to the village of Olga to visit his eldest sister, Rosaline, and her husband, Hugh Kelley. By this time, Rosaline was the mother of half a dozen children. Oliver was greeted by his nieces and nephews, and even got to hold the youngest baby on his lap, the first time he had ever handled an infant. Rosaline prepared a large dinner, and Hugh served wine to complete the specialness of the visit. Oliver had never drunk wine before, not even with his father's card-playing friends. But now he was a man in long pants, out and about in the world. He imbibed freely and talked about his life in the orphan home. After a time he found he had trouble making the words sound right; then his eyes refused to focus. The next thing he knew, it was morning. He had passed out. Rosaline and Hugh, who had realized too late how intoxicated he was, had wrapped him in a blanket with a pillow under his head on the floor. He slept quietly all night. Rosaline fixed a hardy breakfast to counteract any hangover he might have. After a sheep-

32. *Ibid.*, No. 4, p. 1.
33. *Ibid.*, 2.

ish farewell, Oliver headed back downriver on the mail boat, wiser in the effects of wine than he had been before he put on long pants.

When he had been at Port Eads almost a year, Oliver got a job as a messboy helping the cook at the bar pilots' camp. He washed dishes and waited on tables for the pilots, and he was required to live on the premises. It paid more than the job in the store, so he was satisfied. But the easy pace of his life was soon to be thrown out of order. Mary Buras Jackson, the young wife of Oliver's Uncle John, died in childbirth along with her newborn infant.[34] John took their bodies up to Buras Cemetery, between Boothville and Venice, for burial. He was inconsolable. The couple had been married barely three years. Mary, a strikingly beautiful woman, had still been in her early twenties.

John Jackson tried to carry on. But Port Eads was too small. Mary's memory was everywhere. He decided to take the money he had saved to build her a house someday and go up to Algiers. He thought he would open a barroom there. He asked his brother Monroe to come with him. Monroe agreed, and he and Eric packed their few belongings and accompanied John on the journey upriver.

Oliver was left on his own at the bar pilots' station. A few months later, he had an argument with the cook and quit his job. Perhaps his differences with the cook actually went that deep, or perhaps Oliver was simply lonesome for his father and Eric—he had never been separated from his brother before in his entire life.[35]

Whatever his real reason for leaving may have been, Oliver got a ride to Port Eads and boarded the mail boat for Buras, where he caught the train for Algiers. The halcyon days at Port Eads were over. He would never come back to live there again. But he would always remember it fondly. It had been a safe and snug harbor at a crucial time in his adolescence.

34. *Ibid.*, No. 3, pp. 15–16.
35. *Ibid.*, No. 4, p. 3.

5

HARD TIMES IN NEW ORLEANS
1912 – 1914

When Oliver got off the train at the Algiers depot of the New Orleans, Fort Jackson, and Grand Isle Railroad, he walked the few blocks to 419 Patterson Avenue, where his uncle John had opened a barroom. Facing the Mississippi River on Algiers Point, Patterson Avenue was a likely address for such an establishment. It had approximately two dozen saloons strung along its sixteen-block length.[1] Uncle John's establishment, in addition to its liquid refreshment, featured an oyster shop on the premises. After Oliver's arrival in Algiers, he was put to work opening and selling oysters. He also made oyster-loaf sandwiches that his father and uncle sold in the bar and around the neighborhood. Monroe, Sr., was working for John as a bartender.[2]

The saloons on Patterson Avenue catered to thirsty and hungry pedestrians who commuted to and from work via the nearby Canal Street Ferry. Many customers were employed by the nearby United States Naval Station, or by the giant Southern Pacific Railroad or the smaller New Orleans, Fort Jackson, and Grand Isle, both of which had depots and yards along the upper reaches of the riverfront close to Patterson. Numerous small dry docks and coalyards scattered along the Algiers riverfront also supplied patrons for Patterson Avenue establishments.

By 1913 the Jacksons had moved around the corner to 247 Atlantic Avenue, where Uncle John had rented a large two-story house with an upper balcony supported by wooden posts. Customers tied their horses to these posts while they came in for a beer or whiskey—a practice that gave the building something of the appearance of the Old West. Even the policeman on the beat, who rode a beautiful brown horse, stopped in for a

1. David L. Fritz and Sally K. Reeves, *Algiers Point: Historical Ambience and Property Analysis of Squares Ten, Thirteen, and Twenty, with a View Toward Their Archeological Potential* (New Orleans, 1983), 36. Fritz and Reeves prepared this analysis for the U.S. Army Corps of Engineers.

2. Jackson Transcripts, No. 4, p. 5.

beer when he went off duty. The Jackson living quarters consisted of a few rooms behind the bar and had access to a bricked patio in the center of the building.[3]

John and Monroe were in business together as the "Jackson Brothers." They even sold whiskey under their own label. It was purchased in large barrels from a distillery. Oliver and Eric had the task of pouring the liquor into pint and quart bottles, then pasting on labels advertising that the contents were bottled by the Jackson Brothers.[4]

After the oyster shop closed for the evening, Oliver liked to read long into the night. He loved adventure dime novels and sports magazines. *The Wild West Weekly: A Magazine Containing Stories, Sketches, Etc. of Western Life* was his favorite. He bought every new issue. It featured a brawny hero named "Young Wild West"—"Wild," as he was called in the stories—a typically tall, silent, clean-living young westerner who fought rampaging Indians, foiled train robbers, outwitted crooked gamblers, and put claim-jumping prospectors in jail. Some examples of the titles one could read included "Young Wild West's Dangerous Deal; or, The Plot to Flood a Silver Mine"; "Young Wild West and Cayuse Kitty; or, The Queen of the Bronco Busters"; and "Young Wild West's Whirlwind Riders; or, Chasing the Border Thugs."[5]

"Wild" was described in "Young Wild West and the 'Salted Mine'": "Of medium height, perfectly formed and attired in a neat-fitting hunting suit of buckskin, the young fellow made a dashing appearance. A wealth of chestnut hair hung over his shoulders and the sombrero he wore was tipped back on his head in a jaunty fashion."[6] Since Oliver was fond of hats, the rakish sombrero appealed to him, as did Wild's free and easy command of every situation.

Although silent movies existed by 1913, Oliver was not paid much for his chores in the oyster shop. The Jackson brothers' margin of profit was close to the razor's edge, and Oliver's room and board was considered part of his pay. As a result, he was always too out-of-pocket to take in a movie or buy a ticket to the vaudeville or dramatic theaters that flourished in New Orleans. Taking a ride on the First District Ferry (the Canal Street or Algiers Ferry, as it was called) and window-shopping up and down Canal Street on a Saturday night was a diversion he could afford, and one that never seemed to weary him.

3. *Ibid.*, 5–6.
4. *Ibid.*, 5.
5. See, for example, "Young Wild West and the 'Salted Mine,'" *Wild West Weekly*, No. 91 (1904; rpr. Derby, Conn., 1965).
6. *Ibid.*, 9

There was one place where a person with little money could get a couple of beers for a quarter and all the free food he wanted while listening to ragtime and jazz music played all night long. That was in the concert saloons on the fringe of Storyville, the notorious red-light district. When Oliver's cousins Tommy Jackson and Andrew Jackson came up to visit for a few days, Oliver would take them over to the east bank for a night on the town. The three would go into a corner saloon where a jazz band provided music until five or six o'clock in the morning. A table was spread out with food—all kinds of sliced cold cuts (ham, chicken, cheese), pickles, onions, potato salad, and salted nuts. The food was free—for the price of a drink. "You could go in and listen and dance with some of the female customers, buy some beer . . . and eat sandwiches," Oliver recalled.[7] The women customers, he noted, were just that—generally factory girls who came in groups after work to have a few beers and dance—and not prostitutes, who mostly worked Storyville itself.

On their way back to the ferry, the trio might stop off in an all-night photographic studio on Canal Street and have a photo taken as a souvenir of their evening. It was a happy, carefree adventure when Tommy and Andrew came to town. War clouds in Europe, dramatic and tragic changes in their own lives, and the complete destruction of the jaded district they had just witnessed through young, inexperienced eyes were just around the corner. But they didn't know it as they laughed and rode back to Algiers on a late ferry. They were sure there would be lots of other times like this. But the good times came to an end in the summer of 1913.

The barroom on Atlantic Avenue did not make enough profit to keep the Jackson brothers in business. They had so many licenses to purchase—one for cigarettes, one for beer, one for whiskey—that their modest income could not cover these fees plus other expenses in a neighborhood that was already overloaded with saloons. Too few customers selected the Jackson establishment. John and Monroe talked about it, and John concluded: "Well, we just can't keep it up any longer. It's too expensive."[8] So they closed the place.

Uncle John got a job at Todd's shipyard and dry dock. Later, he became captain of one of the transfer ferries that carried railroad cars across the Mississippi River. He also filled out an application with the Crescent River Port Pilots Association to become one of their pilots. These were the men who piloted ships from Pilottown to New Orleans. John and Monroe's brother-in-law George Garrett Vogt, who was married to their sister Ella,

7. Jackson Transcripts, No. 4, p. 10.
8. *Ibid.*, 6.

was a member of the association. He promised to help John get into the group when there was an opening.[9]

Oliver's brother Eric had returned to Port Eads by 1913 to seek a job with the Corps of Engineers. Monroe and Oliver left Algiers and moved to the east bank of New Orleans, looking for work along the river. They drifted up and down the riverfront, taking longshore work for a few days at a time unloading fruit ships. They found cheap rooming houses where they could pay by the night for a bed—twenty-five cents was the usual fee. The duress of job-hunting finally forced them to part company. Monroe found work downtown and roomed nearby. Oliver moved uptown into the Irish Channel, with which he was familiar. He stayed for a while on Laurel Street, near his old orphan home.[10] He got a job as a collier loading and unloading coal for Powell and Company in the 500 block of Carondelet.[11] But the job did not last. Nor did others, as Oliver recalled:

> I just knocked around town. I never had any money. I'd pick up a few dollars here and there maybe doing some little odd work on the riverfront. . . . You'd always get a job on the riverfront. You'd go carry bananas for Vacarro Brothers, and on the uptown side [of Canal Street] was the United Fruit Company—the big white ships. If there were no ships in down there [at the Vacarro Brothers wharf], well, you could go up all the way to Thalia Street and there were always ships laying up there unloading. You could always get a job carrying bananas or sorting out bunches of bananas. . . . It didn't pay much money, but it paid enough to get along, to get by.[12]

Perhaps even this rather dreary picture was a bit too rosy, for Oliver concluded his reminiscence: "It was a hard, hard time. . . . No work. No money. Nothing. I didn't have the second pair of pants, or the second pair of drawers to put on."[13]

The most desperate point in his hand-to-mouth existence came when Oliver went several days without finding work and had dwindled his funds down to about twenty-five cents. He turned from the riverfront to the French Market for possible employment. One of the few things he had kept with him from his days in the oyster shop was an oyster knife. It now proved to be an asset in getting him a job opening oysters at a French Market booth. Even though the other openers used the Boston method of opening oysters, which was with a hammer, Oliver's skill with the knife

9. *Ibid.*, 9.
10. *Soards' New Orleans City Directory, 1914* (New Orleans, 1914), 593.
11. *Ibid.*
12. Jackson Transcripts, No. 4, p. 10.
13. *Ibid.*

convinced the owner of the stall to hire him. He was told to show up the next morning.[14]

With only a quarter in his pocket, Oliver had to make a decision whether to get a bed in a rooming house in Exchange Alley or save the money for breakfast. He decided to keep it for breakfast, which meant he had to find some sleeping place out-of-doors—the first time in his seventeen years of life that he had done this. Walking down the uptown side of Canal Street toward the river, where he thought he might find a spot on the wharves, he noticed a large cardboard box that had been put out on the sidewalk in front of a chinaware store. After examining it, he crawled inside and fell asleep.[15]

Sometime in the middle of the night he was awakened by two policemen. "What are you doing there?" they asked. He explained that he only had twenty-five cents and was saving that for coffee and doughnuts the next morning. He gave them the name and address of the French Market oyster dealer for whom he would be working. "What's that in your pocket?" one of the policemen asked, seeing the bulge of his knife. "That's my oyster knife that I use to open oysters," Oliver replied. They stepped away from him and talked awhile in low tones. Finally, one turned back to Oliver and told him, "All right, go on back in there and go to sleep." Oliver was relieved and grateful. "I'll be out of here by daylight," he promised.[16]

The next morning, Oliver awoke by five o'clock and walked down to the French Market, where the carts and wagons with fresh vegetables and crates of live chickens were beginning to arrive from the country. After his breakfast of café au lait and doughnuts, he went to work opening oysters. He had made it through the night one more time.

The French Market was a complex of buildings dating back to the first quarter of the nineteenth century. Stretching from Jackson Square down to the back of the Old Mint, it had several sections with massive columns and high-pitched roofs. Another section had slim iron posts holding up its roof. The buildings were open on all sides, and a variety of awnings protected the vendors and their customers from sun and rain. By midmorning the market would be bustling with sellers, buyers, and tourists. The sounds of the market combined into an incomprehensible babble of vendors and customers exchanging comments, live chickens, ducks, and turkeys squawking from their crates, and carriages and carts creaking back and

14. *Ibid.*, 7.
15. *Ibid.*
16. *Ibid.*, 7–8.

forth to deliver or pick up produce. There were over five hundred booths in the three main areas of the market—the meat and fish market, the vegetable market, and the dry goods market.[17]

The fish and oysters sold in the booth where Oliver worked were delivered fresh each day from the lower end of nearby Picayune Tier, a landing fronting Jackson Square and running several blocks downriver. It had long been the gathering place for luggers that brought fish, oysters, shrimp, and oranges to the French Market from the Lower Coast and from bayous in southern Louisiana. The part of the wharf given over particularly to the lugger landing by 1913 was at the foot of Ursuline Street. Luggers with their broad four-sided sails were a colorful sight lying side by side along the dock, but their numbers had diminished since the turn of the century.[18]

Oliver kept the job at the French Market for several months. Although he was surrounded by the powerful odor of fish and discarded oyster shells, he liked the parade of humanity the market attracted. It was never boring there. Then his father showed up one day and persuaded him to go back to the riverfront with him and unload bananas. With their combined salaries, they could afford a room in a boardinghouse downtown on St. Ferdinand Street near Chartres.[19]

Unloading bananas was a hot and strenuous job. The hardier and more adventuresome longshoremen were paid extra to go down into the hold of the ship and haul the heavy bunches up to the deck on their shoulders. Others would carry the bunches to the wharf. Going into the hold meant entering the hottest and darkest spot imaginable, where tarantula spiders sometimes nestled among the stacked bananas. Despite the danger and discomfort, Oliver did it for the extra money. On the dock stood wooden barrels filled with river water and big chunks of ice. The banana carriers, streaming with sweat, stopped occasionally to gulp water from these barrels with a cup. When they got a lunch break, Oliver and Monroe might buy a sandwich and a soft drink from a vendor who brought his pushcart out on the dock to sell to the longshoremen.[20]

The two men worked at this job from the hot, humid days of autumn,

17. For descriptions of the French Market, see *New Orleans City Guide*, 151, 255; Jackson, *New Orleans in the Gilded Age*, 12; and Marion S. Oneal, *Garlic in My Shoes* (Philadelphia, 1969), 107–10. The layout of the French Market buildings is in *Sanborn Insurance Map of New Orleans, Louisiana, 1908* (7 vols.; New York, 1908–1909), II, 112.

18. *New Orleans City Guide*, 282. For the location of the lugger landing in the early 1900s, see *Sanborn Insurance Map of New Orleans, 1908*, II, 111.

19. Jackson Transcripts, No. 4, p. 8, 11.

20. *Ibid.*, 10–11.

1913, into early 1914. One night that winter, Oliver began to feel feverish despite the penetrating cold weather. He ached all over and was too weak to get out of bed. Monroe became deeply concerned and went to get a doctor. His eldest son, Monroe, Jr., had died in New Orleans three years earlier, at only twenty-one, from tuberculosis.[21] But Oliver had always been strong and healthy. Monroe was worried seeing him so sick.

The doctor realized immediately that Oliver was seriously ill. "He's got to go to the hospital right away," he told Monroe. They called for an ambulance to take him to Charity Hospital on Tulane Avenue. When it arrived, the driver came up to Oliver's second-floor room and explained the situation: "I have a colored woman in the ambulance down there on my way to the hospital. Now do you want to ride in the ambulance with her or do you want to wait and I'll come back and get you?" Segregation was an ironclad rule, even for the indigent sick, in 1914. But Oliver thought it was nonsense to wait. "No, pick me up and let's go," he told the driver. When they arrived at the hospital, the woman was taken off to a "colored" ward and Oliver was carried upstairs to the isolation ward for infectious diseases. He was diagnosed as suffering from malaria and typhoid fever. His working on the mosquito-ridden riverfront and drinking tainted water—which had been scooped up alongside the dock where ships discharged their wastes—were about to take a heavy toll.[22]

In the hospital, Oliver's fever went up and he became delirious. He drifted in and out of consciousness. His memories of his illness were sketchy: "I was in a room, a ward, and there must have been, I imagine, about twelve other patients. I do remember coming to once in awhile [for] a few hours or a day. . . . I'd see them carrying patients in and carrying them out—dead. They were dying like flies up there. . . . A man died in the bed right next to me. Half of the time I didn't know what it was all about. I was out of my mind there."[23]

Monroe came to the hospital faithfully to check on Oliver's condition, but only once did they allow him into the isolation ward—and then only because they thought Oliver was going to die that night. Oliver was given the last rites of the Catholic church, and the mattress was changed under him. But he held on. By morning he was stronger and his fever began to fall. He was going to make it.

To control his high fever during the crisis period, the nurses and order-lies had taken a bed sheet, dipped it in a tub of ice water, wrung it out,

21. *Ibid.*, 11; Obituary for Monroe Jackson, Jr., in New Orleans *Daily Picayune*, March 4, Sec. 1, p. 4. March 5, Sec. 2, p. 6, 1911.

22. Jackson Transcripts, No. 4, p. 11.

23. *Ibid.*

and wrapped Oliver in it with ice bags under his arms. When the fever finally broke and he regained consciousness, one of the nurses told him, "Your fever was up round a hundred seven a couple of times. I don't know why you're still here. You were pretty bad off. You have a wonderful constitution."[24]

Recuperation took a long time. Oliver spent several months in the hospital:

> I lay in bed and lying in bed so long on my back, I got bedsores and boils that broke out on me. Boils on the side of my hip and then boils came out on the other side—great big boils on both hips. So I had to lay on my stomach for a while and when I was lying on my stomach, I got a couple of boils right on my chest. I'd twist, I'd put my arms underneath to keep from touching the bed. But every once in a while my arms would twist over, and I'd touch the bed . . . it hurt me. Oh, suffer![25]

As the weather got warmer, the large windows were opened to give the patients fresh air. Since there were no screens, insects entered freely. Mosquitoes were kept at bay though the use of mosquito nets on some beds at night. But flies were everywhere in the daytime. To relieve the patients of this nuisance, an old orderly came through the ward with a flyswatter. When he got to Oliver's bed, he would swat the flies even if they were crawling on Oliver's leg or hip or arm. One day he hit one on top of the sheet, but underneath Oliver had a tender bedsore on his leg. Wild with pain, Oliver blew up: "Damn you, don't be hitting me with that damned flyswatter." A Sister of Charity standing nearby heard the altercation and came over to scold Oliver: "Wait a minute! You can't use that kind of language here." "Doggone it," Oliver replied, managing to find a milder expletive, "he's swatting the flyswatter and hitting me and I got my leg and hip that are all sore."[26]

As he grew stronger, he was allowed to sit up in a chair for a short time, which grew longer each day. In time, the nurse began taking him for a short daily walk in the ward. Later, she helped him down the hall and out on the gallery overlooking the courtyard. Finally, he was strong enough to be led downstairs to stroll around the courtyard itself.[27] Although the old hospital, completed in 1832, was crowded and the doctors and nurses were overworked, Oliver received magnificent treatment. The nuns, known as "God's geese" because of their white-winged headgear, were models of

24. *Ibid.*, 12.
25. *Ibid.*
26. *Ibid.*
27. *Ibid.*, 13.

efficiency and dedication in the administration of the hospital. In 1912 a lay administrator had replaced the legendary Sister Stanislaus as superintendent of the hospital. But she and the other sisters were still very much involved in the day-to-day operation of Charity.[28] Oliver was the beneficiary of the combined experience and skills of the medical team working in the isolation ward.

The stronger he grew, the more Oliver looked forward to getting out of the hospital. But going back to his bare room on St. Ferdinand Street was out of the question. To recuperate fully, he would need good food and special attention for several months after he was discharged. Luckily, his aunt Aggie Castell, his father's sister, had moved to New Orleans with her family and was living downtown on Montegut Street. She invited Oliver to come to her house for his convalescence.

The day he was released, Oliver did not contact anyone to help him. His father was working on the docks, and he didn't feel he should bother anyone else. The only clothes he had were the ones he had worn to the hospital when he was admitted. The wool suit hung on him, revealing the many pounds he had lost. His black felt hat came down loosely to his ears—the hospital policy had been to shave his head and keep it shaved even after he became an ambulatory patient; this was done for hygienic reasons—to avoid lice and to bathe and clean him more easily. After a few thank-yous to the nurses who had helped to save his life, Oliver walked out of Charity Hospital and made his way down Tulane Avenue to South Rampart Street. He had come to the hospital without a cent in his pocket; therefore, he couldn't catch the streetcar on Rampart, which would have taken him downtown near his aunt's house. Instead, when he reached Canal Street, he decided to head for the riverfront, where there would be a breeze blowing. He also longed for the sight of the mighty Mississippi. After resting for a few minutes against a showcase at Rampart and Canal, he headed slowly down Canal for the river:

> I'd walk a block and stop. I'd rest a little bit. Then I'd walk a little more. I remember walking out to the foot of Canal Street on the uptown side and sat there . . . on the docks. I got up and crossed over Canal Street to the lower side of Bienville Street. When I got to Bienville Street, I sat down on the docks, and there was a big Morgan ship laying there. I sat down on the docks by the stern, the back part of the ship, looking up at the ship and looking out at the river. . . . I had this winter suit on that fit me like a wrap-around, it was

28. Marjorie Roehl, "Change Is Part of Charity's History," New Orleans *Times-Picayune*, June 7, 1981, Sec. 1, p. 15. For a full account of Charity Hospital, see Stella O'Connor, "The Charity Hospital at New Orleans: An Administrative and Financial History," *Louisiana Historical Quarterly*, XXXI (January, 1948), 5–109.

so big, and this big old felt black hat. All of a sudden, the breeze came along . . . and took it off my head and overboard it went. . . . I sat on the dock and looked down and I didn't know whether to cry or laugh. I could see it—it went into the water—and all of a sudden, it started going down slow, slow, and it went down and sunk. There I was with no hat and bald-headed, like a bald-headed eagle.[29]

After the loss of his hat, Oliver got up again and began walking downtown along the docks as far as Governor Nicholls Street and Esplanade Avenue. There he sat and rested for a long time. When he resumed his journey, he headed down to Elysian Fields Avenue. He knew how to reach his aunt's house by one of the streets that crossed Elysian Fields. But before he reached the desired street, he passed some men working on the railroad track that ran down the neutral ground on Elysian Fields. This was the Pontchartrain Railroad. Its locomotive was known as Smoky Mary and pulled rail cars out to Milneburg, a resort area on Lake Pontchartrain. It was the oldest line in the city.[30]

Oliver never forgot the impression he made on the railroadmen. It remained one of the most painful moments in his life:

There were some men working on the tracks, oh, five or six of them, I guess. They all stopped working and looked at me. I looked over at them, and oh, I felt ashamed. I felt like I could sink through the banquette there. . . . I didn't have a hat on and my hair [was] all shaved off. I guess they thought I was an escaped convict or something or a poor old sick devil—one of the two. I don't know what they thought. But I walked on and I kept on going until I got . . . to my aunt's house . . . and knocked on the door. She came out to the front door and opened it and said, "Where in the name of God did you come from?" And I said, "I come from the hospital." She said, "Who brought you down?" I said, "Nobody. I walked down." "You walked down," she said. "Why didn't you call somebody? You sure got nerve." I said, "Yeah, they discharged me and I walked down. . . . I been a long time coming because I had to stop and rest." And she said, "Come on in here. . . . I guess you're hungry and want something to eat."[31]

Oliver slowly regained some of his energy eating the home-cooked meals of his Aunt Aggie. He counted himself lucky to be alive. The last year, since the summer of 1913, had been one with funereal overtones for the Jackson family. Oliver's eldest sister, Rosaline Jackson Kelley, had died in September, 1913, leaving six young children, who were placed in or-

29. Jackson Transcripts, No. 4, pp. 13–14.
30. *Ibid.*, 14.
31. *Ibid.*

phanages in New Orleans. During Oliver's stay in Charity Hospital, his grandmother, Sarah Celeste Buras Jackson, Captain Andy's widow, had passed away in New Orleans at the home of her daughter, Ella Vogt.[32] She was buried downriver near Buras.

While Oliver was staying at the Castells', he got a letter from his sister Sarah, who was married by this time to a young man named Mike Budenich. Her husband had worked for the Corps of Engineers at Port Eads. Now they were living on Southwest Pass, which the Corps had deepened for larger ship traffic by constructing a jetty system similar to that of South Pass. Sarah invited Oliver to stay with her and her family until he regained his strength.[33] Memories of the sea breeze, the sand and surf, the lazy, cloudless days he had spent at Port Eads made him accept her invitation. In late summer, 1914, Oliver headed back down the Mississippi on the *El Rito*. He left behind bitter experiences of poverty, loneliness, and sickness close to death.

32. Information on Rosaline's death was compiled through several conversations with her daughter, Loretta Armshaw, in 1981. Sarah Celeste's death notice appears in the New Orleans *Times-Picayune*, February 14, 1914, Sec. 1, p. 6.

33. Jackson Transcripts, No. 4, p. 14.

6

WORKING FOR THE BAR PILOTS
Southwest Pass and the *Underwriter*

After Oliver had been living about two weeks at his sister Sarah's house on Customhouse Bayou, a tributary of Southwest Pass, he felt as if he had never been away from the mouth of the river. The desperate struggle of day-to-day existence in New Orleans and his terrible battle to overcome typhoid fever receded rapidly from his conscious mind. He was young and had a basically optimistic disposition. It was a key factor now in his recuperation.

In the peace and quiet of Customhouse Bayou, broken only by seabirds' cries and the motors of occasional Corps of Engineers vessels dredging or doing other work in Southwest Pass, he slept soundly and ate well, went fishing and crabbing, and enjoyed the companionship of Sarah, her husband, Mike, and their three little girls. Mike Budenich was of Croation descent and was one of a number of young men whose fathers or grandfathers had come in the mid-nineteenth century from the coastal area of what was later Yugoslavia and found a life for themselves and their families as fishermen along the Lower Coast of Louisiana. Oliver often went fishing for flounder with his Budenich in-laws.

There were just two houses left standing on Customhouse Bayou in 1914. They were owned by a Mrs. Butcher. The houses were set back on the bayou about a block from the river. Sarah and Mike rented one of them. The old lady herself lived in the other with her widowed daughter. Along the banks of the bayou, Oliver could discern the foundations of former dwellings, only remnants of which were left.[1] Customhouse Bayou itself had been sealed off from the river by the Corps of Engineers as part of their jetty operations, and the bay side of the bayou had silted up so that boats could not come in that way anymore.

In the nineteenth century a revenue station had been built on the bayou near the river—hence the name "Customhouse." Nearby, other buildings, perhaps four to six, had dotted the banks of the bayou.[2] Down

1. Jackson Transcripts, No. 4, p. 14, and No. 5, August 7, 1981, pp. 1–2.
2. *Ibid.*, No. 5, pp. 1–2. For indications of where and how many houses had once been

Southwest Pass about a mile was Pilot Bayou, where a small community of pilots and fishermen had existed from the 1830s to about 1900. In the 1830s it had boasted approximately seventy residents. By 1861 there were some thirty houses along Pilot Bayou, at least seven of them impressive two-story dwellings with upstairs porches protected by overhanging roofs. The settlement had been called "South West Balize" in the 1830s, "Pilotsville" on the 1845 map of La Tourette, and "Pilot Lookout" (Pilot's Lookout) on an 1891 United States Coast and Geodetic Survey map. But it too was in ruins by 1914.[3]

Oliver was impressed by the breath and majesty of Southwest Pass as compared with South Pass. Whereas South Pass was fourteen miles long with its width varying from 530 to 850 feet, Southwest Pass was nineteen and a half miles from the Head of Passes to the Gulf, and its width varied from 1,190 to 4,950 feet. The average width was about 2,000 feet. Its ship channel, however, was shallower than the narrow South Pass.[4] South Pass had a depth of 30.5 feet in its channel by June of 1915. The Southwest Pass ship channel never exceeded 28 feet. The Corps of Engineers, however, considered that their work to create a 35-foot channel (1,000 feet wide) in Southwest Pass was about 69 percent complete by 1915.[5] The large, powerful dredge boat *Benyaurd* and its alter ego, the *New Orleans*, took turns dredging the mouth of Southwest Pass and other strategic sites along the pass and upriver. In the fiscal year 1914–1915, these two dredges removed over 3,800,000 cubic yards of material from the river depths in the lower seven miles of Southwest Pass.[6]

Southwest Pass as a viable entry route for seagoing vessels dated back to the early nineteenth century. Thomas Jackson, the probable founder of Oliver's family in Plaquemines Parish, had received a pilot's license in 1828 from Governor Henry Johnson and in 1833 had purchased a small dwelling with furnishings on Southwest Pass and a whaleboat to take him out to ships waiting to cross the bar.[7] The first lighthouse on Southwest Pass to aid such pilots was built on Waggoner's Island (Middle Ground

---

located on this bayou, see map, *Louisiana West Delta Sheet,* compiled by H. L. Baldwin, Jr., from surveys by U.S. Coast and Geodetic Survey in 1891.

3. Goodwin *et al., Evaluation of the National Register Eligibility of Burrwood,* 80. The Coast and Geodetic Survey map is *ibid.,* 51.

4. *Annual Report of the Chief of Engineers, U.S. Army,* 1915, I, 797, 801.

5. *Ibid.,* 799, 803.

6. *Ibid.,* II, 2565.

7. The pilot license of Thomas Jackson, dated March 31, 1828, is in his succession papers in the Plaquemines Parish Courthouse. So are an 1833 bill of sale by Thomas Holden to Thomas Jackson for a house and its contents on an island off Southwest Pass called Holden's Island, and an inventory, dated July 20, 1834, of the furnishings left in the house after Jackson's death.

Island) at the mouth of the pass, but the ground eroded around it and the structure collapsed into the river in 1838. A second lighthouse was constructed that same year on the west bank of Southwest Pass adjacent to Fitzgerald's Bayou. It settled with the passage of time and by 1914 was an abandoned relic surrounded by water in West Bay. The third lighthouse was built between 1869 and 1871 on Middle Ground Island. Eventually this small island was joined to the main west bank of the pass by the Corps of Engineers through the closing of Nine Foot Channel. The lighthouse was similar in appearance to the one at Port Eads.[8] During his sojourn on Southwest Pass, Oliver became friends with Jake Hanson, whose family lived in the lighthouse and operated it in the early 1900s.

In addition to the lighthouses built to aid navigation in and out of Southwest Pass, the federal government in the nineteenth century attempted to do something about clearing the mudbars that clogged the mouth of the pass at high-water time. In the late winter and early spring, floods from upriver sent millions of tons of silt churning down the river. Some of it settled at the mouths of the passes—enough that Southwest Pass might clog up to a depth as shallow as nine to thirteen feet across the bar. Ships outside the pass were unable to enter, and those in the river attempting to reach the Gulf had to anchor and wait for the bar to erode. Later in summer, when the river was low, the bars might correct themselves. The silt would be carried away, deepening the channel. Then ship traffic was busy going in and out of Southwest Pass.[9]

Despite the self-correcting properties of the bars at the Mississippi's mouth, merchants in New Orleans wanted a river passage open to commerce throughout the year. With the coming of railroads in the 1830s, the business community was apprehensive of losing the city's prominent place as a national port. Railroads might siphon off Mississippi Valley commerce to eastern ports if trading through New Orleans were not made cheaper by assuring ready access through the Mississippi Passes.[10]

In 1836 and 1837, Congress appropriated funds for improving the entrances to the river. The Corps of Engineers was given the task of achieving this goal. In 1837 attempts were made, without success, to deepen Southwest Pass by using a bucket drag. In the 1840s, Pilotsville on South-

8. Goodwin et al., Evaluation of the National Register Eligibility of Burrwood, 82–84. Photographs of lighthouses at Southwest Pass appear in Department of Transportation, U.S. Coast Guard, Lighthouses and Lightships of the Northern Gulf of Mexico (Washington, D.C., n.d.), 34–35.

9. Walter M. Lowrey, "The Engineers and the Mississippi," Louisiana History, V (Summer, 1964), 233–34.

10. Ibid., 238.

west Pass prospered, and smaller ships coming from the western Gulf used this outlet. As Southeast Pass silted and hurricanes decimated the American Balize at its head, some pilots at the Balize moved upriver to Pilottown or to Southwest Pass. The vessel traffic on Southwest Pass increased steadily. In 1852 the federal government entered into a contract with a private company, the Towboat Association, to harrow and stir up the bottom of Southwest Pass to remove silt. The goal was to achieve a channel of 18 feet deep and 300 feet wide. This procedure was successful for a year, but the results were not permanent.[11]

In 1856 another act of Congress authorized the building of a jetty along Southwest Pass. The attempt to construct it failed because the materials used were too fragile and were rapidly undermined by the river. Round pilings were placed in a single line fifteen feet apart, tied together by four-by-eight stringers, and sheeted with tongue-in-groove pine planks to form a jetty out from Southwest Pass. Most of this wall was soon damaged in storms and scattered as flotsam and jetsam down the pass. Sea worms devoured the remaining pilings. To the Corps of Engineers, the very word *jetty* became an embarrassment, and the building of jetties at the river's mouth was a closed matter as far as they were concerned. Fortunately for vessels using it, Southwest Pass scoured its own bar, and the firm that had the contract to build the jetties turned to "stirring up" the silt to achieve eighteen feet of depth. The bar held this depth, with minor fluctuations, until 1859.[12]

The heavy silting of the Southwest Pass mouth in 1859 began two decades of trouble. A mammoth dredge, the *Essayons*, which proved a wretched failure, was built and put into service in 1868. It and other dredges tried unsuccessfully to keep an acceptable depth at the mouths of Southwest Pass and Pass a Loutre, but by 1872 they clearly had failed to keep pace with the silt coming downriver on the spring floods. As a national dialogue developed over which would be better—a canal cut from the Mississippi to the Gulf somewhere near Fort St. Philip or jetties along one of the passes—it seemed at first that most businessmen in New Orleans and most army engineers favored the canal. But one of the engineers, General John G. Bernard, fought for the jetties.[13] The civilian engineer who finally turned the federal government to this point of view was, of course, James B. Eads. As noted earlier, he had at first suggested placing the jetties on Southwest Pass, which was the main pass used by

11. *Annual Report of the Chief of Engineers, U.S. Army, 1915*, II, 1847.

12. See Lowrey, "Engineers and the Mississippi," 240–41, and *Annual Report of the Chief of Engineers, U.S. Army, 1915*, II, 1848.

13. Lowrey, "Engineers and the Mississippi," 242–46, 248–55.

vessels in the 1870s. Congress directed the project to South Pass, which had not been of significance to commerce in the past.

The success of Ead's jetties on South Pass took traffic away from Southwest Pass. The revenue station at Customhouse Bayou was closed and customs facilities set up at Port Eads. By the 1890s, Pilot's Lookout on Pilot Bayou had lost many of its pilots to the other pass or to Pilottown; it became a ghost town. Then, in 1898, Congress directed the Corps of Engineers to study and perfect a plan to deepen Southwest Pass. The board set up to study this problem proposed building jetties on Southwest Pass to create a channel thirty-five feet deep.[14]

Between 1903 and 1913, the jetties were constructed, eleven bayou outlets from the pass were closed, and (in 1908) a wharf and coal-station buildings were set up on the east bank of the lower part of Southwest Pass, forming the nucleus of the community of Burrwood, which became the coaling and refurbishing center for the dredges that worked the pass.[15] By 1915, Burrwood had coalyards, an icehouse, a machine shop, an office, and approximately twenty-six houses for the families of employees of the Corps of Engineers.[16] The floating plant working out of the settlement included the dredges *Benyaurd* and *New Orleans*, the Corps of Engineers tug *C. Donovan*, the survey boat *Picket*, a floating derrick, a pile driver, and numerous smaller boats and barges. Although Southwest Pass had a depth at its mouth of twenty-eight feet by 1915, it was used by only 13 percent of the ships drawing twenty-five feet or more that left or entered the Mississippi; the other 87 percent still used South Pass. The majority of ships traversing Southwest Pass were small cargo vessels drawing less than twenty-five feet.[17]

To handle ships coming up and down Southwest Pass, the bar pilots stationed one of their pilot boats, the *Underwriter*, at the mouth of the pass near the wing dam at the end of the jetties—or simply "the ends," as this location was called by the pilots. In addition to carrying its crew of a captain, deckhands, engine room engineer, oiler, cook, and messboy, the *Underwriter* was home for two weeks at a time to two or three pilots. Their job was to bring vessels up the pass and into the Mississippi River to Pilottown. Like the bar pilots stationed on South Pass, they also boarded

14. *Annual Report of the Chief of Engineers, U.S. Army, 1915*, II, 1850.

15. Department of War, *Annual Report of the Chief of Engineers, U.S. Army, 1916* (2 vols.; Washington, D.C., 1916), I, 852. A full history of Burrwood appears in Goodwin et al., *Evaluation of the National Register Eligibility of Burrwood*, 99–123.

16. *Annual Report of the Chief of Engineers, U.S. Army, 1915*, I, 798; Goodwin et al., *Evaluation of the National Register Eligibility of Burrwood*, 102.

17. *Annual Report of the Chief of Engineers, U.S. Army, 1915*, I, 799, 800.

ships at Pilottown and guided them downriver. If they were needed at the mouth of Southwest Pass, a small launch would bring them down to the *Underwriter*. They worked two weeks on the lower river and had two weeks off. At all times, there were pilots aboard the *Underwriter*, pilots at Pilottown, and pilots at the South Pass Pilot Station. The *Underwriter* carried two yawl boats, hanging one on each side in her davits. Either of them might be lowered for boarding a ship out in the Gulf.[18]

One day after Oliver had been on Customhouse Bayou for over a month, his brother-in-law Mike Budenich asked him if he wanted a job on the *Underwriter*. The bar pilots were looking for a messboy to help the cook, wash dishes, and clean up the galley after meals. Oliver's answer was a definite yes.[19] He was hired and went to live aboard the pilot boat. In addition to a salary of fifteen dollars a month, he got a bunk, a locker for his meager belongings, and all of his meals. More important to Oliver was the chance to watch the bar pilots in action and to participate, however tangentially, in their everyday activities.

Two bar pilots served as alternating captains of the *Underwriter*. The one who was to have a profound influence upon Oliver and prepare him for a career on the river was Captain Albro P. Michell.[20] He or his counterpart served two weeks on the boat with the next two weeks off. If several ships came up the pass in quick succession and all the *Underwriter*'s pilots were engaged, Captain Michell or the other captain (whoever happened to be on board the *Underwriter* at that time) would take the next ship into the pass and up to Pilottown.

After Oliver worked for two or three months as a messboy, he was transferred to the post of watchman. At night he would take a spyglass and station himself in the pilothouse of the *Underwriter*—during warm weather that spring of 1915, he sometimes climbed up on *top* of the pilothouse—to peer out to sea for incoming ships: "When I'd see ship's lights outside in the gulf—you could see them way out, miles out—I'd see them and I'd watch them, and they'd come on in. Sometimes, they'd turn toward us. When I'd see them do that, I knew that they wanted to come into New Orleans, come into Southwest Pass. But if they kept on

18. Jackson Transcripts, No. 5, pp. 4–5. The most complete discussion of the early history and organization of pilots at the Passes of the Mississippi River is in Salomone, "Mississippi River Bar-Pilotage," 39–52. The term *yawl boat* refers to a lifeboat type of craft. In the nineteenth and early twentieth centuries, there were both river yawl boats and deep-sea yawls, which were larger and sturdier. The ones used on the *Underwriter* were of the deep-sea type; they were always referred to as "yawl boats," not just "yawls."

19. Jackson Transcripts, No. 5, p. 3.

20. *Ibid.*, 4.

going . . . to the west, they'd go to Texas."[21] When Oliver spotted a ship making for Southwest Pass, it was his job to awaken the captain and crew. The pilots took turns in boarding the ships at sea, and the captain would rouse whichever pilot was "on turn" next.[22]

The usual distance from Southwest Pass to approaching ships when they became visible to Oliver was between three and four miles. It usually took the *Underwriter* about twenty-five minutes to reach a ship unless it was far out at sea. The pilot boat moved in to about fifty to one hundred feet from the ship. One of the yawl boats was lowered and a boatman and the pilot jumped in. The boatman rowed over to the ship's side, where deckhands lowered a rope ladder for the pilot. The boatman was thrown a single rope to hold onto to secure the yawl boat to the side of the ship while the pilot climbed the ladder.[23]

The boatman now let go of the ship's rope and rowed briskly back to the *Underwriter*, where he threw the painter (a rope secured to the bow of the yawl boat) to the deck. Immediately, a man on deck threw down the block and tackle—this was one of Oliver's tasks when he was watchman— which the man in the yawl boat grabbed and hooked to his craft. This procedure had to be accomplished while the tug and the yawl boat were going down into the trough of a wave. The boatman jumped out of the yawl boat onto the deck of the tug before it was lifted by the next wave; meanwhile, the men on deck rapidly secured the boat and hoisted it with the block and tackle.[24] This was an extremely precise operation that had to be carried out in exact timing with the wave motion. It required men who were exceptionally quick, strong, and well coordinated.

Most of the boatmen who worked for the bar pilots were natives of the lower river who had worked with boats all their lives. But Oliver was eager to row the big yawl boats. He had gotten his strength back, his hair had grown out, and he was putting on weight. By early summer of 1915, he was promoted to boatman, a job that earned him the sum of thirty-five dollars a month and built his physique into that of an athlete. Once when he went to New Orleans to visit relatives, his Aunt Nan asked him, "What's wrong with your arms? They're all swelled up." He just laughed and told her, "That's muscle from pulling boats for the bar pilots."[25] The pitiful convalescent who a year earlier had wandered down Elysian Fields Avenue and stopped men at work with his appearance was only a memory.

21. *Ibid.*, 5.
22. *Ibid.*, 6.
23. *Ibid.*, 6, 11.
24. *Ibid.*, 11–12.
25. *Ibid.*, 7, 12.

Besides his duties as boatman, Oliver also had to help keep the pilot boat in spit-and-polish condition when there were no ships to board. A more arduous task, which took a rugged half a day about once a month, was loading the coal that fired the *Underwriter's* boiler:

> The *Underwriter*, she burned coal. We'd have to load her with coal. We'd make a trip over to South Pass. We'd . . . make the trip outside since it wasn't too far to go—out in the Gulf. . . . We'd come into South Pass . . . and at the pilot station they had a great big coalyard where the boats brought a coal collier and a whole big barge loaded with coal. They'd bring it down from New Orleans. That coal collier would have a great big chute way up high and they'd bring the coal up and dump it in that chute and shoot it out into the yard. Then they'd always have a lot of coal. Well, we'd go on over there and we'd . . . load the *Underwriter* with coal on one side and fill her up. You'd use a slice bar and slice the coal and make room for more coal coming in. Then they'd turn her around—Captain Albro [Michell] would turn her around. Instead of being level, . . . the *Underwriter* would be listed over . . . all on one side. You had to put coal on the other side. So they'd turn around and when they did, she'd be up high and boy, we'd roll the coal out of the coalyard in a wheelbarrow, each of us would have a wheelbarrow. Sand flies would be eating you up and it would be hot—especially in summer time—and you'd be wiping your face off—it was awful. . . . We'd have to shove those wheelbarrows up a "hill" and then dump that coal in and that's exercise. . . . Finally, we'd get that side filled and the boat would sit straight then.[26]

During 1915 the Corps of Engineers accomplished a number of tasks on Southwest Pass that were to be of crucial importance later in the year. A wooden bulkhead of creosoted pilings and lumber was constructed at Burrwood along the entire length of the station facing the pass, 3,763 feet. Its purpose was to guard against erosion of the bank and give some protection in stormy weather. A second improvement was the filling-in of the Burrwood station with river sand pumped from Southwest Pass by the dredge *Ram.* Begun in December, 1914, this landfill work was complete by April, 1915, and raised the upper half of Burrwood to an elevation of four feet above mean high water. A small levee was built at the back and to the sides of the community to prevent the new earth from washing away into the marshes. The bulkhead served the same purpose fronting the river. A third measure was the building-up of the concrete and stone capping of the jetty superstructure, which had been settling and could be swamped at high tide by water intruding from the Gulf. This work was contracted out to a New Orleans firm in 1914 and completed by June, 1915.[27]

26. *Ibid.,* 8.
27. *Annual Report of the Chief of Engineers, U.S. Army, 1915,* II, 2563–66.

These protections for the little settlement and the jetties at the mouth of Southwest Pass proved invaluable just a few months later—in September to be exact—when a killer hurricane came ashore, bringing a four-foot tidal wave with it up Southwest Pass.

Late summer of 1915 had been a stormy season altogether. Three major storms entered the Gulf of Mexico, eventually striking either Florida or the Texas coast. In the last days of September, the weather bureau at New Orleans began to issue warnings of another tropical storm, which had been spawned in the vicinity of Barbados.[28] At first it had headed into the Gulf traveling west-northwest toward Mexico. Suddenly it turned north and aimed its fury straight for the Louisiana coast and the Mississippi River Passes. The renowned meteorologist Dr. Isaac M. Cline, who had predicted the 1900 hurricane at Galveston, was district forecaster for the United States Weather Bureau in New Orleans. He had messages sent to outposts all along the Louisiana coast warning of the approaching storm. The *Times-Picayune* noted later that "never before, perhaps, in the history of the Weather Bureau, have such general warnings been disseminated."[29]

Burrwood received these weather advisories, and the bar pilots were likewise informed of the impending rough weather, on Tuesday, September 28. The Corps of Engineers prepared for the big blow by filling both its dredges that were then in the pass with river sand and water so that their weight would hold them steady and solid.[30] Then the families living at Burrwood and along Southwest Pass and its little blind outlets were evacuated to these two dredges to wait out the storm. Some others sought shelter in the Southwest Pass lighthouse.

As the tides grew higher and the seas became rougher, the *Underwriter* stubbornly held to its post alongside the jetty wing dam until the dawning of Wednesday, September 29. A small cargo ship had raced ahead of the storm and wanted to enter the pass. The *Underwriter* sailed out into the towering waves and gale to meet her. Oliver served as boatman to row the pilot to the steamer. The waves he had to battle were ten to twelve feet high. Walls of angry gray water rose up and collapsed before and behind him as he struggled to row the yawl boat back to the *Underwriter*. The pilot boat was pitching and rolling violently in the mammoth waves.

28. New Orleans *Times-Picayune*, September 29, 1915, Sec. 1, pp. 1–2. In this issue is a story detailing the weather bureau's early warnings. A map showing the progress of the storm across the Gulf of Mexico from about September 23 through September 29, when it hit Louisiana, is in the October 1, 1915, issue of this paper, Sec. 1, p. 14.

29. New Orleans *Times-Picayune*, September 30, 1915, Sec. 1, p. 2.

30. *Ibid.*, October 1, 1915, Sec. 1, p. 2.

Oliver still did not know how to swim, but this was no time to think about that. He timed his leap and landed safely on the heaving deck.[31]

The *Underwriter* was not built for such seas. Only the skill of the captain and crew got her home. But that was the end: they could not stay moored at the entrance to the pass to face the hurricane. Winds of seventy-five to eighty-five miles an hour—hurricane strength—were predicted. Such forces and the flood tide they brought could easily hurl the little boat onto the stone capping of the jetties and sink her within minutes.

With this in mind, the captain gave an order to head straight up Southwest Pass for Pilottown. Once there, however, he found no safe anchorage. Crowds of other boats had berthed at the Pilottown dock to ride out the storm, and the captain feared the high winds and churning currents of the swollen river might smash them together. He elected to push farther upstream and across the river to the west bank, where he entered the Jump, an opening the Mississippi had cut in the nineteenth century. It led to a network of bayous that eventually found their way to the Gulf. The *Underwriter* went down the main channel, called Grand Pass, and dropped anchor in a secluded spot where there were no other boats or even signs of habitation.[32] The marshes stretched out all around, swollen with rising tides that reduced the landscape to a plain of pulsating dark water. Here and there little islands of high ground could be seen on which marsh creatures tried to take refuge.

The worst part of the storm hit the lower Louisiana coast between 7 A.M. and noon on Wednesday, September 29. Down at Southwest Pass a four-foot tidal wave swept in, covering the newly raised jetties and inundating the little community of Burrwood.[33] No lives were lost there, however; the weighted dredges held steady in the ship channel without incident, and the lighthouse stood firm. Although all of the houses and other buildings received water and some wind damage, the bulkhead and the back levees were a significant factor in keeping the site from being completely eroded. Water was bailed for days and repairs made to houses and levees, but the inhabitants were safe. The *Underwriter* also survived, sturdily remaining afloat in the deepest channel of Grand Pass. Aside from several hours of lurching up and down with the whitecaps in the bayou and get-

31. Jackson Transcripts, No. 5, p. 9.

32. *Ibid.*

33. Goodwin *et al.*, *Evaluation of the National Register Eligibility of Burrwood*, 106. The person interviewed for this study by Goodwin was Eric Jackson, Oliver's nephew and the son of his brother Eric. He remembered his mother, Dora Williams Jackson, who was at Burrwood in 1915, describing the tidal wave, which today would be called a "storm surge."

ting thoroughly drenched while some of them worked on deck to secure the yawl boats and check the boat's general condition, the crew came through unscathed.

Rain and brisk winds continued into the night. It was Thursday, September 30, before the captain felt safe enough to take the *Underwriter* from its refuge in Grand Pass and return to the Mississippi for the journey downstream. The sight that greeted Oliver and his companions was awesome. The river was swollen to the top of the levee, licking menacingly at the willow trees growing along its banks down to Head of Passes. High on the current of the wild river, the men on the *Underwriter* could see over the levees to the floodplain on both sides. Navigation lights and markers along the river were blown down, and finding the true channel was tricky work. Since few inhabitants lived right above the Passes, no one could tell how persons on land had fared; the crewmen could only speculate from the flooding beyond the levees that conditions on both sides of the river above the two forts must be desperate.[34]

Another ominous sign was the debris floating down the river from upstream. It included pieces of fencing, bits of houses, and dead animals—cattle, hogs, and chickens. Large "rafts" of driftwood and dead plants that had piled up along the riverbank were now being swept downriver. On one such raft, Oliver made out a family of raccoons clinging sad-eyed to high branches protruding out of the water.[35] They were doomed—heading for a rendezvous with the open Gulf. It was a poignant reminder of the toll the river could take in flood and storm season on the fragile creatures, both human and animal, who inhabited the marsh along its lower reaches.

The *Underwriter* made Southwest Pass and anchored across from Burrwood near the lighthouse until the weather calmed and the floods subsided, making it possible for the pilot boat to return to its station at the jetties' opening.[36] Getting ships up and down the pass for the next week was a difficult task because the storm and the flooding had obliterated markers along the banks and most lights were out at night.

As ships that had entered the river the day of the hurricane and boats from the Lower Coast arrived at New Orleans, disturbing reports began to be made public about the storm's havoc on the lower Mississippi. The captain of the Southern Pacific Line vessel *Proteus,* which arrived in New Orleans late Thursday afternoon—the day after the storm—told the *Times-Picayune* that his ship had reached the mouth of the river early that

34. Jackson Transcripts, No. 5, p. 10.
35. *Ibid.*
36. *Ibid.*

morning, having dropped into the wake of the storm at an early hour on Wednesday and trailed it toward the coast. The captain described what he had seen at the entrance to the Passes: "At the mouth of the river everything was tangled up and at least two vessels that I know of were stuck fast on the mud banks. Several other ships were riding at anchor, awaiting an opportunity to proceed to sea. The *Mar Cantabrico*, a Spanish vessel, was stuck hard in the mud, and no doubt will require the assistance of at least two powerful tugs to float her. Another vessel which was tossed on a sand bar was the United States Lighthouse boat, but I believe she is not damaged to any extent."[37]

Persons from New Orleans trying to reach Plaquemines Parish by automobile on the east bank got about as far as Caernarvon, where they encountered high water. Some turned back; others took to small skiffs to search for their relatives and friends. One man found two mules to pull his car through the floods. From Caernarvon to English Turn, two or three feet of water covered the road. The living quarters of a prison camp at Caernarvon had been blown down and several of the prisoners had escaped. But the remaining convicts helped in shoring up the precarious levees in the vicinity of the camp.[38]

The quickest way to reach the Lower Coast was by boat. By Thursday night, September 30, the *El Rito*, the Spicuzza Brothers Transportation Company's packet boat, returned to New Orleans with the first full account of the situation down the river. The *El Rito* had left Burrwood at the height of the storm, "after the wind had swung to the southwest and in the face of the storm proceeded up southwest pass." The newspaper account of this dangerous passage gave credit to the resourceful captain: "It was only the cool headedness and able seamanship of Capt. Tom Spicuzza, in command, that saved the vessel, her crew and passengers, and brought them all to a safe harbor near Fort Jackson just alongside the Southern Pacific steamer *Creole*, which had also sought refuge there."[39]

On the morning after the storm, the *El Rito* returned downriver to Venice to see if any assistance was needed. It made stops all along the river checking on damages and human injury—at Boothville, Olga, Buras, Ostrica, and the Doullut Canal area.[40] Everywhere, Captain Spicuzza found communities flooded. Many persons were marooned on high ground or rooftops with only the clothes on their backs. All were wet and hungry. Some needed medical treatment. Local grocery stores to which Spicuzza

37. New Orleans *Times-Picayune*, October 1, 1915, Sec. 1, p. 14.
38. *Ibid.*
39. *Ibid.*, Sec. 1, p. 2.
40. *Ibid.*, October 2, 1915, Sec. 1, p. 4.

delivered supplies along the Lower Coast were either destroyed or badly flooded, with little or no food to offer storm survivors. Each community had a few dead and missing to report. The oyster-canning factory at Ostrica was severely damaged, and all of the summer camps on Bay Adam and the houses along the Doullut Canal were destroyed or flooded. The railroads on both sides of the river were out of commission. As the day drew to a close, Captain Spicuzza realized that he had done what he could to check on the desperate conditions along the river. He headed for New Orleans to make the facts known to the press and to gather food and other supplies to take to the refugees of the storm.

The next day Captain Spicuzza steered back downriver with the precious supplies and clothing. A reporter who accompanied him, Bill Keife, wrote a compelling account of what he saw on this mission of mercy:

> Levees have crumbled away, homes are wrecked, orange groves, rice fields and truck farms are devastated, many head of stock have been drowned and human life has paid a toll in practically all that section of the lower Mississippi coast lying between Myrtle Grove and Buras on the west side of the river and Poydras and Neptune on the east side, as a result of the storm.
>
> For miles and miles, especially on the west bank of the river (which side, incidentally, suffered considerably more than the opposite shore), a thin strip of land, narrowing in spots to a few scant yards, is all that separates the river from the waters of the gulf, which have backed up from behind.
>
> Marooned families, with the live stock which weathered the storm, can be seen on this bit of land. Boats owned by most of these families either have been blown away or sunk. All are cut off from communication and the great majority of them are in need of help, or will be. . . .
>
> Below Buras and Neptune conditions are far better. Probably this section was missed by the fury of the hurricane, or again probably the dense thickets of willow trees which grew on both sides of the levees between Buras and Port Eads broke the force of the wind.[41]

At Pilottown, Keife interviewed Crescent River Port pilot Captain Joseph P. Loga, a native of the Lower Coast and a pilot for twenty-four years. Captain Loga had just brought the United Fruit ship *Abangarez* down from New Orleans to Pilottown. The devastation he had encountered prompted him to tell Keife: "Never before have I ever seen anything to equal it and I live in hopes of never seeing this storm duplicated." On its journey down to Pilottown, the *Abangarez* had passed Captain Spicuzza aboard the *El Rito*. The crew of the big United Fruit vessel had lined the deck to cheer the gallant captain. He and his men were dispensing food and clothing

41. *Ibid.*

and attempting to move refugees to higher ground. Spicuzza was later credited with saving two hundred storm victims after the 1915 hurricane.[42] In one of the darkest hours of its existence as a workhorse packet boat, the faithful *El Rito* had become a legend, and her captain and crew heroes.

While the remote rural areas of the Lower Coast and southwest Louisiana were suffering from floodwaters, New Orleans was also cleaning up after the storm. Hundreds of homes and businesses had been damaged, and a number of small boats and barges lay sunk or disabled in the harbor. The wharves were missing parts of their siding or roofs. The Canal Street Ferry house had partially collapsed, and three men were killed.[43] The outer wall of a veterinary hospital had also collapsed on Rampart Street, killing two men. A third man had been walking by when the wall gave way. An open window fell around him, and he stepped out of the debris unhurt.[44]

Some of the canals in the city had overflowed. Telephone and telegraph service were temporarily cut off. Many city streetcars, as well as trains bound in and out of New Orleans, were at a standstill. One group of passengers on a Southern Pacific train that had been crossing the Mississippi at Avondale aboard the train transfer ferry *Mastodon* were swept downriver with the ferry and stuck on a sandbar almost all day Wednesday before three tugs pulled the transfer boat free and escorted it, with its load of railroad cars and passengers, to a safe landing.[45] Across Lake Pontchartrain on the North Shore, the little community of Frenier was wiped out by the cruel storm. Twenty-five persons died. Most of the dead lost their lives when the depot in which they had sought shelter was demolished. Some survivors had taken refuge in boxcars or, as a last resort, in trees.[46]

As all of the drama and tragedy of the storm was revealed in newspaper articles and through word of mouth, relief funds were raised, and volunteers aided state, parish, and city officials in a cleanup effort. The passes at the lower river were remarkably intact, considering that they had faced the brunt of the storm as it made landfall.

For the remainder of 1915 and on through 1916, Oliver continued to work as a boatman. He also learned to steer the pilot boat under the direction of Captain Albro Michell. Although he had come aboard the *Underwriter*

42. *Ibid.* See also "Funeral of Boat Operator Today," clipping from Centennial Edition, New Orleans *Times-Picayune*, January 25, 1937, Sec. 1, p. 6, in Louisiana Scrapbook 28, 96 (Port), Howard-Tilton Memorial Library, Tulane University, New Orleans.

43. New Orleans *Times-Picayune*, October 1, 1915, Sec. 1, pp. 13–14.

44. *Ibid.*, September 30, 1915, Sec. 1, p. 1, October 1, 1915, Sec. 1, pp. 5, 13.

45. *Ibid.*, September 30, 1915, Sec. 1, pp. 1–2, 6, October 1, 1915, Sec. 1, pp. 1, 13.

46. *Ibid.*, October 1, 1915, Sec. 1, p. 2, October 2, 1915, Sec. 1, p. 5.

with no experience or knowledge of boat or ship handling, the years with the bar pilots proved a valuable education to him. He learned how to handle lines in casting off and tying up, how to splice rope and wire, tie knots, sound the passes, read a compass, steer the boat, and follow the range lights and buoys in and out of the pass. Mastering the yawl boat had been a physical challenge, but one that he enjoyed. The true love of the river and its navigation had taken hold of him just as it had possessed his grandfather, old Captain Andy. By the beginning of 1917, when he was twenty years old, Oliver was a first-rate deckhand whose knowledge of the river and the boat made him a good candidate to become a pilot. With the encouragement of his mentor Captain Albro and some of the other pilots, he began to study maps and charts of the river, hoping to pass the examination for a river pilot's license.

With the entry of the United States into World War I in April, 1917, the country went on a defense-preparedness program. The *Underwriter* was converted to military service, and the bar pilots had to find another pilot boat. They purchased the motor yacht *Kiva* from a doctor in Greenport, on New York's Long Island. Two pilots and a crew were chosen to go to New York and bring the vessel back. Oliver was named one of the deck-hands, along with his friend Tim Lincoln. In addition to the pilots and the deckhands, there were an engineer and a cook.[47]

In July, 1917, the week before the group left by train for New York, Captain Albro escorted Oliver up to New Orleans to the United States Custom House to take the examination before the State Board of Local Inspectors for a pilot license on the lower Mississippi River. It was a written test involving queries about the rules of the road on the river and the location of lights and markers along the banks. Oliver passed and received his license on July 20, 1917.[48] Now he had a vocation and a chance to make something of himself. He was a licensed river pilot. Ironically, the terrible sickness that had almost destroyed him in 1914 had been responsible for sending him down to Southwest Pass to recuperate. By doing so, it had changed his life for the better. Without that turn of events, he might have been trapped in the drudgery of the city docks for the rest of his days.

During this time of change, Oliver had encouragement from another source besides his friends at the bar pilots'—his brother Eric. After returning downriver, Eric had eventually moved to Southwest Pass to work for the Corps of Engineers, and he and Oliver saw each other frequently. Eric

---

47. Jackson Transcripts, No. 6, August 7, 1981, p. 4.
48. *Ibid.*, No. 5, p. 13; No. 6, p. 7.

was grown now—much taller and heavier than Oliver. He did not need his big brother to look out for him anymore. But the two remained close, with a special bond reaching back to their childhood. In October, 1916, at age eighteen, Eric had married a native of the Southwest Pass area, Dora Williams. They would live at Burrwood and in its vicinity on the west bank for the next fifteen years.[49]

As soon as Oliver got his pilot license, one of the bar pilots took him to Pointe a la Hache to see the clerk of court, Frank Lobrano, who was also head of the local draft board. The bar pilots requested that Oliver Jackson be exempted from the draft because he did work vital to the nation's welfare—aiding the pilots in getting ships in and out of the Mississippi River. The request was granted, and within a few days Oliver was on his way to New York to bring back the *Kiva*.[50]

The trip was a broadening experience for Oliver. He had never been outside Louisiana except for his brief stay in Biloxi as a child. He watched the countryside avidly as flat cottonfields turned into the Blue Ridge Mountains. Later, the industrial complexes of the eastern seaboard came into view. Greenport was a beautiful nautical town. The crew stayed there for about ten days getting the yacht ready for the trip home. While the *Kiva* was tied up at the wharf, a group of local girls asked if they might come aboard and dive from the deck. The captain gave permission. Tim Lincoln went swimming with the girls. Oliver, the nonswimmer, watched forlornly from the deck. Finally he could stand it no longer. He called out, "Tim, I'm coming in," and dived from the ship. As he bobbed up to the surface, he began kicking his feet and flailing his arms and spitting out water. Tim quickly swam to a skiff tied to the yacht and rowed to Oliver. "Hold on to this and kick your feet," he directed. Within a day or two, Oliver was swimming well enough to be a part of the bathing parties.[51]

When the *Kiva* left Long Island on July 31, 1917, it followed the Intracoastal Canal down the East Coast. It was a beautiful route and a leisurely one. In Georgia, the bar pilots hired a pilot who knew the area to guide them for a brief stretch. When the *Kiva* reached Jacksonville, Florida, the captain took her outside into the Atlantic Ocean. Oliver was given the job of steering as they rounded the Florida Keys. It was not an auspicious

49. Eric Jackson and Dora Williams were married in a civil ceremony on October 14, 1916, according to their daughter, Ethel Jackson Miller. The location of their house on Southwest Pass is shown on U.S. Coast and Geodetic Survey map, Register No. 4044, of Southwest Pass. Compiled from photographs by Naval Air Service between April and May, 1922.

50. Jackson Transcripts, No. 6, p. 4.

51. *Ibid.*, 4–5.

turn at the helm. The *Kiva* was gasoline powered, and a stern wind was wafting the fumes up to the deck. The sea was rough and the ship was rolling from side to side on heavy swells. The combination of motion and fumes took its toll. Oliver managed to hold out until the boat pulled into Key West. Then he fell into his bunk wretchedly seasick. The cook mixed up his special concoction for the malady and forced him to swallow it. Whatever was in it—the cook wouldn't say—it worked. This was to be the one and only time in his life that Oliver suffered from seasickness. He always blamed it on the gasoline fumes. The *Kiva* reached Southwest Pass on September 4, 1917.[52]

Oliver got his first chance to pilot a ship on Southwest Pass one day when all of the pilots, and finally Captain Albro, had boarded ships to take up the pass. The captain left Oliver in charge and told him that if a small ship came along and wanted to follow the pilot boat in, he could lead it up Southwest Pass. If it drew more than twenty-five feet of water, however, the captain admonished him to send it over to South Pass. Within a short time a ship was sighted out in the Gulf. The pilot boat headed out to meet it. Oliver shouted over a megaphone that there were no pilots to put aboard, but that the captain could follow the *Kiva* into the pass if he wished. The ship was small enough to qualify for this treatment. The captain agreed. Oliver guided the pilot boat down the ranges and into the pass with the ship following close behind. When they got almost up to Head of Passes, the pilot launch from Pilottown came downriver with several pilots aboard. One was put on the ship; the others, including Captain Albro, came aboard the *Kiva*. Oliver was congratulated on the job he had done. His first piloting experience had been by remote control—but a total success.[53]

Unfortunately, being a pilot was not merely a matter of having experience and a license. One also had to belong to the pilots association—and in that respect a problem soon arose. In early 1918 two men from New Orleans came to work aboard the *Kiva*. One was an experienced pilot who had worked with the Local Inspectors in testing candidates for river pilot licenses. The Coast Guard was about to take over that chore, and he was looking for other employment. He was obviously being groomed to become a bar pilot. The other man had no boat experience at all. But he did have political ties to Mayor Martin Behrman and the New Orleans political machine, which the other young men working for the bar pilots lacked. Oliver was certain that this man also would be made a pilot in the

---

52. *Ibid.*, 5–6.
53. *Ibid.*, No. 5, pp. 14–15.

near future.[54] Oliver himself had been promoted to first mate of the *Kiva*, and he aspired to be a regular bar pilot. But whereas the bar pilots sometimes took qualified young men with no blood connections into their limited ranks, they more often trained and elected members of their own families. Now Oliver was torn between his desire to be a pilot and his despair that it would never happen because he did not have the family ties or political connections that might aid in his selection.

He was not the only young crew member disturbed by the arrival of the two newcomers. About four men quit. Oliver debated with himself what he should do. He went to see the president of the bar pilots, old Captain Ben Michell, Captain Albro's father. Oliver asked him point-blank if he had a chance of getting elected a bar pilot. "I don't want to be working here half of my life for nothing," he added. "I want to make something of myself." Captain Michell answered: "You stay here and work and you'll have a chance. It's got to take time."[55]

Oliver interpreted this to mean that he was viewed as too young to be chosen yet. After all, he was only twenty-one and had held his pilot's license for barely a year. But if he took Captain Michell's advice and stayed on the *Underwriter* as its first mate, many more years might go by before his chance came to be elected into the association.

After four years of complete satisfaction with the life on Southwest Pass, Oliver suddenly felt the urge to break away. He had spent over half of his life in orphanages or the remote communities of Port Eads and Burrwood. Now he wanted to seek opportunities in a broader world. He made up his mind to quit. Captain Albro was sympathetic and tried to persuade him to stay. When this failed, he suggested that Oliver might get a mate's ticket and go to sea for a while. "Then come back later," he said. Oliver decided to take this course.[56]

Another factor that probably influenced Oliver's decision to leave was a breakup with his first love. On his days off, Oliver visited his father or brother on South and Southwest passes, made an occasional visit to New Orleans, or caught a pilot's launch up to Pilottown, where he could stay at the bar pilots' quarters. It offered the companionship of other young men working for the pilots with whom he went fishing, and there were also invitations to parties and dances at the homes of Pilottown residents. It was at such a gathering that he met a young girl named Jessie, one of six children of a widowed mother. He began spending most of his free

54. *Ibid.*, No. 5, pp. 15–16.
55. *Ibid.*, No. 5, p. 16.
56. *Ibid.*

time courting her and actually began to think of marriage. The romance soured when Jessie balked at going steady. She was not ready for a serious commitment to Oliver. The two quarreled and ceased seeing each other. The breakup with Jessie would have given Oliver one more reason to leave the lower river.[57]

Oliver had once had his fortune told through a palm reading by the *Underwriter's* cook, a Frenchman who at one time had been a chef at the Roosevelt Hotel in New Orleans. He predicted that Oliver would indeed be a river pilot one day—but not with the bar pilots. Instead he would be farther upriver. He also predicted entanglements of the heart with a dark-haired girl, which would end in disappointment, and with a fair-haired girl, which would be a turning point in his life.[58]

Now Oliver caught a ride on the mail boat to Buras and boarded the train for Algiers. He rode up with one of the bar pilots, Captain Steve Gusina, who tried to persuade him to take a holiday in the city and then go back downriver. This veteran pilot, who had known his grandfather and father, advised him, "Come on back, and don't get mad and quit."[59] Oliver listened respectfully, but his mind was made up. He was determined to find out what going to sea involved. Later, he promised himself, he would return to Southwest Pass and the bar pilots.

That return would never take place. Instead, Oliver was moving toward the future the old French cook had predicted. His years on Southwest Pass had not been wasted, however. The work with the bar pilots and the special tutelage of Captain Albro Michell had taught him the craft of being a river pilot. He had learned the art of guiding a ship into the tricky currents of the river and keeping it in the channel. He had come to love the exhilaration of piloting, of setting the course of a vessel on the mighty Mississippi where the river runs deep.

57. Interview by Michael Steimle with Edna Smith on history of Pilottown, May 1, 1992, Oral History Collection, Southeastern Louisiana University Archives, Hammond; *Thirteenth Census, 1910: Population,* Plaquemines Parish, 61; Author's conversations with Oliver D. Jackson and Alice O'Brien, New Orleans, in the 1970s.
58. Jackson Transcripts, No. 6, pp. 3–4.
59. *Ibid.,* No. 5, p. 16.

Undated view of the Balize at the junction of Balize Bayou and Southeast Pass.
Courtesy of the LaVerna R. and Edwin A. Davis Collection, Southeastern Louisiana
University Archives

"Pilot-Town" in an 1871 sketch by Alfred R. Waud.
Courtesy of the Historic New Orleans Collection, Museum/Research Center, Acc.
No. 1974. 25. 30. 133

Port Eads and the construction of the jetties on South Pass, as drawn by
Frank H. Taylor and published by *Harper's Weekly* in 1878.
Courtesy of the Historic New Orleans Collection, Museum/Research Center, Acc.
No. 1974. 25. 30. 739

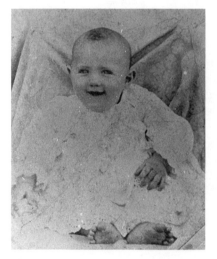

Oliver Jackson at the time he was
baptized by a Methodist minister visiting Port Eads.
Courtesy of the author

Canal Street in New Orleans, *ca.* 1905.
 Courtesy of the LaVerna R. and Edwin A. Davis Collection, Southeastern Louisiana
 University Archives

St. Joseph Orphan Asylum, where Oliver and Eric lived from 1906 to 1910.
 Courtesy of the Redemptorist Fathers

Oliver when he was confirmed in the
Catholic faith, May, 1910.
Courtesy of the author

The *El Rito,* on which Oliver and Eric returned to Port Eads in 1910. The boat
became famous for its rescues during the 1915 hurricane.
Courtesy of the Louisiana Collection, Howard-Tilton Memorial Library, Tulane
University

Monroe Jackson, Sr. (left), and Henry Morgan when they were Customs Service boatmen who rowed the quarantine doctor to and from ships at Port Eads; this was at about the time that Oliver and Eric came back to live with their father.

Lugger Landing. New Orleans, La.

Picayune Tier, the landing in New Orleans where luggers from the Lower Coast of Plaquemines docked to unload fish, oysters, and oranges for the French Market, where Oliver worked.

Courtesy of the Louisiana Collection, Howard-Tilton Memorial Library, Tulane University

"Mastodon," Southern Pacific Ry. Barge, New Orleans, La.

The *Mastodon*, a Southern Pacific Railway transfer ferry at New Orleans. Before the first Mississippi River bridge near the city was completed in 1935, train cars had to be ferried across the river. Oliver's uncle John worked on transfer ferries and probably captained the *Mastodon*.

From the collection of Tom Davidson

The pilot boat *Underwriter* at the bar pilots' wharf on South Pass. Oliver worked aboard the *Underwriter* from 1914 to 1918.
Courtesy of Gilbert Manson, Jr.

Oliver at eighteen or nineteen, when he was working for the bar pilots at Southwest Pass.
Photo by C. Bennette Moore. Courtesy of the author

The *Underwriter* rides a storm. The New Orleans *Times-Picayune* dates the photograph to 1907, but Oliver and at least one other pilot, Captain Jacques Michell, always thought it showed the 1915 hurricane.
Courtesy of the New Orleans *Times-Picayune*

Oliver's brother Monroe Jackson, Jr. (right), not long before his death from tuberculosis. With him are his wife, Louise Pratt, and her brother, name unknown.
Courtesy of the author

Captain Albro Michell, a bar pilot who served as captain of the *Underwriter*. Captain Michell was a friend and teacher to Oliver and encouraged him to learn the profession of piloting.

Courtesy of Albro Michell (nephew)

Oliver in 1921, during his merchant-seaman days. The photo was taken in a park in Honduras.

Courtesy of the author

Oneida Drouant in 1923, at about the time she married Oliver Jackson.
Courtesy of the author

The Venus Street house the Jacksons built in New Orleans in 1925.
Courtesy of the author

Neda and Joy, 1928.
Courtesy of the author

Joy at the beach, about five years old.
Courtesy of the author

The *Inspector* in the crevasse in the levee at Junior Plantation, 1927.
Courtesy of the National Archives, No. 77-MRF-177

The *Corona*, Oliver's favorite among the tugs he captained.
From *History of W. G. Coyle and Co., Inc.*, (N.p., n.d.). Courtesy of Bailey T.
DeBardeleben

Oliver aboard the *Corona* in the mid-
1930s
    Courtesy of the author

The *Donie* navigating the Intracoastal Canal with a tow, 1937.
From the Joseph Merrick Jones Steamboat Collection, courtesy of the Special Collections Division, Howard-Tilton Memorial Library, Tulane University

Eight of the nine New Orleans–Baton Rouge pilots receive state pilot commissions from State Senator Lionel Ott in 1942. Left to right: (seated) Oliver Jackson, Alex Chotin, James Roberts, Harry Koch; (standing) Adolph Schwalb, Charles Jackson, Charles Lauterbach, Eugene Higbee.
Courtesy of the New Orleans *Times-Picayune*

Oliver in his Coast Guard uniform.
Photo by C. Bennette Moore. Courtesy of the author

New Orleans harbor in the 1950s.
Courtesy of the LaVerna R. and Edwin A. Davis Collection, Southeastern Louisiana
University Archives

The giant Standard Oil (now Exxon) refinery on the river at Baton Rouge.
Courtesy of the LaVerna R. and Edwin A. Davis Collection, Southeastern Louisiana
University Archives

Oliver at sixty-seven, when he
retired.
    Courtesy of the New Orleans *Times-*
    Picayune

Oliver fulfills a lifelong dream at
seventy-five: the footbridge spans the
Mississippi River at its headwaters,
Lake Itasca, Minnesota.
    Courtesy of the author

7

THE FLYING DUTCHMAN YEARS
1918 – 1923

When Oliver reached New Orleans, he arranged to board with the Peter Borcich family. Mrs. Borcich, whose maiden name was Mary Denesse, was his cousin. Her father was the half brother of his mother Eliza. The Borciches lived at 2105 Bienville Street. Oliver stayed with them for about two months while he attended a navigation school on Royal Street to prepare himself for a life at sea. After he had learned enough about navigation to apply for and receive a third mate's license, he joined the seamen's union and secured a third mate's job on a ship sailing out of Mobile.[1]

He took a train to Mobile and found the ship to which he had been assigned. The master of the vessel, a Captain Fonton, was a big, husky, friendly man who had been a sailing-ship captain most of his career. But with sail giving way to motorized power almost completely by the second decade of the twentieth century, he had become captain of a steamship engaged in the sugar trade between Cuba and New York. One small hitch developed: Captain Fonton needed a second mate before he could set sail. Nearby was berthed a small Norwegian ship that carried bananas from Central America to the United States. Fonton offered the first mate of the Norwegian vessel the job of second mate on his ship. Since the job would pay him three times what he was making, the man, a native Swede, accepted the offer even though he had been sailing on the little Norwegian ship for almost twenty years. Since he was a foreigner from a foreign-registered vessel, he had to get a special "red ink" license to serve aboard the American ship.[2] Once that detail was out of the way, Oliver's first voyage to sea began:

> We left Mobile and sailed down to [Havana] Cuba. We loaded sugar and we came out [into the open sea]. A storm blew up and got pretty bad and we put into a port in the southern part of Cuba and spent a half a day there. It looked

1. Jackson Transcripts, No. 5, p. 16.
2. *Ibid.*, 16–17.

like the thing had blowed over. So we came on out and came around the southern part of Cuba. We headed for New York and boy, it was rough. I'd never seen it so rough! The water was washing all over the deck of the ship, and the ship was bouncing up and down. Loaded with sugar, there was no way of dumping anything overboard—big sacks of sugar, you know. I was just hoping that it wouldn't start leaking. The water washed from one side of the ship to the other side. But the captain, he knew his business, and he knew how to hold the ship to the sea. All day long we fought in that sea—rolling and pitching around—she was a small ship, one of those "lake" ships. Anyhow, we ran out of it, and we sailed on up and got to New York and went up to Yonkers and discharged the sugar.[3]

Later, the Swedish second mate found out that his former ship and all of his shipmates had been lost at sea in the same storm.[4]

After unloading, the ship went to a shipyard in Brooklyn for a routine overhaul. Oliver's salary was $163 a month, and he was given an additional $5 a day for meals and $1.50 for a room if he wished to go ashore and live while the repairs were being made.[5] The work would take several months to complete. He chose to stay on the vessel and save the room rent. But he did have to find his meals ashore, as well as occasional entertainment after his daily watch aboard the idle ship was over.

One night Oliver decided to take in an amateur night at a local vaudeville theater in Brooklyn. It was a spectacle he never forgot. A performer would come out on the stage and begin singing. If the audience didn't like the hapless amateur, they threw tomatoes and other vegetables on the stage. As Oliver recollected one performer's fate, "A poor devil came out and started singing and all of a sudden the orders [from the audience] were 'Pull him off!' They threw something at him—a piece of cabbage or a tomato or something. The fellow offstage, behind the curtain to one side, would take a great big hook and hook the singer around the waist and pull him off the stage."[6] Oliver was overwhelmed with laughter at the bizarre byplay between the audience and the performers. It was obvious that the hook was the real star of the show.

As October came and the weather began to get nippy, Oliver decided that he didn't want to remain in the North through the winter. He had no clothes for cold weather and would have to buy a whole new wardrobe.

3. *Ibid.*, No. 5, p. 17, No. 6, p. 1.

4. Oliver Jackson told this to the author after the tape recorder was turned off on August 7, 1981. Thus this information is not in Transcript No. 6, but the author made a note of it at that time.

5. Jackson Transcripts, No. 6, p. 2.

6. *Ibid.*

He also was getting homesick for New Orleans and the Mississippi River. Captain Fonton was sorry to see him leave, since Oliver was a willing and steady worker, but he understood how the young greenhorn felt. He paid him and let him catch a train for home. Oliver felt proud of the stake of cash he had accumulated from his voyage. He was determined to save as much as he could and bought only a day-coach seat on the train, sitting up all the way from New York City to New Orleans.[7]

Once there, he went to spend some time with his sister Sarah and her husband, Mike Budenich. The two had just moved to the city from Southwest Pass. They were living at 3214 Marais Street, downtown in the Ninth Ward.[8] Mike was working as a carpenter for the Corps of Engineers at their headquarters on the New Orleans riverfront at the foot of Prytania Street. Oliver was surprised to hear that his youngest sister, Viola, whom he regarded as still a child, had married a young man from down the river, Robert Barrios, known familiarly as "Boy" Barrios. Viola, taken out of an orphanage in New Orleans as a baby by her sister Alvaretta Nicholson, had stayed with the Nicholsons until she reached her teens. Then she had returned to New Orleans to live with other relatives.[9]

Now all of his surviving brothers and sisters were married—but not Oliver. He was the rover, the Flying Dutchman, who seemed destined never to settle down. Although he was a hard worker who did his job well, he was struggling to find a path that would someday lead to a position he could be proud of. He was also alone, with no family and no home—a handsome young man whom all the girls loved to talk to or dance with, but one who still hadn't found the special girl he wanted to marry.

After New Year's of 1919, Oliver was ready to set sail again. He went to the seamen's union hall and signed up for a job as third mate aboard the Sinclair oil tanker *Northwestern*. In the latter part of 1919, the *Northwestern* got an assignment to carry fuel oil from Port Arthur, Texas, to United States Navy destroyers at the navy yard in Pensacola, Florida. The voyage to Pensacola was uneventful. When the *Northwestern* reached its destination, it anchored off the dock. Two destroyers at a time came out and pulled up on each side—starboard and port—to take on fuel oil.[10] Since the fueling operation would take several days, Oliver had hopes of going ashore. He had a particular reason for shore leave—his sister Alvaretta, whom he hadn't seen since his mother died, was married and living in Pensacola. He wanted to visit her.

7. *Ibid.*, 2–3.
8. *Ibid.*, 3; *Soards' New Orleans City Directory, 1920* (New Orleans, 1920), 265.
9. Jackson Transcripts, No. 6, p. 3.
10. *Ibid.*, 7.

On the brief voyage from Port Arthur, Oliver had told the chief mate about his sister. "I haven't seen her since I was a little fellow, eight years old, when we were put in the orphan home."

"What's her name?" the chief mate asked.

"Nicholson. Her husband's Tom Nicholson."

The chief mate replied, "I know a Tom Nicholson. His wife's name is Retta."

"Yes—Alvaretta."

"She's a black-haired woman," the chief mate recollected.

Oliver was excited by this recognition and answered, "That's right. I'm told she has long black hair down to her ankles."

The chief mate smiled and said, "When we get there, you go and catch a cab and go out and see her. I'll take care of your watch." [11]

Oliver's watch was twelve to four in the morning. The chief mate's favor would allow him to stay overnight with his relatives.

Alvaretta, who had been sixteen years old when their mother Eliza died in Biloxi, had gone to Florida to live with their aunt Louise Loar Williams. Aunt Louise's husband, Richard Williams, was a professional fisherman who had met and married her at Port Eads but later moved to Florida and settled near Destin. Alvaretta had married her husband a year after coming to Florida, and they now lived in Pensacola, where Tom Nicholson ran a "fish house," a combined wholesale icehouse and processing plant for the catch of commercial fishermen. [12]

Oliver took a cab to the Nicholsons' house, asked the cabbie to wait until he was certain he was at the correct address, and knocked on the door. A tall, blue-eyed young man with dark hair opened the door. It was Tom Nicholson. Oliver told him who he was and asked to see Retta. Tom assured him he had come to the right house and that he was his brother-in-law. Oliver waved to the cabbie to drive off. Then Tom said, "Wait a minute. Don't say anything." He called to his wife to come to the door.

As Retta confronted Oliver, her husband asked her, "Do you know this man?" Retta sensed something special about the stranger, but she failed to recognize him. "No, I don't know him," she answered. Tom couldn't keep the suspense going any longer and burst out, "That's your brother Oliver!" Retta threw her arms around Oliver and started crying. [13] The years had changed Oliver from an eight-year-old to a muscular young seaman of twenty-three and Retta from a sixteen-year-old to a thirty-one-

11. *Ibid.*
12. *Ibid.*
13. *Ibid.*, 8.

year-old matron and mother. Late into the night they tried to make up for lost time by reminiscing and catching up on each other's activities since they had parted. Oliver stayed over with the Nicholsons and went back to his ship the next day.

After a few days in Pensacola, the *Northwestern* sailed to Port Neches, Texas, to pick up a load of asbestos for Rhode Island. But the ship was never to leave port. The night before they were due to sail, Oliver and several of his shipmates went ashore. When they returned late that evening, they could smell smoke and see the orange glow of fire long before they reached the dock. It was the *Northwestern*. The fire was all over the ship, burning out of control. Several small tugboats were alongside pumping water onto the hapless vessel, but it was obvious to Oliver and the other crew members that the ship's interior would be a total loss. After dawn, when the fire had finally been extinguished, Oliver realized that he had lost everything he owned—his clothes, his sextant, his pilot license, some books, and a picture of his mother that Retta had just given him. The only thing he salvaged was his overcoat, which the wireless operator had managed to grab from his cabin and carry off the ship.[14] Oliver had to go into Port Arthur and get a notarized statement concerning his license. It read:

> State of Texas, This county of Jefferson, city of Port Arthur. Be it remembered that on this 13th day of February 1920, before me the undersigned authority, personally appeared Oliver D. Jackson and being by me first duly sworn according to law deposed as follows: That he was third officer on board the steamer *Northwestern* on the 11th day of February 1920 on which date the said steamer was destroyed by fire at Port Neches, Texas. That on the said date his license as first class pilot on the Mississippi River from New Orleans, Louisiana to sea and third mate on any ocean tonnage was destroyed by said fire. Subscribed and sworn to before me at my office in the city of Port Arthur, Texas on this the 13th day of February 1920.[15]

The cause of the fire, as far as Oliver knew, was never discovered.

With the *Northwestern* a burned-out shell, the crew was discharged with the promise that the company would make amends for their lost personal property (it never did). Oliver returned to New Orleans to look for another ship. For a time he sailed to Central America aboard the *Panuko*, which was carrying fuel oil to factories in Mexico, Honduras, and Cuba. By the end of 1920, he had moved up to second mate. From January to July, 1921, he served in that rank on the oil-carrying vessel *Harry*

14. *Ibid.*
15. Notarized statement of Oliver D. Jackson, February 13, 1920, Port Arthur, Texas, in Oliver D. Jackson Papers.

Farnum, another Sinclair ship.[16] But by the summer of 1921, when Oliver returned to New Orleans from his stint aboard the _Harry Farnum,_ his flirtation with the sea was coming to an end. He was twenty-five and still a Flying Dutchman without any permanent home or human relationship of substance. He decided to find a job in New Orleans and settle down.

The New Orleans of 1921 was a changed place from the pre–World War I port city whose docks Oliver had worked in 1914. In 1914 automobiles were just beginning to appear on the streets of the Crescent City; in 1921 parked cars lined the curbs of Canal Street and motorized vehicles outnumbered wagons and other horse-drawn conveyances in all parts of the city. New Orleans' famously languid pace of life would never be quite the same.

A change that many New Orleanians found harder to accept was the coming of Prohibition. At almost every intersection in working-class neighborhoods, there was a small grocery on one corner and a neighborhood barroom on another. There had been such a bar across from the Jacksons' oyster shop in Algiers when Oliver was a small boy. Later he had helped his uncle and father in their oyster bar and saloon. Now these working-class bars, along with the famous bistros in the French Quarter, were serving only beer and preparing to go out of business.

Prohibition had come to New Orleans on July 1, 1919, under the Wartime Prohibition Act. Hard liquor was definitely against the law. But local breweries continued to experiment with their brewing processes to produce a "near beer" that might be legal. In January, 1920, Prohibition as mandated by the Eighteenth Amendment and defined by the Volstead Act (any substance with more than one-half of 1 percent alcohol was illegal) went into effect.[17]

In the month before the official Prohibition era began, whiskey exports from the port of New Orleans increased phenomenally. Exporters of hard liquor had been given until January 26, 1920, to ship their stock to foreign markets. Between mid-December, 1919, and mid-January, 1920, 99,991 gallons of whiskey and 1,332,380 gallons of pure alcohol were shipped out of New Orleans, mainly to South America.[18] Wealthy citizens who felt compelled to follow the exodus of alcoholic spirits booked pleasure cruises to Havana. Some of the steamship lines carrying passengers had long waiting lists of such travelers.[19]

16. Letter of Recommendation of O. D. Jackson from Sinclair Oil Co. Manager, July 16, 1921, in Oliver D. Jackson Papers.

17. Joy Jackson, "Prohibition in New Orleans: the Unlikeliest Crusade," _Louisiana History,_ XIX (Summer, 1978), 264–66.

18. New Orleans _Times-Picayune,_ January 16, 1920, Sec. 1, p. 14.

19. _Ibid.,_ February 1, 1920, Sec. 3, p. 6.

In 1921 New Orleans became the scene of the first federal judicial injunction in the nation upholding the Volstead Act. On June 24 six local breweries were shut down and their stock of thousands of bottles of beer, valued at $35,000, was seized by Prohibition agents. The alcoholic content of the beer was considerably higher than 0.5 percent. The breweries raided were the American, National, Standard, Columbia, Dixie, and Union. A compromise was later achieved by which the breweries were allowed to reopen but had to pay penalties in excess of $100,000 and obey the injunction of Judge Rufus Foster of the United States district court to conform to the Volstead Act or face permanent closure.[20] This order was issued in July, 1921—the month that Oliver came back to town. While the breweries complied, backyard home brewing and clandestine bootleg stills sprang up all over the city and its outskirts.

Oliver had experienced searches of his quarters aboard ship by Prohibition agents every time he had returned from a voyage. Like the rest of the crew, he had borne the invasion of his privacy with cynical amusement and suppressed aggravation. What he missed in 1921 was not the hard liquor that was no longer legally available, but the camaraderie of a night on the town with his country cousins, going to concert saloons to listen to jazz music, have a beer, and eat the free lunch offered to patrons. Now the concert saloons were closed. The jazz musicians had scattered, many of them going upriver to Memphis or Chicago to spread the sound of their music. The Jazz Age had begun, and the New Orleans of 1914 was gone forever. (One of the cousins with whom Oliver had enjoyed the city in its pre-Prohibition days was gone too. Tommy Jackson had been drafted during World War I and stationed at Camp Beauregard, Louisiana, for training. There he contracted spinal meningitis and died before he could ever go overseas.)

Not every change in the city had been as disruptive as Prohibition. The riverfront, for example, had undergone noticeable improvement since Oliver's longshoreman days. Its upgrading was part of a continuing metamorphosis that had started in 1896, coincidentally the year Oliver was born. That year the state legislature created the Board of Port Commissioners of the Port of New Orleans.[21] The act was amended in 1900 to

20. *Ibid.*, June 26, 1921, Sec. 1, pp. 1, 4, June 27, 1921, Sec. 1, p. 2, June 28, 1921, Sec. 1, p. 9, July 1, 1921, Sec. 1, pp. 1, 3, July 10, 1921, Sec. 1, p. 11, July 12, 1921, Sec. 1, p. 18; Jackson, "Prohibition in New Orleans," 270–71.

21. H. S. Herring, *History of the New Orleans Board of Trade Limited, 1880–1930* (New Orleans, 1930), 57; Board of Commissioners of the Port of New Orleans, *A Long-Range Program for the Development of the Port of New Orleans* (New Orleans, 1978), 1; James H. Gillis, "Port's Facilities, Foreign Shipping Show Huge Gains During 100 Years," Centennial

give the agency, which became known as the "Dock Board," complete control of New Orleans' port facilities when the private lease that controlled the city wharves expired in 1901.[22] By 1921, the Dock Board had altered the city waterfront dramatically.

In the late nineteenth century, the riverfront had consisted of wooden docks with little covered shed space. Most cargo was simply piled on the open docks. Fire protection for merchandise and for the wooden wharves themselves was thus limited. Night lighting along the docks was inadequate, as was access to them—the hole-pocked streets that connected them to the city could not be traversed in rainy weather for fear of breaking an axle or injuring the horse or mule drawing the wagon. Even the river traffic had about it an air of the worn and outdated. Steamboats dominated the docks from Girod Street all the way downriver to Canal. Luggers with colorful sails berthed along the Picayune Tier in front of Jackson Square and the French Market.[23] All of this began to change after 1901.

Within twenty years after assuming control of the port, the Dock Board had upgraded more than six miles of wharfage on the east bank and had constructed several modern warehouses, nineteen large steel sheds, new wharfage for the eight grain elevators, and other facilities such as a cotton terminal that could store 400,000 bales of cotton at once and 2 million bales a year. A coal storage and handling plant was almost complete by 1921, and the Industrial Canal locks were formally dedicated on May 2 of that year. The canal itself was completed and opened in 1923, connecting the river to Lake Pontchartrain. Ultimately, it would serve as a link with the Intracoastal Canal, which was being extended by this time along the Gulf Coast, and would offer additional wharfage and warehouse space along its five-and-a-half-mile length.[24]

Edition, New Orleans *Times-Picayune,* January 25, 1937, Sec. K, p. 2; Jackson, *New Orleans in the Gilded Age,* 320.

22. Herring, *History of the New Orleans Board of Trade,* 57; Board of Commissioners of the Port of New Orleans, *Long-Range Program for the Development of the Port of New Orleans,* 1.

23. Herring, *History of the New Orleans Board of Trade,* 30–31; R. W. Bradbury, *The Water-Borne Commerce of New Orleans,* a publication of the Bureau of Business Research, Louisiana State University (Baton Rouge, 1937), 9–10; Gillis, "Port's Facilities, Foreign Shipping Show Huge Gains During 100 Years," Centennial Edition, New Orleans *Times-Picayune,* January 25, 1937, Sec. K, p. 2; *New Orleans City Guide,* 282.

24. Department of War, *Annual Report of the Chief of Engineers, U.S. Army, 1921* (Washington, D.C., 1921), 933–34; James P. Baughman, "Gateway to the Americas," in *The Past as Prelude: New Orleans, 1718–1968,* ed. Hodding Carter (New Orleans, 1968), 264–65.

Railroad operations on the riverfront had been integrated through the creation in 1904 of the Board of Commissioners of the Public Belt Railroad. Partial construction on the public belt line began in 1905 with modest funds from the city council. In 1908 the state legislature authorized the city to issue a two-million-dollar bond issue subject to voter approval (which was achieved) to fund the complete project of sixty miles of public rail lines along the river—trackage badly needed to move cargo coming and going through the port. Roads leading to and from the docks were paved and kept in repair for the new motorized vehicles as they multiplied in the post–World War I era. Finally, the muscle of longshoremen alone was no longer the only way to load and unload boats and ships: the Dock Board and private shipping firms built and operated such handling devices as banana conveyors, floating derricks, magnets, escalators, and electric trucks, almost all of them put into operation after 1914.[25]

Foreign trade through New Orleans, both export and import, steadily expanded in the early twentieth century, but it was apparent that this trade was becoming monopolized by foreign carriers. The American merchant fleet was shrinking. Along with this shrinkage was the disappearance of the steamboat as the common carrier on the Mississippi River. Railroads transported directly to the East Coast commodities from the Mississippi Valley that steamboats had hauled down to New Orleans in antebellum days.[26] The river-borne commerce of the tributaries of the Mississippi and of the great river itself had almost died out by 1914. Only little local steamboats that carried food and dry goods to the Lower Coast of Plaquemines Parish or to remote bayous or rivers with few or no highway outlets were still plying their trade.

World War I revived river commerce in a remarkable way. As early as 1916, members of a prominent New Orleans businessmen's organization, the Board of Trade, advocated the forming of a commercial corporation to operate boats and barges up and down the Mississippi. Their plan envisioned commercial organizations like their own in towns throughout the Mississippi Valley joining together to revitalize river traffic by investing in the corporation. Business interests in St. Louis pledged their support to the project, but before it could be put into operation, the United States entered the war. The need for swift movement of military supplies made government officials adopt the concept of a Mississippi River barge line. The nation's railroads, which had been taken over by the federal govern-

25. Herring, *History of the New Orleans Board of Trade Limited*, 58–62; *Annual Report of the Chief of Engineers, U.S. Army, 1921*, p. 934.

26. Gillis, "Port's Facilities, Foreign Shipping Show Huge Gains in 100 Years," Centennial Edition, New Orleans *Times-Picayune*, January 25, 1937, Sec. K, p. 2.

ment as a wartime measure, simply could not move all of the goods and raw materials needed for the war effort. A New Orleans shipping official, M. J. Sanders, who was also president of the Board of Trade was appointed the first federal director of the Mississippi-Warrior Service, which was created through an act of Congress in 1918. It was designed to operate barge service on the Mississippi River and the Warrior River in Alabama. In 1920, when railroads were returned to their private owners, the barge corporation was kept under federal control and the Inland Waterways Corporation was created to operate the system, which became known as the Federal Barge Line.[27]

With this government-operated company to lead the way, private barge lines sprang up by the early 1920s, and towboat and barge caravans on the Mississippi River took the place of the old-time steamboats. Rates were competitive with rail lines, and service was fast enough to attract a steadily increasing list of customers.

Oliver was thus returning to the New Orleans harbor at a time when river traffic was renewing itself, but at first he did not try to get work on the river. He had decided to find a land job instead—one that would assure him of regular hours and not send him out of town anymore. He applied for work as a streetcar conductor and was hired on a probationary basis.[28] Taking instructions from a veteran driver on how to stop and start properly, he tried so hard to get the knack of it that his instructor told him to loosen up: "You're going to stop the car in the middle of the block." Oliver finally learned, but his heart wasn't in his work. After a couple of weeks on the job he felt he was wasting his time. The streetcar was too constrained. It followed the same track, back and forth, without deviation. He longed for the freedom of the river, for the fresh river breeze blowing across the bow of a tug. He quit the streetcars and headed for the waterfront. Within a week, he had a job as a deckhand aboard the *Port Sulphur*, a tug in the harbor of New Orleans.

Oliver found lodgings in Algiers on Patterson Avenue, near Algiers Point. At various times he had boarded with relatives, but now he felt he should be on his own. He was far from being alone, however. Most members of Captain Andy's family had left Port Eads by this time for the city. Aunt Nan and her sister Pearl Ronquillo were living in the same block of Delachaise Street, across from the St. Joseph Orphan Asylum. Aunt Aggie Castell and her family were on Port Street, below the French Quarter. Uncle John was remarried to a young woman named Annie Goff and

27. *Ibid.*; Herring, *History of the New Orleans Board of Trade*, 62–67.
28. Jackson Transcripts, No. 6, p. 10.

lived on Elmira Avenue in Algiers.[29] He had become a member of the Crescent River Port Pilots Association. Oliver's father came up to New Orleans sporadically, although he preferred to live at the mouth of the river, fishing and oystering. Eric, his wife Dora, and their children still lived on Southwest Pass.

As Oliver settled into his routine on the tug, he used his time off to visit his relatives and get acquainted with their friends and neighbors. At his Uncle John's he met a young woman named Vera, with thick dark hair and a gentle demeanor. She was a native of Algiers who lived with her parents in the older section of that suburb. Oliver began calling on her and taking her out to silent movies, to dances, or just for Sunday strolls. Within a few months, the lonely young man asked Vera to marry him. She accepted. Oliver began planning for the future. Vera began embroidering linen for her hope chest.

That, however, was the high point of the relationship. Whenever they discussed life after marriage, Vera's plans were different from what Oliver wanted. She was totally dedicated to living in the large two-story house owned by her family. She and Oliver would occupy an apartment above her parents and next door to her married sister. Oliver felt suffocated at the idea of so many in-laws so close by. The two argued, but Vera was adamant in her conviction that she could not leave her parents. Oliver, who had been thrust out into the world on his own since he was eight, did not understand or wish to share such a married life. After one soul-searching discussion in which neither would yield, Oliver told Vera that if she really would not move at least a few blocks away to a more private residence after they were married, he would walk out and never return. Their engagement would be ended. Vera was as proud and stubborn as Oliver. She did not yield to the ultimatum.[30]

Each of them may have thought when they parted that time would make the other relent and everything would turn out happily in the end. But time was against them. Oliver not only did not come back to Vera, he moved from Algiers to the New Orleans side of the river to board again with his cousins, the Borciches. And there Antonia Borcich, Peter and Mary Borcich's daughter and Oliver's second cousin, became a match-maker.

In 1921 Antonia was working for the Commercial Credit Company, where she had made friends with a petite blonde girl, Oneida Drouant. Oneida (she pronounced it O-need-a) was a self-reliant, energetic, quick-witted young woman who came from a family of four boys and two girls.

29. *Soards' New Orleans City Directory, 1921,* pp. 328, 413, 928, 1276.
30. Jackson Transcripts, No. 6, pp. 11–12.

Her sister Leonora—"Nora"—was the eldest child in the family. Next came John Joseph (Joe), then Oneida, and her three younger brothers, William Lloyd, Elmer Richard, and Sidney Herman. Although born in New Orleans, Oneida had spent much of her childhood in Abita Springs on the North Shore of Lake Pontchartrain in St. Tammany Parish. Her father moved there from New Orleans to engage in a well-digging business, which failed and left him struggling to support his family from a number of odd jobs. As a child, she had earned the nickname "Cat" because of her quickness and agility in climbing, running, and jumping. After her family returned to New Orleans and she grew to young womanhood in the era of World War I, Oneida, or "Neda" as her family called her, enjoyed attending plays or going to neighborhood dances. There were dances at fraternal or church halls almost every weekend, and every other family had a piano in their parlor that served for home parties. Neda loved to attend such gatherings. She was a friendly girl who knew many of the neighbors. At the time she met Oliver, she lived nine blocks from the streetcar, which she took every day to work. Walking to and from this streetcar, Neda became acquainted with residents in every block. People sat outside or stood in their doorways to catch a breath of air. Neda's friendliness was a natural part of life in her neighborhood. Essentially domestic, she loved to cook and sew. An accomplished seamstress by the time she was seventeen, she made most of her own clothes and sewed delicate baby clothes and children's dresses for her younger cousins. Skilled also in decorating hats, she once thought of becoming a milliner. Instead she had chosen what seemed a more practical course, taking lessons at a business school to learn typing, shorthand, and bookkeeping. The latter subject was a favorite of hers.

Sometime shortly after Oliver came to board with the Borciches, Antonia introduced Oliver to Neda Drouant.[31] As her friend, Antonia wanted Neda to meet Oliver. Oliver was getting over his broken engagement, and Neda was trying to forget a former suitor whom she was not seeing anymore. Neda was bitter and felt she would never marry. But after Oliver and Neda met, they both forgot their past disappointments very quickly.

Oliver and Neda found that simple pleasures satisfied them deeply. When they were together everything they did seemed special. They enjoyed dancing. They loved to window-shop, walking ten or fifteen blocks after taking in a movie, and they both had hopes of getting ahead in life. Neda introduced Oliver to her dream of someday owning a home and living in a suburb with green lawns and an automobile in the garage.

31. *Ibid.*, 12.

Somehow, when this intense, slim girl with the large blue eyes and soft hair that looked like a golden halo talked about the possibilities of the future, Oliver felt he was finding a direction for his own dreams. In the summer of 1922 he asked Neda to marry him. She accepted.

In hopes of making a bigger stake than he could earn as a deckhand, Oliver quit the harbor tug and went downriver to join his father for several months of oystering. The venture was not as successful as he had anticipated, but what little profit he made, he sent to Neda to put in the bank. She was saving her income as well. At Christmas, 1922, Oliver returned to New Orleans. He spent some of his modest savings to buy Neda a Christmas present of a silver-and-bone comb, brush, and manicure set.[32]

Oliver now got a job working on a seagoing tug between Mobile and New Orleans. His employer was the W. G. Coyle Company, whose tugboat yard was located above Algiers Point. In addition to long-distance hauling to Mobile or Pensacola, Coyle tugs mainly carried coal to ships and industrial plants along the riverfront. They also did general work in the harbor and up and down the river to the Passes moving ships and barges. Occasionally Coyle tugs assisted ships that were caught on sandbars.[33]

Oliver and Neda's plans for an October wedding in 1923 intermingled with planning for their first home. Neda owned a vacant lot, and she sold it to add to their savings. With their combined funds, they put a down payment on a new house on Verbena Street. It was a few blocks from the Drouant home on Lavender Street in the new suburb of Edgewood. The house cost a total of $2,500. It had four rooms, a wood stove in the kitchen, and an outhouse in the backyard.[34] But it seemed like a dream house to the happy couple.

Rain fell most of the day on October 17, 1923, but stopped late in the afternoon, just in time for the Drouant-Jackson wedding. Neda's brother Joe was best man. Her maid of honor was a close friend, Carrie Weber. There were two bridesmaids, two groomsmen, and a flower girl, who was related to Uncle John Jackson's wife. Horse-drawn carriages were still used for wedding parties, but unpaved Lavender Street in front of the Drouant house was too flooded and muddy for the carriages to approach. Neda and her family had to walk to the corner to get in. The wedding took place in Mount Calvary Lutheran Church on Grand Route St. John.[35]

32. *Ibid.*, No. 7, August 9, 1981, pp. 1–2.
33. Centennial Edition, New Orleans *Times-Picayune*, January 25, 1937, Sec. K, p. 14.
34. Jackson Transcripts, No. 7, p. 2.
35. *Ibid.*, 3; Interview with Oneida Drouant Jackson by Joy Jackson, Hammond, La., June 23, 1987; Marriage Certificate for Oneida Christina Drouant and Oliver Daniel Jackson, October 17, 1923, Mt. Calvary Lutheran Church, New Orleans, in Oliver D. Jackson Papers.

Neda's mother, Josephine Koester Drouant, was the daughter of German Lutheran immigrants. She had raised her children in the religion of her ancestors, although her husband was Catholic. Neda's father, John Joseph Drouant, was the eldest son of immigrants. His father and mother were from Alsace-Lorraine. The Drouants were all ingenious, and vitally creative in their work and leisure activity. Like Oliver, they were proud individualists who worked hard to accomplish what they wanted, and they believed their goals were achievable. Oliver felt comfortable with this family. His values and personality fitted well with theirs. "Oliver" seemed too formal a name to his new in-laws. They began calling him "Jack" (short for Jackson), a name that even Neda soon adopted permanently. His own family continued to call him "Oliver," whereas to the men with whom he worked on the river he was "O. D."

Uncle John and his wife, Annie, attended the wedding as did Sarah and Mike Budenich, the Borciches, and Oliver's aunts. They were all touched and happy to see the half-orphan boy grown up and finally settling down. It seemed he had found a snug haven at last. Most of the guests, however, were friends of the large Drouant family, folks whom Oliver did not know. The reception was held at the Drouant home on Lavender Street. When it was over, Neda changed from her chic short-length wedding gown into a simple house dress. Oliver exchanged his tuxedo for everday pants and shirt. Then they took their leave of the Drouants and, accompanied by Nora and her husband, Joe Rupp, walked toward their new home, carrying their wedding clothes in a package. At the corner of Verbena, the Rupps said goodnight and turned to go their way. Neda and Oliver walked alone down Verbena to their new little house and the beginning of their life together.

8

SAFE HARBOR
1923 – 1928

The winter of 1923–1924 was a time of quiet happiness for Neda and Oliver. She put up curtains, kept house, and started a garden. He went to work by streetcar and ferryboat, and made several trips a month aboard the Coyle steamer *DeBardeleben,* carrying coal and other cargo between Mobile and New Orleans. Although he liked working for the Coyle Company, being away from his new wife and home for five days or more on these trips made Oliver decide to seek a harbor job again. He left Coyle and went to work temporarily at the Jahncke Drydock and Ship Repair Company on St. Maurice at the riverfront.[1] Later he got a permanent position as a deckhand on the *Egyptian Prince,* a harbor tug that was part of the Federal Barge Line fleet. Its job was to pick up barges brought downriver by towboats and deliver the barges to ships waiting to take on their cargo. After they were unloaded, the *Egyptian Prince* would take the empty barges to other ships, where they would be loaded with cargo going upriver. Completing the circle, Oliver's tug would then shift the loaded barges to a Federal Barge Line towboat ready to head upstream.[2]

In 1923, a total of 710,431 tons of cargo had traveled up or down the Mississippi River between New Orleans and St. Louis in barges towed by Federal Barge Line boats. The line made three sailings a week in each direction. Its fleet included forty recently built 2,000-horsepower towboats. It had also added forty new barges, each with 2,000 tons deadweight carrying capacity.[3] Both additions represented impressive improvement over the first operations of the government-sponsored towing line, which at its inception in 1918 had consisted of five small towboats, two 1,000-ton barges, three 600-ton barges, and twenty 450-ton barges that belonged to the Corps of Engineers. The first three barges, handled by the towboat *Nokomis,* left St. Louis on September 28, 1918, to the sound of harbor

---

1. Jackson Transcripts, No. 7, pp. 5, 17, 18.
2. *Ibid.,* 5.
3. Centennial Edition, New Orleans *Times-Picayune,* January 25, 1937, Sec. K, p. 6.

whistles. The towboat and its load of grain arrived in New Orleans on October 10, during the brutal 1918 influenza epidemic. On the two previous days, 1,108 new cases of influenza had been reported in the city. At least 8,000 cases existed in New Orleans, according to Dr. Oscar Dowling, president of the State Board of Health. State and city officials had taken measures to limit large public gatherings. Schools, churches, movie theaters, and dance halls were closed. Under the circumstances, the *Nokomis'* arrival was not heralded by a large public celebration; nevertheless, it marked the turning point for declining river traffic.[4]

By the end of 1923, nonperishable goods could be transported downriver as rapidly by Federal Barge Line as by railroad car. The upriver traffic was also surprisingly strong, almost as heavy as the downriver flow of goods. (The actual split for the year was 390,870 tons downriver, 319,561 tons upriver.) This flourishing trade encouraged the construction and use of new facilities at small towns up and down the Mississippi. Commercial life along the great river was reviving after a Rip Van Winkle sleep of several decades.

Oliver enjoyed his work on the *Egyptian Prince*. He learned a lot about the harbor of New Orleans and the operation of a tugboat in the busy port. In addition to his deckhand duties of tying and untying the tug and barges, keeping the tug cleaned, the paint fresh, and the brass polished, he sometimes served as helmsman. This allowed him to learn the tricks of the current along the various city docks, and how to dock and undock the tug and maneuver its barges properly. A deckhand's job was a hurry-up-and-wait occupation. There were times when he had to work fast and hard—when the tug was engaged in tying up to a wharf or a ship, or when he had the tricky, dangerous job of securing barges to the tug's side or reattaching one whose cables had broken loose. Then the deckhand had to be swift, strong, and careful not to lose a finger to a tightening cable. Stepping back and forth on the barges took agility and timing; one wrong move could put a man in the river, maybe even—a deckhand's nightmare—under the tow. Working with ropes and cables that secured barges or large ships to the little tug required a knowledge of how to tauten and tie them so that they would hold but could be released quickly if necessary. Deckhanding was primarily outdoor work. Winter cold and rain, the heat and humidity of summer were part of the elements that had to be endured. But when a job was complete, there was always some leisure time while

4. *Ibid.*, Sec. K, p. 1, and October 10, 1918, Sec. 1, pp. 1, 10, October 11, 1918, Sec. 1, p. 14. For a detailed description of the Board of Trade's part in initiating this barge line, see Herring, *History of the New Orleans Board of Trade*, 62–67.

the tug cruised back to its dock or waited there for the next call. Then the deckhands gathered, usually in the pilothouse or galley with the captain and mate, to swap stories. Everything from river experiences to barroom brawls to women was discussed.

Just as the Jacksons seemed to be settling into a pleasant, predictable routine, a double crisis confronted them: Neda contracted pneumonia and became so ill that she went into unconsciousness with high fever; and on about the second day of her sickness, Oliver lost his job: the *Egyptian Prince* was taken out of service, the Federal Barge Line officials having decided to turn over harbor work to the private tugboat lines operating in the city and concentrate on their long-haul towboats.[5]

With no paycheck coming at the end of the week, Oliver could not afford to put Neda in the hospital. As a result, her doctor refused to treat her any longer, saying he did not want to be responsible if she died at home. Neda's mother, who had come to care for her the first day she was sick, found another doctor who was willing to treat Neda at home and would wait until the Jacksons could pay him. One night he stayed until after 2 A.M. watching over his comatose patient. In order to keep his wife from worrying about his unemployment, Oliver and his mother-in-law conspired to keep the bad news from her during her brief waking moments. Every morning for several days, Oliver got up, dressed, ate breakfast, and went out the front door as if he were going to work, then he sneaked around the house and reentered the kitchen through the back door. He kept busy by helping Mrs. Drouant with household chores and running errands to the drugstore.[6]

He was desperate to get a job as soon as possible. By the end of the week after she had fallen ill, Neda had improved slightly. She was going to get well. With this encouragement and the knowledge that he wasn't needed at home anymore, Oliver headed downtown to look for work. He rode the streetcar to Canal Street and walked to Monkey Wrench Corner—the nickname for Royal and Canal streets—where rivermen had congregated and talked since the golden age of steamboats. Oliver saw several fellows he knew and told them he was looking for a job. They advised him there was no work to be found, but one of them suggested he go to the Dock Board headquarters at the foot of Canal Street, put in an application for work, and then wait to be called. Oliver thought that such an application would be filed away and forgotten. He replied that he was going to talk directly to the captain of the Dock Board's dredge boat. The

5. Jackson Transcripts, No. 7, p. 6.
6. *Ibid.*, 5–6.

denizens of Monkey Wrench Corner rejected this idea as futile. But Oliver was determined.

He caught the Magazine streetcar and rode up to Napoleon Avenue. In brisk step, he walked from Magazine to the riverfront, where the dredge was anchored. Going aboard, he talked to the captain and described his experience and credentials. The captain was impressed by Oliver's ability to splice wire as well as rope. He needed a man with this skill. Oliver was hired on the spot. The only catch was that he would have to work the night shift, beginning at eleven o'clock the next night. But Oliver was satisfied—he had a job again. When he came back down to Canal Street, the same bunch of men were still standing on Royal and Canal. They would go around the corner and get a drink in a speakeasy hidden from public view and Prohibition agents, then come back to their favorite haunt to talk awhile. When Oliver told them he had a job beginning the next night, they were momentarily startled into silence. "Well, I'll be doggoned," one of them finally said, apparently expressing the general sentiments of the group.[7]

The job aboard the dredge was placid. The most difficult part was adjusting to the night hours, but Oliver had the ability to fall asleep almost immediately when he reached home after a long night watch. As a deckhand, he did the splicing the captain had needed and helped with docking and undocking and operating the dredge bucket. The restless Mississippi was constantly piling silt against certain banks and cutting away at others. The Dock Board floating dredge migrated slowly around the New Orleans harbor scooping up the silt wherever it was hindering ships from docking. The silt was then dumped into the deepest part of the central river to be churned down toward the Passes and the Gulf. Usually, the dredge operated in one location for a week or two, then moved on. Once a day, the crew cleaned out the large bucket of the dredge to keep the silt from caking and clogging it. Sometimes they found odd articles caught in it—coins, old shoes, and once several bottles of unopened whiskey that may have been hurriedly thrown off a ship being inspected by Prohibition agents.[8]

Oliver worked on the dredge for a few months, until a job aboard the Dock Board's fire tug, the *Deluge*, was offered to him in 1925. He took it. The work was still on the night shift, but it was quite different from dredging. The major job of the *Deluge*, which was tied up at the foot of Jackson Avenue, was to be on call to fight any fires aboard ships or along the

7. *Ibid.*, 7.
8. *Ibid.*, 7–10.

docks. Oliver was trained to work the powerful hoses, which could spray out huge volumes of water in high arcs. Some of the other crewmen were trained in fire-fighting techniques for boarding burning ships to fight the blaze by hand. The normal night for the *Deluge,* though, was quiet, with no emergencies. Oliver fought only one big fire while he was employed aboard the tug. It was on a Morgan line steamship that caught fire while alongside the wharf. The blaze was quickly extinguished, but the ship suffered extensive damage.[9]

While working nights aboard the fire tug, Oliver also had a day project. He and Neda decided to buy another lot and build a double house. They planned to live in one side and rent the other. Building and buying of real estate was a mania sweeping the country in the mid-1920s. Optimism in the future and the firm belief that owning real estate was the way to riches was the credo of the decade. The young Jacksons were in step with the times. Neda searched the neighborhood and found the perfect site—a lot on Venus Street two blocks from Gentilly Boulevard and one block from Franklin Avenue. It was high ground sloping down to the street and located in the true Gentilly Terrace area: although only four or five feet above sea level, this was one of the highest natural ridges in New Orleans.

Once the lot was purchased, the Jacksons needed a contractor. With the confidence of youth, they chose Neda's youngest brother, Sidney, an eighteen-year-old who had been working for a contractor, learning the building trade. He had a gift for carpentry and was more than willing to help his sister and brother-in-law build their dream house. Relying on imagination and talent for design in lieu of experience, he drafted the plans for the house and began building it. Neda bought all of the lumber, bricks, wiring, hardware, and other materials. The Jacksons did not have an automobile, and she had to travel by streetcar and bus to the lumber-yards and hardware stores. She also engaged the subcontractors and kept records in a ledger of all transactions and purchases.

The house was built of high-grade cypress, with pine flooring and wood-work. Oliver worked with Sidney during the day, after he had caught a few hours of sleep. Neda helped also. As Sidney finished laying the narrow pine-board flooring, Neda and Oliver took bricks wrapped in sandpaper and got down on their knees and sanded the floors by hand. They did the same to the woodwork—the doors and window frames. Finally, they varnished the woodwork and the flooring.

On each side, the house had a living room, dining room, hall, indoor bathroom, bedroom, and kitchen; the kitchen opened onto a back porch.

9. *Ibid.,* 11.

There was a front porch covered by a roof extension. Building inspectors who checked the house expressed astonishment at its quality and the skill of the youthful contractor. To Neda and Oliver, building it had been a true labor of love—it was fitting that it should be located on Venus Street. The house took three or four months to build. The Jacksons and their first tenants occupied their new home by the end of 1925.[10]

Early in March, 1926, Oliver was offered work delivering a coal tender from Key West to Frontera, Mexico, for a company that was digging a canal. It would be a well-paying job, but only a one-trip engagement. He decided to take it. Traveling by train to Key West, he joined the other crewmen aboard the small seagoing tug *Alvarado*. Their agenda called for a stop at Havana to pick up coal, a second brief stop at Progreso on the tip of the Yucatán Peninsula, and finally arrival at Frontera on Campeche Bay midway between Campeche and Veracruz in the state of Tabasco.

After leaving Havana, however, the tender caught stormy weather, and the crew had to follow the buoys of a small Cuban port into its harbor. Lying at anchor there for several days, they used more water than they had anticipated and needed to go ashore for more. A native took them in his motorboat up a river to a spot in the interior where fresh water ran down from the hills. He towed their lifeboat along as a floating water tank. They partly filled it with fresh water and towed it back to their tug. They transferred the fresh water by the bucketful from the lifeboat to containers on deck. Thus resupplied, the *Alvarado* sailed for Progreso. By the time she arrived, the storm had turned to follow her, and the heavy winds blew her against the dock: "It got so rough that the boat was running up and down and rubbing on a concrete piling. So we had to let the boat come up [toward the shore] until she touched bottom. Then when the water got a little higher, we got further in and we had to tie her up. But she had already made a bad spot on the side. . . . When the weather started getting good [by the next day], we went out to try to get the boat . . . back out to deep water. But she wouldn't move, she was grounded."[11]

The captain went ashore and called the home office of the company that owned the coal tender. After explaining the situation, he was instructed to get rid of the coal the tug was carrying. This would lighten the vessel and allow it to float free. The captain found a bakery in Progreso that was willing to purchase the coal. After the tug was freed and its damaged wooden hull was patched by a local ship's carpenter, the journey resumed. At Frontera, a village of simple huts near several banana plan-

10. *Ibid.*, 11–12.
11. *Ibid.*, 13–14.

tations, Oliver and another crewman had to wait several days in the small local hotel until a ship came by that could take them back to New Orleans.

Despite the relative primitiveness of Frontera, Oliver enjoyed walking around viewing the houses and marketplace. He had also enjoyed the brief stay in Progreso, a large and cultivated town. Every evening he had walked down to the central part of town, where a band played nightly public concerts in a beautiful park. He was intrigued by the longshoremen in Progreso, who were allowed to work only half a day. He was told that so many men sought work that they were divided into two shifts—morning and afternoon. That way more people got work, even if it only brought a half day's wages.[12]

In mid-March, 1926, Oliver returned to New Orleans aboard a banana boat that had picked him up at Frontera. He had given up his job aboard the *Deluge*, and now that he was finished with the construction of his house, he didn't want to work at night anymore. He decided to try W. G. Coyle Company again. He took the Canal Street Ferry and walked several blocks to the tugboat yard. Coyle's superintendent remembered "O. D." from his service on the *DeBardeleben* in 1924. He told Oliver to come to work the next morning and to report to Captain Adolph Schwalb.[13] Schwalb was a native of Algiers. Tall, lean, and quick-moving with dark straight hair and china-blue eyes, he was a man of strong convictions and loyalties—a tugboatman of superb skill—the kind of riverman who inspired legends.

But the next morning when Captain Schwalb looked up from the report he was writing on the past day's work in the wheelhouse of the *Corona*, he was not happy to see this stranger coming aboard his tug. Oliver greeted him and explained that the superintendent had sent him to work as mate on the tug. Schwalb was not impressed and seemed to be angry. "I'll see about that," he replied. After checking with the office, he reluctantly accepted Oliver as a crew member. The reason for his displeasure had to do with the man Oliver was replacing, who had been fired. Although there had been sufficient reason for the dismissal—absence and drunkenness—the man was a lifelong friend of Schwalb's and a fellow native of Algiers. Schwalb felt a loyalty to him and thought he should have been given a second chance.[14]

In the next few weeks, Oliver proved invaluable to Schwalb. Although

12. *Ibid.*, 16.
13. Jackson Transcripts, No. 8, June 6, 1982, p. 1.
14. *Ibid.*

the captain had been sullen at first, he came to depend on his hard-working mate and finally to like him—the beginning of a deep friendship that would last a lifetime between the two rivermen.

Oliver left home in Gentilly Terrace around 4:30 A.M. and reported to work aboard the *Corona* by 5:30. All day, as mate, he was constantly at the captain's call for help in steering the tug. When Captain Schwalb got off at 3 P.M., O.D. stayed on as acting captain. His day was officially up at 6:30 P.M., but he was called upon to work longer if Coyle needed a tug to assist a ship in docking or undocking, or to tow a vessel or barge from one location to another. Sometimes he worked as late as 10 or 11 P.M. His regular workday was thirteen hours; he did not collect overtime until he worked past 6:30. When he had to work very late, he called Neda to tell her he would sleep on the tug. After all, if he got off at eleven and reached home by midnight, he would have only four hours' sleep before he had to rise and start the journey back to Coyle's. If the crew worked until 9 P.M., they got to order a night lunch—coffee and ham—to be brought aboard (the *Corona* had its own cook, but he ordinarily worked only days, fixing breakfast and lunch aboard the tug). Oliver's salary was $75 a month, but he usually worked enough overtime to bring it up to $100.[15]

The Coyle Company yard was located astride the levee above Algiers Point. Part of it flowed over onto the batture—the strip of land between the levee and the waterline—where the tugs tied up. There was an office for the dispatchers and their personnel, and a naval stores and grocery commissary for the company tugs. The yard was always a busy place, with men coming and going to work or helping to dock or undock the tugs or just standing around laughing and talking on payday. Coyle's tugs all had a yellow smokestack with a black stripe at the top and a white C on the yellow background. There were two types of tugs: the harbor tugs, about one hundred feet in length, and the larger and heavier oceangoing tugs.[16]

In addition to its main tugboat yard, Coyle's had a coalyard downriver in Chalmette. The DeBardeleben family, who owned Coyle Company, had made their fortune from coal mines in Alabama. They brought coal from these mines by large seagoing tugs down the Warrior River in Alabama to Mobile and then to New Orleans. In the 1920s most ships were

15. *Ibid.*, 1–2.

16. Descriptions of Coyle Company's yard at the foot of Eliza Street in Algiers, its equipment, and its operations are given in Jackson Transcripts, No. 8, p. 2; *History of W. G. Coyle, Inc., and DeBardeleben Coal Corporation* (N.p., n.d. [but apparently published between 1923 and 1934]); and Charles L. Dufour, *The Story of Coyle Lines Incorporated* (New Orleans, 1965), 19.

converting to oil as their fuel, but some still operated on coal. Coyle tugs would go down to the Chalmette coalyard with several barges to be loaded with coal, then tow them back to the yard in Algiers. When a ship requested coal, one of the tugs, perhaps the *Corona*, took a barge of coal and the Coyle collier and tied the collier alongside the ship with the coal barge on the outside of the collier. Then the collier transferred the coal into the ship's bunkers. Some of the names of the Coyle tugs— *Corona* and *Sipsey*—were types of coal processed by the DeBardeleben mines. Other boats—the *H. T. DeBardeleben*, the old *W. G. Wilmot*, and the *Donie*—were named for persons. In addition to the coal deliveries, Coyle tugs towed barges, both empty and filled with cargo (usually grain, sulphur, oil, or boxed machinery), to waiting ships in the harbor or to Federal Barge Line towboats waiting to go back upriver. They also assisted ships to dock or undock. Sometimes, their task might be out of the ordinary. Just a few months after Oliver came to work at Coyle's, in April, 1927, Coyle tugs were called upon for just such a job.

In the spring of 1927, the seasonal rise in the Mississippi River was higher than average. By late April there was widespread flooding of farmlands in Arkansas and Mississippi, and the highs for Louisiana were yet to come. On April 23 the first major break in the Mississippi River levee system below Red River occurred at Junior Plantation in Plaquemines Parish. The molasses tanker *Inspector*, of the Dunbar Molasses and Syrup Company, was proceeding downriver hugging the west bank. Attempting to negotiate a bend in the river between Myrtle Grove and Diamond, forty miles below New Orleans, the ship sheered suddenly to the right and rammed the levee. The contact occurred at a point where caving of the bank had brought the current up to the toe of the levee. A crevasse opened and the Mississippi began to pour through. Ironically, the levee had been scheduled to be strengthened within a few days.[17]

The pilot aboard the *Inspector* swung it around to deflect the brunt of the current, and kept the ship in position while emergency measures were put into operation on shore to close the crevasse. The Corps of Engineers and the Lafourche Basin Levee Board were called into action. Within hours, hundreds of men were rushed aboard the New Orleans and Lower Coast Railroad, a subsidiary of the Missouri Pacific, from Algiers to the scene to fight the break. A second train of this same line came up from Buras with additional men and equipment. The trains also brought sand-

17. See New Orleans *Times-Picayune*, April 24, 1927, Sec. 1, pp. 1, 6; New Orleans *States*, April 24, 1927, Sec. 1, pp. 1, 8; and New Orleans *Item-Tribune*, April 24, 1927, Sec. 1, p. 1, for first news of the break at Junior Plantation by the *Inspector*.

bags, lumber, and other supplies. Workers attempted to close the gap from behind the levee with a box levee, but it was washed away. Late that night the Coyle tug *Adler* arrived with a 124-foot barge loaded with stones, but efforts to wedge this barge into the crevasse also failed. The tug attempted the maneuver several times unsuccessfully, finally returning to New Orleans on Sunday night, April 25. By that time the crevasse had grown to about a hundred feet wide by fifteen feet deep.[18]

Fortunately, there was no loss of life. As the *Times-Picayune*'s account of the accident on April 24 noted:

> The break was thought at first to have endangered approximately 150 passengers who left New Orleans over train number 5 of the New Orleans and Lower Coast railroad for Buras, Myrtle Grove, Grand Isle and other Lower Coast points. . . . Aside from cutting off communication between the towns of Diamond, Buras, Empire and other points below Junior Plantation and New Orleans, the crevasse was expected to result in small danger to residents or live stock or damage to property, according to those familiar with the locality.
>
> The section is principally marshland and inhabited sparsely by fishermen and trappers, all of whom have built homes high above the high tide level.[19]

The population in the area behind the crevasse was estimated at about one thousand. The railroad track, which lay near the levee and ran parallel to it, was flooded with three to four feet of water. The entire area affected was described in an April 25 account in the *Times-Picayune* as "a stretch of land between Myrtle Grove and Magnolia eight miles wide . . . inundated from two to four feet deep."[20]

The biggest loser was John Bonura, who operated a number of truck farms on Junior Plantation. He estimated his losses to be around $100,000. Shrimp and oyster fishermen who worked the back bays that would be outlets for this fresh water rushing toward the salty Gulf also suffered from the disaster.[21]

The frantic attempts to close the levee break were abandoned within forty-eight hours after the accident, all having failed. One final effort had been to construct bulkheads from both sides of the levee and fill the gap with rocks and sandbags. The river quickly swept the rocks and sandbags away.[22] The *Inspector* had originally crashed into the levee with its prow. It had pulled back and attempted to shield the break and slow the water.

18. New Orleans *Times-Picayune*, April 24, 1927, Sec. 1, pp. 1, 6, April 25, 1927, Sec. 1, pp. 1–2; New Orleans *States*, April 25, 1927, Sec. 1, p. 7.

19. New Orleans *Times-Picayune*, April 24, 1927, Sec. 1, p. 6.

20. *Ibid.*, April 25, 1927, Sec. 1, p. 1.

21. *Ibid.*

22. *Ibid.*, Sec. 1, p. 2.

Unfortunately, when "attempts were made to hold the bow in the crevasse to stop the water, . . . the current caught its stern and swung it around—pulling the bow through the levee and enlarging the break." The captain then beached his ship with the port side to the break. On April 26 three tugs were sent to try to pull the *Inspector* out of the crevasse. It had slipped fifty feet into the opening. On April 27 the tug fleet was increased to six, and the *Inspector* was sixty feet into the opening.[23]

Almost all of Coyle's harbor tugs were involved in this operation. Captain Schwalb, Oliver, and the *Corona* were among the men and boats trying vainly to dislodge the grounded ship. Several cables they attached to the *Inspector* snapped. This was a risky business. The tug itself could be swung against the bank and grounded when a cable broke. Meanwhile, the *Inspector* could be damaged from the constant pulling and tugging. As the tugs worked doggedly for several days with no success, it became apparent that the rescuers would have to wait for the Mississippi to crest before the ship could be freed. But a crest was still weeks away.

The efforts to free the *Inspector* were front-page news in New Orleans and called the attention of local citizens to other stories about flood horrors upriver—people marooned on rooftops, families swept away and drowned, thousands of cattle stranded on levees from Illinois to Mississippi. Oliver began to follow these stories more carefully after his personal encounter with the crevasse at Junior Plantation.

Two days after the *Inspector* struck the levee, the mayor of Chicago and a party of businessmen from the Windy City arrived in New Orleans aboard the steamboats *Cincinnati* and *Cape Girardeau* on a goodwill visit. The official purpose of the visit was to celebrate the passage of federal legislation for waterways connecting Chicago to the Mississippi and thus to New Orleans. The Chicago mayor, William Hale Thompson, however, was more vocal about the distress he had seen in flooded areas as he traveled down the Mississippi than he was about river commerce. After alighting from his steamboat at the foot of Canal Street to official greetings from New Orleans mayor Arthur J. O'Keefe, the cheers of a throng of greeters, and the sounds of several local bands, Thompson expressed his conviction that the federal government had to take the responsibility for better flood control along the river.[24]

On the front page of the *Times-Picayune* along with the story on Thompson's arrival was an account of a very different kind of steamboat

23. *Ibid.*, Sec. 1, pp. 1–2, April 26, 1927, Sec. 1, p. 1, April 27, 1927, Sec. 1, p. 2.
24. *Ibid.*, April 25, 1927, Sec. 1, pp. 1, 9; New Orleans *Item*, April 26, 1927, Sec. 1, p. 1.

arrival at Greenville, Mississippi. It was a story of the rescue made by the workhorse steamboat *Wabash*, whose captain had reacted to the sound of gunfire set off as a distress signal by black refugees caught along a narrow drainage canal that connected the small community of Wayside to the Mississippi River about fifteen miles above Greenville. When the flood swept over Wayside, five hundred persons were caught on the levee at the head of the canal. They had no food or clean water and had to scoop drinking water from the muddy flood around them. Three of them died from exposure, and one man was suffering from the bite of one of the numerous snakes that shared the high ground (he survived). The *Wabash* tore away its guardrails in negotiating the narrow canal. But it reached the flood victims and evacuated all of them. Tired, hungry, and homeless, they were nevertheless jubilant. They crowded the deck of the steamboat, according to the newspaper account, and sang plantation songs and spirituals in thanksgiving as the *Wabash* carried them to dry shelter in a refugee camp on the Greenville levee.[25]

The federal government could not ignore the mass destruction and human misery the flood was creating in the Mississippi Valley. In the last days of April, President Calvin Coolidge sent his secretary of commerce, Herbert Hoover, who was famous for his efficient relief work in Europe after World War I, to tour the areas under flood and report back to him. What was intended to be only a brief trip for Hoover turned into a series of constant journeys up and down the river and stopovers at locations on inland tributaries also affected by the flood. Hoover found himself taking on an active role in marshaling the relief forces in Tennessee, Arkansas, Mississippi, and Louisiana to set up refugee camps, house, feed, clothe, and provide medical care and vaccines for the flood victims.[26]

In Louisiana, as the Mississippi River rose steadily toward a threatening high, Governor O. H. Simpson named former governor John M. Parker to head the state's flood-relief program.[27] He also issued a proclamation on April 26 explaining the necessity for cutting the levee somewhere below New Orleans to save the city from flooding. It read in part:

> An unprecedented flood now holds in its grip the Mississippi Valley. Large areas of the state of Louisiana and the entire city of New Orleans, are seriously threatened.

25. New Orleans *Times-Picayune*, April 25, 1927, Sec. 1, p. 1.
26. *Ibid.*, April 24, 1927, Sec. 1, pp. 1, 20; New Orleans *States*, April 25, 1927, Sec. 1, p. 4.
27. New Orleans *Times-Picayune*, April 28, 1927, Sec. 1, pp. 1, 3; New Orleans *Item*, April 27, 1927, Sec. 1, p. 1.

The levees of this state are now holding, but the strain to which they will be subjected in the next fifteen days seriously aggravates the present danger, and imperatively demands that drastic steps shall be taken to avert the menace.

The Mississippi River Commission believes that the creation of an artificial break at some appropriate point will reduce the flood waters at New Orleans and for miles above, thus avoiding great loss of life and property. The state board of engineers of the city of New Orleans and of the dock board concur in this view and recommend immediate action.[28]

The point chosen for the cut was the Poydras levee in St. Bernard Parish. A crevasse at this point in 1922 had lowered the river more than two feet at New Orleans.[29] Now inhabitants of the area were ordered to evacuate as quickly as possible. Although the truck farmers and trappers living in the vicinity were distressed by the news, most accepted it stoically and began the exodus. In New Orleans, quarters were prepared for them in the Trade Exhibit Building and at the Fairgrounds Racetrack.[30] In Plaquemines Parish, the Celeste Sugar Company offered St. Bernard Parish evacuees free temporary occupancy of houses and shelter for their livestock on 210,000 acres of company land at Myrtle Grove that had not been touched by the Junior Plantation crevasse flood.[31] The Louisiana National Guard was called out to patrol St. Bernard Parish and assist the evacuation. Some units were also put on alert in other parts of the state as the raging river threatened north Louisiana.[32]

Vigilantes atop the St. Bernard levees had been firing guns to warn ships they thought were getting too close and threatening to cause another crevasse like the one at Junior Plantation. Now these men abandoned their posts. The crevasse they had feared was to become a reality by official order of the governor. Long lines of St. Bernard residents moved slowly up the highway toward New Orleans. They were described by one reporter as "a highway of humanity on trucks, in pleasure cars, on wagons, horseback, muleback, afoot, on oxen, goading cattle, leading cattle."[33] Children brought a favorite toy or clutched a puppy, cat, or chicken. A young boy led a scrawny calf on a frayed rope. Another had a small pet alligator. What to take and what to leave behind was an agonizing decision. One woman pulled up a favorite rosebush and wrapped it in newspaper. Some

28. New Orleans *Times-Picayune*, April 27, 1927, Sec. 1, p. 1; New Orleans *States*, April 27, 1927, Sec. 1, p. 10; and New Orleans *Item*, April 27, 1927, Sec. 1, p. 8.
29. New Orleans *Times-Picayune*, April 27, 1927, Sec. 1, p. 1.
30. *Ibid.*, Sec. 1, p. 12, April 29, 1927, Sec. 1, p. 10.
31. *Ibid.*, April 28, 1927, Sec. 1, p. 1.
32. *Ibid.*, April 27, 1927, Sec. 1, p. 1–2.
33. *Ibid.*, April 28, 1927, Sec. 1, pp. 1, 6; April 29, 1927, Sec. 1, pp. 1, 10.

families took furniture or farm implements. The farther a community was from the river, the harder it was for the inhabitants to accept the decision that they had to evacuate. Some threatened to stay and fight the government. Mosquito-bitten and sunburned, angry trappers clenched their fists at the orders to leave. But as the hour of demolition on the levee grew near, they all gave in.[34] Before they left, though, they thought of the hapless wild animals that were their livelihood and devised a clever scheme to help them survive. With help from the state Department of Conservation, trappers built rafts for the muskrats and stocked these with various roots and grains favored by the animals. Then they waited for the levee cut.

The levee was assaulted with multiple dynamite charges at twelve noon on Friday, April 29, at Caernarvon near Poydras. But the mud blasted into the air only fell back down again into the same place it had occupied before. When nothing but a weak trickle resulted from this operation, a diver was sent into the river to plant a charge under the batture in front of the levee. This time the explosion brought on a rushing flood that quickly spread over the land behind the levee.[35]

As muddy yellow-brown waters flowed massively into the countryside, trappers in boats, pulling the rafts they had built, entered the flooded backcountry and moored the rafts to trees. Desperate muskrats swimming for their lives sought this refuge—as many as 150 might huddle together on one raft. The trappers, aware that the greedy might try to take advantage of the animals' misfortune to gain their pelts, patrolled the flooded areas in boats to warn off human predators.[36]

While St. Bernard received a vast inundation reaching back to Delacroix Island and Shell Beach, New Orleans was safe. Secretary of Commerce Hoover had issued a public statement on the eve of the Caernarvon cut: "Cutting the levee line so as to lower flood levels at New Orleans will entirely change the situation here. It is a measure that relieves us considerably."[37] The grateful city became a center of activity for raising funds, gathering food, clothing, and bedding, and marshaling a fleet of boats to

34. Ibid., April 28, 1927, Sec. 1, p. 6; New Orleans Item, April 27, 1927, Sec. 1, pp. 1, 8.

35. New Orleans Times-Picayune, April 30, 1927, Sec. 1, pp. 1, 2, 10; George W. Healy, Jr., "A Newsman Who Covered It Recalls the Drama of the 1927 Flood," Dixie Roto Magazine, ibid., May 6, 1962; New Orleans Item, April 29, 1927, Sec. 1, pp. 1, 6, April 30, 1927, Sec. 2, p. 3; New Orleans States, April 29, 1927, Sec. 1, pp. 1, 7, April 30, 1927, Sec. 1, pp. 1, 2.

36. New Orleans Times-Picayune, May 5, 1927, Sec. 1, p. 11.

37. Ibid., April 28, 1927, Sec. 1, p. 12.

help the flood victims. Benefit performances to aid flood relief were held at local theaters. The Louisiana Historical Society in New Orleans and its counterpart in New York agreed to donate $500 collected for a memorial statue of the founder of New Orleans, Jean-Baptiste Le Moyne, sieur de Bienville, to the flood-relief drive. This is what Bienville would have wanted, they explained.[38]

The New Orleans Clearing House Association, representing the city's banks, put up $200,000 to fund loans to St. Bernard residents whose property was damaged by the Caernarvon crevasse. The loans would be repaid later by the state of Louisiana after the borrowers had posted claims for indemnification.[39] Governor Simpson called upon the Board of Liquidation to petition the legislature for the power to borrow $300,000 to fight the flood and its consequences.[40]

Federal agencies did their part also—official representatives of the Commerce, War, and Navy departments, the Veterans Bureau, the Coast Guard, and the Public Health Service had met with Secretary Hoover at Memphis to plan relief measures when he first arrived in the Mississippi Valley on April 26.[41] The Coast Guard rushed its vessels into service; everything from rowboats to lighthouse tenders to the big, fast rum-chasing boats that prowled the Gulf of Mexico now came up the Mississippi to New Orleans ready for action.[42]

Oliver visited the Junior Plantation site only occasionally after the first desperate days' work trying to pull the *Inspector* out of the crevasse. The later trips downriver were to bring supplies to the men aboard ship. Throughout the last days of April and early May, as the flood menace upstream grew more severe, the men working on Coyle's tugs observed the many relief vessels steaming upriver, and in New Orleans crowds congregated on Audubon Park's batture and at the foot of Canal Street to keep watch on the river's rise. High water and the swift current made working in the harbor more hazardous. But Coyle's crews were experienced and had no accidents. Down at Junior Plantation, the Lower Coast Railroad

38. *Ibid.*, April 27, 1927, Sec. 1, p. 12, April 28, 1927, Sec. 1, p. 3, April 29, 1927, Sec. 1, p. 3, May 23, 1927, Sec. 1, p. 1, May 25, 1927, Sec. 1, p. 1, May 27, 1927, Sec. 1, p. 2.

39. *Ibid.*, April 28, 1927, Sec. 1, pp. 1, 6.

40. *Ibid.*, April 26, 1927, Sec. 1, p. 1.

41. Pete Daniel, *Deep'n as It Come: The 1927 Mississippi River Flood* (New York, 1977), 10; New Orleans *Times-Picayune*, April 24, 1927, Sec. 1, pp. 1, 20, April 25, 1927, Sec. 1, p. 1, April 26, 1927, Sec. 1, pp. 1, 3, April 27, 1927, Sec. 1, p. 2, April 29, 1927, Sec. 1, p. 3.

42. New Orleans *Times-Picayune*, April 27, 1927, Sec. 1, p. 2, May 1, 1927, Sec. 1, pp. 1, 17.

line kept serving its customers by engaging boats to link Myrtle Grove to Buras.[43] Some rivermen who passed by the crevasse wondered if the unfortunate *Inspector* would survive if the ship were not removed before the waters began to recede. It might end up a cracked hulk.

By the time of the Caernarvon crevasse, the Mississippi had begun to rise menacingly in north Louisiana. A break at Cabin Teele, Louisiana, on May 3 resulted in the flooding of more than six million acres and uprooted some 277,000 persons.[44] In mid-May, the bayou country south of the Red River was inundated when crevasses along Bayou des Glaises caused the collapse of the bayou's levees, and breaks occurred along the Atchafalaya River at Melville and at McCrea, Louisiana. The floodwaters moved southward, endangering Opelousas, Lafayette, and New Iberia. There were some crevasses and flooding along the Mississippi between New Orleans and Baton Rouge—at Geismar, for instance—but in general the worst flooding was on the west bank and flowed away from the river at Pointe Coupee Parish and down into southwest Louisiana. A mammoth rescue effort was undertaken on behalf of human victims of the flood and their farm animals. Large refugee camps grew up almost overnight to shelter them until the emergency was dissipated by receding waters.[45]

The *Inspector* was finally dislodged from the levee at Junior Plantation on June 9, seven weeks after its accident. The honor of freeing it went to the *Robert W. Wilmot,* a tug owned by the Bisso Towing Company. The *Wilmot* succeeded where other tugs had failed by pulling the vessel stern-first downriver out of the crevasse, even though this left the ship facing upriver. The *Inspector* had been going downriver at the time of its impact with the levee, but the current had shifted the imprisoned ship so that the stern lay downstream. Since the vessel had to return to New Orleans anyway for repairs to its capstans and bitts and to have a hole in the stern closed, the *Wilmot* was really pointing it in the right direction.[46] The *Inspector*'s ordeal was over, but the levee at Junior Plantation would have to wait another two weeks before the river would fall low enough to make work on it practical.

By the end of June, the river was returning to a more normal course and the long work of reconstruction lay ahead for refugees returning home.

43. *Ibid.,* April 25, 1927, Sec. 1, p. 3.

44. Daniel, *Deep'n as It Come,* 9.

45. For maps of the flooded area, see Daniel, *Deep'n as It Come,* 85, and *Map of the State of Louisiana, Alluvial Lands in the State Flooded by High Water, 1927,* in Southeastern Louisiana University Archives and Special Collections. On refugee camps in Louisiana, see Daniel, *Deep'n as It Come,* 88–111.

46. New Orleans *Times-Picayune,* June 10, 1927, Sec. 1, p. 3.

The flood of 1927 would be remembered in Louisiana as the worst since European settlement on the lower Mississippi had begun, in the early eighteenth century. Through it all, Oliver had come to work in the morning and gone home at night with no fear that the floodwaters would endanger the New Orleans harbor or his bright new home on Venus Street. The Canal Street Ferry missed its landing once or twice due to the fury of the high water and swift current, but always made it after two or three tries. Oliver did not let such a minor inconvenience disturb him—that could happen any spring.

He had reached a high ground in other areas of his life as well. He had a wife, a new home, and a steady job with a company he liked. What else could he possibly want? Neda supplied the answer the next year, 1928, when she gave birth to what would be their only child, a girl they named Joy. The baby was born in their bedroom, delivered by Neda's mother, Josephine, who was a midwife. The family cycle had repeated itself. Oliver, who had been part of a big family, then half an orphan and alone for many years, was now part of a family again. When he saw his daughter for the first time, she was quietly sleeping with her left hand against her face and the little index finger stretched out against her cheek.[47] *So perfect!* he thought, and was overwhelmed with the miracle of life renewing itself. Oliver tiptoed out of the bedroom after seeing his wife and daughter and tried to tell his brother-in-law, Joe Drouant, what he was feeling at that moment. But his emotions choked him. He couldn't say a word. Joe sat him down at the kitchen table and poured him a stiff drink of whiskey. Words weren't necessary.

47. The daughter of Oliver and Oneida, Joy Juanita, was born on October 8, 1928, at about 1 : 30 P.M.

9

CAPTAIN OF THE *CORONA*
Tugboating at Coyle's, 1928 – 1934

By the time Oliver's daughter was born in 1928, a decade had passed since he left the employ of the bar pilots. During those ten years he had gone to sea and worked at a variety of jobs in the harbor of New Orleans. But he had never once considered going back to Southwest Pass to ask for his old job. What had seemed a reasonable prospect in 1918—that he would eventually return—had receded from his thoughts and finally, after he married, had been rejected altogether. He did not want to return to the isolation of that job without a guarantee that it would lead someday to membership in the Associated Branch Pilots. But he still hoped to become a river pilot someday. His uncle by marriage, Garrett Vogt, a member of the Crescent River Port Pilots Association, had died, but Uncle John, also a Crescent River Port pilot, promised to sponsor Oliver for election to this prestigious association, whose members piloted large vessels between Pilottown and New Orleans. Before Oliver could be seriously considered, however, John died in 1932. It was a tragic loss of a very gifted pilot in the prime of his life.

Oliver continued to hope that he might win a berth among the Crescent River Port pilots as their business increased and they had to take in new members, but he knew that it would be difficult without a relative to sponsor him. Most of the members had kin of their own whom they wished to offer for election. Also, after years of steady growth, the magic prosperity of the local port and of the rest of the nation came to an end in 1929. The aftermath of the stock market crash lessened the need for new pilots. As the Great Depression settled over the port of New Orleans in the early 1930s, Oliver was caught in an endless cycle of long hours and hard work with little indication that he would ever advance. Nevertheless, he was grateful that he had a job, a regular salary, and a work atmosphere he liked on the Coyle tugs.

Actually, as far as the port of New Orleans was concerned, the progression from prosperity to depression began in the last two years of the 1920s. The impact of the 1927 flood upon farmers' ability to plant and harvest crops in the Mississippi Valley slashed into the port's business in 1928 and 1929. The negative effect was reflected in the 1929 annual report of the Dock Board, which covered September, 1928, through August 31, 1929. The report recorded the smallest operating gain for the port in a decade and cited as the cause "a financially disastrous year at the public grain elevators" and the second smallest amount of business at the public cotton warehouse since its opening in 1916.[1] Obviously, the great flood had affected the grain and cotton production in the two years following its occurrence and probably accounted for a share of the deficits in receipts at both the local grain elevators and the cotton warehouse.

Another sign of economic unrest was the report in the *Times-Picayune* on January 1, 1930, that deposits at seven local banks were down 5 percent from 1928. This percentage was also reported as the approximate rate of decline in local business activity. The causes included labor troubles, threats of high water in the spring of 1929, and of course, the shock of the stock market crash in October.[2] Despite these signs of a troubled economy, Canal Street was crowded on New Year's Eve, 1929, with holiday celebrants who welcomed in 1930 with noisemakers and laughter.[3]

Among the most symbolic casualties of changing times and economic reverses were the traditional steamboats that had proudly lined the docks of New Orleans in the nineteenth century. By 1930 the Bienville Street Wharf offered the last glimpse of cargo-carrying steamboats near Canal Street. In the first week of 1930, the Dock Board announced its plans to move the steamboat landing away from Bienville, probably to the area of Press Street, many blocks downriver. A young *Times-Picayune* reporter, George Healey, noted bitterly in a front-page story that the steamboats were literally being sold down the river:[4]

> Almost all of the old steamboats . . . are gone. Of the 2000 "floating palaces" built between 1860 and 1900 none plies the Father of Waters from New Orleans. . . . The *Tennessee Belle*, operated by the Bradfords to Vicksburg . . . and Captain Cooley's *Ouachita*, formerly the *George Prince*, are the largest steamboats operating from New Orleans today. Neither can compare in size with the "floating palaces" of 50 years ago. A score of smaller boats operate from the Bienville street wharf up the Mississippi and along the Louisiana bayous, but the line seen from the Canal street ferry today is pitifully thin in

1. New Orleans *Times-Picayune*, January 1, 1930, Sec. 1, p. 1.
2. *Ibid.*
3. *Ibid.*, Sec. 1, pp. 1, 3; New Orleans *Item*, January 1, 1930, Sec. 1, p. 1.
4. New Orleans *Times-Picayune*, January 5, 1930, Sec. 1, pp. 20–21. A follow-up story appeared *ibid.*, February 8, 1930, Sec. 1, p. 9, on possible sites for the steamboat landing below Canal Street.

comparison with the long rows seen along the levee in the early eighties. . . .
Not a single passenger steamboat line is operated to the North, although the
Cape Girardeau at Carnival season brings revelers to New Orleans from St.
Louis and the Ohio river cities.[5]

There was one notable exception to the disappearance of the steamboats: the large excursion steamer *President*. From its dock at Eads Plaza
near Canal Street, almost directly across from Coyle's yard, the *President*
churned up and down the river with tourists in the daytime, calliope too-
tling happily (Oliver, who saw the boat every day, could hear it all the
way across the wide harbor); on weekend nights, festooned with strings of
lights, it offered live band music for couples who came aboard to dance
on "moonlight cruises." A prime attraction to out-of-towners and young
Orleanians alike, it also became, as the years passed, a kind of floating
landmark for veteran rivermen and others who remembered the all-but-
vanished era it represented.

At the same time that the Dock Board recommended the removal of
the steamboats from the prime area of the Bienville Street Wharf, it announced plans to improve facilities for handling barges and cargoes of the
Federal Barge Line. As the steamboats faded downstream, towboats and
their barges were recognized as the economic hope of the future.[6]

Such changes as the disappearance of the steamboat landing and the
general economic decline made Oliver realize that the future seemed less
rosy than it had in 1924. Worried about how this turn of the economy
might affect them, the Jacksons decided in late 1929 to move to Algiers
into half of a rented double house and rent out both sides of their Venus
Street home. They would receive more rent than they paid, and they
hoped to apply the balance to their house notes. Also, Oliver would be
close to his work. Neda sorely missed her Venus Street house, but she
believed that the move represented a wise course that would allow them
to return someday after her husband got a raise.

A bizarre problem that plagued Oliver at this time was a case of mistaken identity. Prohibition was still the law of the land in the early 1930s,
although the public as a whole was completely disillusioned with it and
was beginning to demand that it be scrapped. Oliver found to his chagrin
that he had the same initials and last name as the major official in charge
of Prohibition operations in Louisiana—O. D. Jackson. Many times in
the late twenties and early thirties he was contacted by phone by someone
who wished to report the whereabouts of a whiskey still or a shipment of

5. *Ibid.*, January 5, 1930, Sec. 1, p. 21.
6. *Ibid.*

rum and gin from Cuba. No matter how sincerely he tried to convince the callers that he was not the man they wanted, they always brushed off his protestations as subterfuge and insisted he investigate their accusations. Awakened one night after a particularly hard day on the river by a call of this sort, Oliver gave up trying to persuade the caller that he was not a Prohibition officer. "All right," he told her. "I'll have some agents check out your tip first thing tomorrow." Happily for the Jacksons, these messages stopped in 1933 with the repeal of the Prohibition amendment.

Despite the hopes of the public and the predictions of the newspapers at the beginning of each new year, the commerce of the river decreased rather than increased during the early 1930s. The first five years of the decade were the most difficult of the depression for the port of New Orleans. As a barometer of economic well-being, the figures for the total water-borne commerce of New Orleans compiled by the Corps of Engineers in its annual reports reveal that annual tonnage totals between 1930 and 1935 were all below the figure for 1929. Even in 1936, when both the tonnage and its value increased considerably over what it had been in the previous five years, both were still slightly lower than in 1929. In 1929 water-borne commerce through the port amounted to 15,995,374 tons valued at $908,536,416. It fell each year until it reached 10,491,084 tons in 1932 valued at $468,898,262, a decline of one-third in tonnage and almost one-half in value.[7] That same year, the total value of water-borne commerce passing through the port of New Orleans was lower than it had been since 1916. By 1936, more prosperous times were returning to the port. Among other reasons, the Italian-Ethiopian hostilities in North Africa stimulated European demand for scrap iron, grain, cotton, and other products from the United States.[8]

During the hard times, tugboat companies such as Coyle's had to cut back on their crews and vessels. But Coyle's had a policy of keeping its experienced tugboatmen—even if they had to be put to work painting tied-up tugs or helping around the yard. In the grim days of the 1930s, Oliver didn't get many raises, but he kept his job—maybe one week a captain and the next week a deckhand or yard worker. At year's end, the Coyle Company tried to reward its employees with bonuses according to their safety records. Oliver was fortunate enough to receive a bonus every year at Christmas during his tenure at Coyle's.

The Coyle tugboat yard at the foot of Eliza Street in Algiers was a

7. For statistics on the decrease in imports and exports through the port of New Orleans between 1930 and 1935, see Bradbury, *Water-Borne Commerce of New Orleans*, 14–15.

8. *Ibid.*, 12.

landmark of long standing in the New Orleans harbor. Its two-story white wooden office topped by a large sign displaying the name—W. G. Coyle Company—across the entire length of the building's shallow roof could be seen from across the river. Tugs and barges lined its docks, which ran for several blocks in front of the yard where workers parked their automobiles. A tall flagpole with the United States flag displayed daily graced the center of this shell-filled yard.[9] In 1930, W. G. Coyle Company was already sixty-five years old, one of the oldest tugboat companies in the city. It was founded in 1865, the year the Civil War ended, by a Confederate veteran, William G. Coyle.

William G. Coyle was an epic figure in the history of the port of New Orleans in the late nineteenth century.[10] A native of England, born on January 1, 1836, he migrated to New Orleans early in life with his parents. When they died, he was adopted by the Reverend Dr. Charles Goodrich, rector of St. Paul's Episcopal Church. As a youth, he went to work for the prestigious local jewelry firm of Hyde and Goodrich. With the outbreak of the Civil War, he enlisted at age twenty-five in the Washington Artillery, 3d Company. He had a brother, Frank, who also joined this fighting unit, which became famous for its valor and achievement in battle. The Coyle brothers saw much action. Frank was killed at Petersburg.

By the time Lee surrendered at Appomattox, Bill Coyle had risen to the rank of sergeant. He formed part of the escort that rode with Confederate president Jefferson Davis as he made a vain effort to escape capture by the Federal forces. At Washington, Georgia, a week before Davis' capture, the escort party were each paid $26 in gold or silver coins from Confederate Treasury funds Davis and his cabinet were carrying with them.

After Davis' capture on May 10, 1865, Coyle returned to New Orleans. In his search for employment there, he became aware of large surpluses of coal owned by the federal government and piled at various locations on the city's levees. With the war at an end, the United States Navy did not need the stockpiles, and the government offered the coal at auction to the public. Coyle managed to put together enough cash (perhaps including the coins Davis had given him) to purchase some of the surplus coal and go into the coal business locally. The W. G. Coyle Company was founded through this action in 1865.

9. See *Sanborn Insurance Map of New Orleans, Louisiana, 1937* (9 vols.; New York, 1937–40), VII, 711, for location and layout of the Coyle Company's tugboat yard in Algiers.

10. Descriptions of W. G. Coyle and the operations of his company in his lifetime are taken from Dufour, *Story of Coyle Lines*, 1–6; W. G. Coyle obituary in New Orleans *Daily Picayune*, February 18, 1914, Sec. 1, pp. 7, 8; and John E. Land, *Pen Illustrations of New Orleans, 1881–82* (New Orleans, 1882), 90.

Within a year, Coyle had made connections with Simpson R. Horner of Pittsburgh, who had supplied coal to the United States government during the war. Horner wished to continue his trade downriver to New Orleans and was impressed with the initiative of young Coyle. He offered and Coyle accepted the proposition that they become partners. Horner supplied coal by barges down the Ohio and Mississippi rivers. Coyle sold it in New Orleans and to maritime customers on the river. The firm of W. G. Coyle as a partnership venture of Coyle and Horner prospered and remained in existence until Horner's retirement about 1886. At that time Coyle's son Charles Goodrich Coyle entered the business.

In addition to their many coalyards scattered around the Crescent City supplying coal to industrial and household customers, the Coyles had a number of tugboats that towed barges and colliers to vessels in the harbor to restock the ships' supplies of coal. The tugs also did general harbor work needed by shipping firms. The Algiers tugboat yard was the main yard throughout the company's entire existence, but there were also branch yards upriver at Plaquemine and Baton Rouge. The business office was located at 323 Carondelet Street.

Another venture of W. G. Coyle Company was the operation of the steamer *New Camellia*, which at first carried freight and passengers between New Orleans and Bay St. Louis, Mississippi. Later shifted to Lake Pontchartrain, it acted as an excursion boat between New Orleans and Mandeville, Louisiana, across the lake. In connection with this steamer, Coyle Company served as the agent of the Abita Company to advertise and make travel and hotel arrangements for tourists wishing to visit Abita Springs in St. Tammany Parish, just a short distance from Mandeville.[11]

Coyle's son Charles died in 1910, and the company was incorporated in 1911. The original founder remained active in the business until his death on February 17, 1914, but his surviving children, two daughters and a son, had no desire to operate the firm personally. A year after the death of William G. Coyle, the company was acquired by the DeBardeleben Coal Company of Birmingham, Alabama. The guiding force behind DeBardeleben Coal was an Alabama native, Henry T. DeBardeleben, whose father had been one of the founders of the city of Birmingham.[12] Under his guidance, the W. G. Coyle Company continued its service to the New Orleans harbor. The coal handled by Coyle Company now came from the DeBardeleben mines in Alabama. It was shipped both by rail and by barge

11. Land, *Pen Illustrations of New Orleans*, p. 183.
12. On Henry T. DeBardeleben, see *National Cyclopaedia of American Biography* (New York, 1951), XXXVII, 320.

from the Warrior River in Alabama. Seagoing tugs were added to Coyle's fleet to aid in this endeavor.[13]

At the end of World War I, DeBardeleben's son Henry Fairchild De-Bardeleben, who was returning from the war with the rank of sergeant, went to work at Coyle's, starting as a deckhand. He served in numerous other jobs to learn the business from the bottom up. After three years he was made office manager at Coyle's. In 1924 he moved up to manager of operations. Through his family connections, he held a number of additional positions of importance in the DeBardeleben company and its subsidiaries. But his major work in the 1920s and 1930s was done at Coyle's, which served as his base of operations. As his involvement in other of his family's companies became more necessary, he divided his time among New Orleans, Birmingham, and Tampa. He became president and general manager of Coyle Company in 1937, and chairman of the board of both DeBardeleben Coal and the Coyle Company in 1949. He was succeeded as president of Coyle Company by his brother Bailey T. DeBardeleben. Later he was named chairman of the board of the DeBardeleben Marine Corporation and its subsidiaries, and finally, president of Tampa Marine Company and its subsidiaries. By the time of his death in 1964, Henry F. DeBardeleben headed eight corporations in his family's coal and maritime empire.[14]

Throughout his life, DeBardeleben was dedicated to river and canal trade in the Gulf Coast area and participated in national movements and government programs to promote it. In his personal relations, he was a friendly, outgoing individual who had a genuine rapport with the men working under him. At Coyle Company he knew most of the employees by their first names. He made it a practice to take an occasional ride on one of the tugs and talk with the men and listen to their problems. When he could help in some labor dispute or personal emergency, he did it promptly and without any fanfare. Oliver admired DeBardeleben as a man of integrity and considered him the finest boss in the New Orleans harbor. Henry F. expected hard work, long hours, and loyalty from his tugboatmen but was capable of compassion and loyalty when the economic outlook on the river was clouded by the Great Depression.

The men who worked for Coyle Company in the 1930s were an especially skilled group. Some came to the company with their pilot licenses and considerable experience on tugs. Oliver fit into this category. Others,

13. Dufour, *Story of Coyle Lines*, 6.

14. *Ibid.*, 6–10; New Orleans *States-Item*, April 8, 1964, Sec. 1, p. 10; New Orleans *Times-Picayune*, April 9, 1927, Sec. 1, p. 7.

like Captain Adolph Schwalb, had family members with a background in tugboating or came out of the navy and added to their extensive knowledge of naval craft what they learned about tugboats at Coyle's. After a few years of working thirteen-to-fifteen-hour shifts, all of the Coyle tugboat captains who survived were masters of their trade. Many went on to become river pilots, either in the Crescent River Port Pilots Association or in the upriver organization, the New Orleans–Baton Rouge Steamship Pilots Association.

In the 1930s, some of the men who served as tugboat captains at Coyle's were Adolph Schwalb, Oliver Jackson, Gilbert Manson, Sr., Gilbert Manson, Jr., George George, William Henley, Walter Wright, A. Warren Whiteman, Adolph Clark, John Lingoni, J. E. Mitchell, and William Short. Engineers on the tugs were also of vital importance and had to know their business to keep the tugs' engines fired up and running properly. Coyle engineers of the 1930s included Richard H. Buras, Sr., who worked with Oliver and became a close friend of his; Eric Jackson, Oliver's brother, who came to town from Burrwood in the mid-1930s and got a Coyle job through Oliver's recommendation; James Talbot; Eugene Cadro; Peter Algero; and Earl Sutherland. Other employees were Thomas St. Germain, fireman and oiler, and deckhands Stanley Huber, Jerry Diket, Godfrey McNeeley, and Charles Fink. The majority of this last group of men moved up to the rank of captain, and some became pilots in later years. In the tugboat yard, Captain Charles T. Kight served as yard superintendent, Phillip Sunseri ran the company's grocery store, and Neil Watson was the company machinist.[15]

The tugs in service at Coyle's during the 1930s varied in size, age, place of origin, and purpose. The *Adler*, 146 feet in length, was built in Pensacola, Florida, in 1921 and was the only tug of its power and capacity in United States waters; the *Adler* was designed for both harbor and deep-sea work. The *DeBardeleben*, 150 feet in length, was another deep-water craft, built in Elizabeth, New Jersey, in 1919. The third powerful seagoing tug was the *Sipsey*, 123 feet long and built in Ferrysburg, Michigan, in 1905. The *W. G. Wilmot*, 110 feet and named for an old-time tugboat owner in New Orleans, was designed especially for the Mississippi River and had been built in West Bay City, Michigan, in 1892. The *Corona*, 100 feet, was the oldest of Coyle's tugs, built in Camden, New Jersey, in 1886.

15. Interview with Richard Buras, Jr., by Joy Jackson, September 26, 1987, Hammond, La.; Richard Buras, Jr., to Joy Jackson, October 22, 1987, in possession of the author; *Soards' New Orleans City Directory, 1933*, (New Orleans, 1933), 756.

Despite its age, it was seaworthy as well as harbor oriented. Equipped with wrecking, towing, and fire-fighting devices, as were most of the other tugs, the Corona was remarkably agile in handling and was a favorite with Oliver, his friend Adolph Schwalb, and chief engineer Richard Buras.[16] Buras, whose pastime was making model tugboats, carved over fifty models of this beautiful tug out of driftwood cast up on the riverbank near Coyle's yard.[17] Oliver and Richard probably spent more time on the Corona than they did on any other Coyle tug. She was the first of the company's tugs on which Oliver got to act as captain. As a result, he felt a special pride in being her master, even after he had captained a number of the other tugs (Coyle's captains were moved about from one tug to another to fit the company work schedule). Somehow Oliver always felt he had come home again when he transferred back to the Corona.

Other Coyle tugs basically of the same type as those just described were the H. T. DeBardeleben and the White Water. Rounding out Coyle's fleet were three large canal towing steamers, the Donie, the Helen, and the Clara, which saw much of their service after the opening of the segment of the Intracoastal Canal between New Orleans and Galveston, Texas, in 1934.[18]

One unorthodox crew member aboard the Corona when Adolph Schwalb and Oliver were alternating as her captain was the pride of the Coyle yard. He was a clever fox terrier called Jimmie. A short-haired white dog with a few black spots, Jimmie wandered into the yard as a pup and was promptly adopted by Schwalb, a tenderhearted pushover for small children and animals. Adolph brought the little canine aboard the tug, which quickly became his home when he wasn't roaming along the levee in Algiers or hanging around the Coyle yard. A born sailor, Jimmie learned to climb ladders and once followed Captain Schwalb right up to the pilothouse of a ship—the Corona's crew extended a wooden ladder from the deck of the tug to the ship's deck for him. Schwalb shouted directions through a megaphone from the bridge of the ship to Oliver, who guided the Corona and the attached ship away from the dock. Jimmie sat alongside Schwalb high up on the ship's bridge looking down.[19]

The little dog loved to sit on the deck of the tug while it steamed down the river. He would sniff the breeze with his head held forward, a seasoned

16. *History of W. G. Coyle and Co., Inc., and DeBardeleben Coal Corporation* (New Orleans, n.d.), 6–15.

17. Interview with Richard Buras, Jr., September 26, 1987.

18. Dufour, *Story of Coyle Lines*, 11, 13.

19. Jackson Transcripts, No. 9, June 7, 1982, p. 6.

old river dog savoring his territory. One of Jimmie's most traumatic adventures came about when Oliver, serving as captain of the *Corona*, was ordered to Chalmette to deliver a barge filled with oil to a sugar refinery:

> While we were tied up and pumping oil, Jimmie went ashore, I don't know where, and when we got ready to leave, we didn't know where he was. I tooted the whistle a couple of times. No Jimmie. . . . I couldn't wait. I pulled away and came back up to town . . . and about a week afterwards, we went down there to deliver some more oil to the refinery. I figured if Jimmie was around anywhere, he'd hear the whistle and he'd recognize it. So before I began rounding to, I blew "Beeeeeep, beeeeeep, beeeeeep. Toot. Toot. Toot." I rounded the barge around, and as I was going alongside the dock and tying up to the dock, here came Jimmie. He was running like Hell! He ran and ran down onto the barge, and he crossed the barge to the tug. He went to me, and he went to Richard Buras, and he just bawled out all of us. He was barking and barking and barking. Oh, he was something. He was one more dog![20]

As surefooted as Jimmie was on the tugboat, he was no match for the swift movements of the motor vehicles in the Coyle parking lot. He was killed by an automobile that backed up suddenly. His passing left a small empty spot on the deck of the *Corona*.

Although Coyle tugs daily crisscrossed the Mississippi in all kinds of weather, often towing barges loaded with hazardous substances such as fuel oil, accidents were relatively rare and usually minor. But in 1934 there were two serious accidents involving Coyle tugs. Although neither was the fault of Coyle's captains, the second of them proved costly to the company; fortunately, neither involved loss of life.

The first incident occurred in February, 1934, when the Dock Board fire tug *Samson* collided with a barge being towed by the Coyle tug *Sipsey* near the entrance of the Industrial Canal. A deep hole was torn in the port side of the *Samson*, sinking the fire tug within ten minutes. Its crew dived overboard and swam safely to shore. The *Sipsey* managed to control its tow and deliver the damaged barge to the Poland Street Wharf. After considerable struggle, divers and a crew with salvage equipment were able to raise the sunken vessel from the entrance of the canal.[21]

Oliver had not been aboard the *Sipsey* when it collided with the *Samson*. But less than two months later, he took part in a rescue operation that had disastrous consequences for Coyle's. On Friday, the thirteenth of

20. *Ibid.*

21. New Orleans *Times-Picayune*–New Orleans *States*, Sunday combined edition, February 25, 1934, Sec. 1, pp. 1, 13; New Orleans *Times-Picayune*, February 26, 1934, Sec. 2, p. 13.

April, a Japanese freighter and passenger ship, the *Rio de Janeiro Maru*, went aground on a sandbar at the mouth of South Pass. Freeing it would be no easy task. The ship weighed 9,627 tons and was stuck fast. The agent for the ship's company requested tugs from Coyle Company to extract it. He also sent a launch down to the ship to remove thirty-one of the forty-four passengers aboard. They were taken to Buras, where they transferred to a bus and were driven to New Orleans and housed in a downtown hotel.[22] The ship's crew and the thirteen passengers who opted to remain with the grounded vessel hoped that Coyle's tugs would do a quick job of freeing them from the silt of the Mississippi.

The three tugs sent to help refloat the *Rio de Janeiro Maru* were the *Sipsey*, the *Adler*, and the *H. T. DeBardeleben*. They reached the mouth of the river Saturday afternoon and worked into the night pulling on the ship.[23] Oliver served as captain of the *Adler*, considered a uniquely powerful tug, with no equal in the United States. Aboard the *H. T. DeBardeleben* was the company's general manager and vice-president at that time, Henry F. DeBardeleben, as an observer. The strategy of the Coyle captains was to deploy their tugs on either side and to the rear of the ship and endeavor to pull it sternward into deep water.

Each tug had one or two lines attached to the ship. Night came and they continued their efforts with only a minimal shifting of the formidable vessel. Suddenly a bitt on the port side of the *H. T. DeBardeleben* gave way without warning. This threw the tension between the tug and the ship, which had been shared by the port and stern bitts, onto the stern bitts alone. The tug's captain, J. E. Mitchell, gave a hurried order to loosen the stern line to disengage the tug from the ship, but before this could be done the loss of leverage swept the *H. T. DeBardeleben* out of control into the shallow water of the sandbar. A swell from the Gulf picked the tug up and then set it down with a bang on the bottom. The plates of the hull sprang, and the boat started taking water.[24]

Oliver, aboard the *Adler* nearby, reacted quickly to the disaster:

> They hollered to me what the trouble was, so I hurried up and let my hawser go. I had the big twelve-inch hawser I was pulling along. . . . I got men to turn it loose altogether—I just let it go overboard. It was made fast to the ship. . . .

22. New Orleans *Times-Picayune*–New Orleans *States*, Sunday combined edition, April 15, 1934, Sec. 1, pp. 1, 18; New Orleans *Times-Picayune*, April 16, 1934, Sec. 1, pp. 1, 10.

23. New Orleans *Times-Picayune*–New Orleans *States*, Sunday combined edition, April 15, 1934, Sec. 1, p. 1; New Orleans *Times-Picayune*, April 16, 1934, Sec. 1, p. 1; Jackson Transcripts, No. 9, p. 1.

24. Jackson Transcripts, No. 9, p. 1.

I hurried as fast as I could get to them . . . but in the meantime while I was letting go of my line, they [the men aboard the *H. T. DeBardeleben*] hollered to the Japanese ship. . . . Right away they [the Japanese] lowered a yawl boat— a lifeboat—and by that time I got around and I was drawing more water than the *DeBardeleben*. My tug was drawing twenty, twenty-one feet of water. So I couldn't take a chance of going in too close because I'd hit bottom myself. But I put my search light on them, a big powerful search light. . . . I put that on and I could see Captain Mitchell and the deckhands . . . all standing on the tug. The tug hadn't gone down yet all the way. Her decks were still out of the water, and they were standing on the deck of the sinking tug waiting for the Japanese. I threw the light on them, and the Japanese had plenty of light then. They pulled quick over there and picked them all up, and as they picked them up, I kept holding the light on them until they were up on the ship. . . . When I saw they were safe, then I backed down, spun around, and picked up my line again. . . . The tug, the *H. T. DeBardeleben*, kept going down, down, and the swell knocked her smokestack off . . . just the masts were standing up [above the water].[25]

Another perspective of the accident was given many years later by Captain Gilbert Manson, Jr., who was a young crew member on the *H. T. Debardeleben* in 1934. He remembered the shock of the initial impact with the sandbar and the realization that the tug was sinking. Manson rushed to a locker to get a lantern to help with evacuation of the stricken vessel. As he opened the locker door, the tilt of the sinking tug caused a can of red paint to turn over and spill on his head. Abandoning the search for the lantern, he returned to the other crew members on deck to await evacuation. When Manson climbed the ladder to the deck of the *Rio de Janeiro Maru*, his paint-spattered head was visible to the small group of passengers still left on the ship, who were crowding the rail watching the rescue. A woman passenger fainted at the sight of Manson. She thought that the red paint was blood.[26]

Henry F. DeBardeleben made a ship-to-shore call from the Japanese ship to his office to inform them of the sinking of the tug. It must have been a bitter experience for him to watch the tug named for his father sink beneath the water at the mouth of South Pass. Efforts to free the ship continued the next day. Bisso Towing Company sent down their old reliable *Robert W. Wilmot*, the tug credited with pulling the *Inspector* out of the Junior Plantation crevasse in 1927. The *Adler*, which had taken the wrecked tug's crew to New Orleans, also returned to help. It was a week

25. *Ibid.*, 1–2.
26. Statement of Captain Gilbert Manson, Jr., to Joy Jackson on June 30, 1984, at the Jackson residence in Hammond, La., during a visit to Oliver Jackson.

before the ship was freed from the sandbar. The *Adler*, with Oliver as its captain, and a small ship sent down to South Pass by the St. Clair Line finally dislodged the captive vessel.[27] The *H. T. DeBardeleben*, however, was a permanent loss. It joined a list of shipwrecks off the coast of the Passes dating back to the eighteenth century.

27. New Orleans *Times-Picayune–New* Orleans *States*, Sunday combined edition, April 15, 1934, Sec. 1, p. 1; New Orleans *Times-Picayune*, April 16, 1934, Sec. 1, p. 1; Jackson Transcripts, No. 9, pp. 2, 3.

IO

STORM CLOUDS AND RAINBOWS
NEW ORLEANS, 1935 – 1937

On the New Orleans waterfront, the early 1930s was a stormy time for those seeking employment or trying to hold a job. The docks were haunted by hollow-eyed men looking for work and angry union men caught in labor disputes. Oliver and Neda had moved back to the east bank in 1932 and into their Venus Street home in 1934. Each morning when Oliver caught the Canal Street Ferry, he was greeted on the Algiers side by a line of shabby wanderers with bundles of clothes and, sometimes, small children. They had just gotten off a Southern Pacific freight train in Algiers and were waiting to board the ferry for the trip to the east side.[1] Boxcar passengers, they had hopes of finding work in New Orleans. Remembering his own hard times in New Orleans back in 1913 and 1914, Oliver always felt a tightness in his throat when he passed such newcomers.

The unemployed were pathetic, but the dock workers, frequently on strike, were frustrated. Each year they found their pay decreasing and their grievances ignored. For a brief interval in 1934, it appeared that all labor grievances had been set to rest when two of the major longshoremen's unions signed an agreement with the New Orleans Steamship Association.[2] But on October 1, 1935, the labor-management breach reopened again when the International Longshoremen's Association called for a strike against the shipping companies.[3] In their attempts to picket wharves and prevent strikebreakers from taking over their jobs, dock workers resorted to name calling, pushing and shoving, fighting, and sometimes, fatal violence.

In late October, a white farmer and his black helper who had been in New Orleans selling vegetables out of their truck were pelted with brickbats as they drove to the Jackson Avenue ferry landing. The victims tried to explain that they were not strikebreakers, but to no avail. Finally, the

1. Jackson Transcripts, No. 9, p. 5.
2. New Orleans *Times-Picayune,* February 27, 1934, p. 17.
3. New Orleans *Times-Picayune*-New Orleans *States,* Sunday combined edition, October 20, 1935, Sec. 1, p. 20.

farmer pulled his gun from under his seat and fired out the window above the heads of the assailants. They fled, leaving him with ten dollars' worth of damage to his truck.[4]

Shipowners tried to prevent incidents by posting copies of two federal injunctions against interfering with peaceful commerce.[5] This had no effect. In early November two homeless men who had spent the previous night at the Baptist Rescue Mission in the French Quarter walked down to the docks at Elysian Fields Avenue looking for work on the banana wharves. They were challenged by two other men, one of whom pulled a gun and shot one of the transients in the chest. As the gunman and his companion fled behind freight cars on the railroad tracks nearby, a harbor patrolman arrived and found the victim dead.[6]

Some owners, determined to keep their ships moving but worried about the confrontation between strikers and the men hired to replace them, arranged to bring the strikebreakers to their ships by river barge. That way they would not have to pass the picketers walking the streets leading to the wharves. Arrangements were made with Coyle Company to tow barge-loads of the temporary workers to designated ships. One morning when Oliver came to work, he was handed a slip with his assignment—take a barge loaded with about two hundred men to specified ships to report for longshore duties. Police would be stationed on the docks to keep strikers from confronting these men once they began the work of loading or unloading. There were no union men at Coyle's at this time, and Oliver had allowed his seaman's union membership to lapse in the 1920s. So he faced no conflict in transporting the strikebreakers.[7]

Oliver was captain of the *Corona* at this time, and his mate was John Lingoni. As they pulled away from the Coyle yard, Lingoni went up to the pilothouse to handle the tug while Oliver ate breakfast. Oliver recalled the run:

> We started up the river and when we got abreast of Thalia Street, . . . I heard some shots ring out and I realized that somebody was shooting at us. So I ran quickly away from the table and left my breakfast . . . and jumped . . . over the rail to the wheelhouse. Because the pilot had to protect himself, he left the wheel. They were hitting too close to him. He was lucky he didn't get hit. So I took the wheel and kept going upriver. I got to the landing and put the longshoremen off at their different ships and later came on back to the yard.

4. New Orleans *Times-Picayune*, October 26, 1935, Sec. 2, p. 13.
5. *Ibid.*, November 5, 1935, Sec. 1, p. 2.
6. *Ibid.*, November 7, 1935, Sec. 2, p. 23.
7. Jackson Transcripts, No. 9, pp. 14–16.

Henry F. DeBardeleben called the police and an investigation of the incident was conducted. Nothing ever came of it.[8] The strike was settled eventually, and the docks calmed down again to normal workday activities.

The year 1935 brought two historic accomplishments on the Mississippi River at New Orleans. One was the completion of the Bonnet Carré Spillway above the city to aid in flood control. The other was the opening of the Huey P. Long Bridge, the first bridge across the Mississippi in the vicinity of New Orleans.

After the flood of 1927, the Corps of Engineers and the Mississippi River Commission began putting into effect a comprehensive plan to avoid future natural catastrophes connected with flooding up and down the Mississippi Valley. As part of that plan, the Corps chose to safeguard New Orleans by building a spillway at Bonnet Carré, about twenty-five miles upriver. This spillway would drain water along a lowland floodway from the Mississippi to Lake Pontchartrain, a distance of over five miles.

The location was a natural basin for floodwaters. Twice in the nineteenth century—in 1850 and again in 1874—crevasses had broken the levee at Bonnet Carré and Mississippi River water had flowed north to the lake. The Bonnet Carré Spillway dike stretched for 7,698 feet along the Mississippi with 350 weirs that were electrically operated by a crane. The spillway's capacity was 250,000 cubic feet per second, and the cost of the project was over $13,000,000.[9]

The Airline Highway Bridge across the floodway was opened at the same time that the spillway was dedicated, on December 13, 1935. Three railroad bridges were already in operation. After the dedication, the dignitaries and many members of their audience walked to an L and N train that took them to Kenner, where they boarded the Streckfus Steamers, Inc., steamboat *Capitol*, ordinarily used for harbor tours and moonlight dance cruises, for the trip down to New Orleans.

The *Capitol*'s berth was the foot of Canal Street at Eads Plaza. On the day of the spillway dedication, a lavish celebration was planned in the plaza. As the *Capitol* approached its landing, a twenty-one-gun salute was fired by members of the Washington Artillery to commemorate the completion of the flood-control project. The men working at Coyle's, a short distance upriver on the west bank, could hear the commotion and see the smoke from the gunfire. After the *Capitol*'s passengers had disembarked and joined the crowd in the plaza, they were treated to band music,

8. *Ibid.*, 16.
9. Hansen, ed. *Louisiana: A Guide*, 526–27.

a patriotic pageant, and speeches once again by federal, state, and city officials.[10]

Three days later the Huey P. Long Bridge, just above New Orleans, was also dedicated and opened to the public. Forty-three years of planning had become reality.[11] At the time of its dedication it was the longest railroad bridge in the world, besides holding roadways for motor vehicles. It was a cantilever bridge with eight spans, the center section extending for 790 feet 135 feet above the river. Built at a cost of $13,000,000, it had taken three years to complete. It greatly facilitated railroad travel across the river, eliminating the old railroad ferries, such as the *Mastodon*, that had shuttled trains back and forth in sections across the Mississippi (Oliver's uncle John had worked as captain of one of these ferries for several years before becoming a river pilot).

First to consider building such a bridge had been the Southern Pacific Railroad in 1892. But the nationwide economic panic of 1893 caused the railroad line to drop the project. In 1904 the idea was revived when the Public Belt Railroad Commission came into existence to supervise the public rail lines along the riverfront. Despite discouragements and setbacks, the Public Belt officials persisted in their dream of building a bridge. In 1924 the noted architect Ralph Mojeski was engaged to draw up new plans after the War Department turned down earlier ones the Public Belt Railroad Commission had submitted. The first bridge permit was obtained in 1926, a second in 1927 (after improvements to the plan were made), and the final permit in 1930. The stock market crash and the financial crisis that followed delayed the funding arrangements for the bridge, but by the end of 1932 the Reconstruction Finance Corporation arranged to take over the entire issue of the Public Belt Railroad Commission's bonds. The state of Louisiana contributed funds to keep the bridge toll-free, and the Southern Pacific agreed to a rental contract for its use of the span.[12]

First-day celebrants drove across the bridge in automobiles or rode in the special train that carried more than a thousand guests from the east bank to the west bank and back again. Neda and some of her relatives

10. On the building and dedication of the Bonnet Carré Spillway, see New Orleans *Times-Picayune*, October 26, 1935, Sec. 1, p. 3, October 30, 1935, Sec. 1, pp. 1, 3, November 14, 1935, Sec. 1, pp. 1, 3, December 13, 1935, Sec. 1, pp. 1, 3, and December 14, 1935, Sec. 1, p. 3.

11. *Ibid.*, December 16, 1935, Sec. 1, p. 15, December 17, 1935, Sec. 1, pp. 3, 4.

12. On the building and dedication of the Huey P. Long Bridge, see New Orleans *Times-Picayune*, October 20, 1935, Sec. 1, p. 1, December 14, 1935, Sec. 1, pp. 1, 13, December 15, 1935, Sec. 1, pp. 1, 15, December 16, 1935, Sec. 1, p. 10, December 17, 1935, Sec. 1, pp. 3, 4, 6, and *New Orleans City Guide*, 371.

were among the many who drove across that day.[13] Boat whistles blew, bands played, and airplanes flew overhead to commemorate the great occasion.[14] Tugboat and towboat crews passing under the high-rising span during its last months of construction had been impressed as they looked up at its progress. The bridge had become a part of the river landscape. Boats and ships would have to come to terms with it in good weather and bad, in high water, and in dangerous fog. Despite its element of hazard to river traffic, the bridge did facilitate increased shipments by rail into New Orleans, and since most of these were headed for the riverfront, tugboat and towboat companies and shipping lines benefited. After its long-awaited completion, the bridge was like a rainbow stretching from shore to shore.

Traffic crossing the river in the heart of the city was not much affected by the bridge. Ferries continued to thrive—the bridge was too far upriver greatly to reduce their vehicular business as yet. Besides, automobiles were in general not as heavily relied upon as they are today. For example, by 1935 Oliver and Neda had both learned to drive a car and owned a modest coupe, but Oliver did not drive it to work. He considered that the cost of gasoline and the ferry charges twice a day would be too expensive, and driving up to the Huey P. Long Bridge would be too long a trip. He continued to commute by streetcar and ferryboat.

Oliver always broke his early morning journey to work by stopping at Gluck's Restaurant, 124 Royal Street, for a cup of coffee and a sweet roll. He left home about four-thirty and got off the Royal streetcar when it reached Canal Street, usually just before five. The Gluck's on Royal was one of several restaurants by that name in the city. The Royal Street version was a twenty-four-hour establishment. It had a large section with tables, a counter section with stools, and a bar. Oliver always sat at the counter.[15]

The morning after the dedication of the Huey P. Long Bridge, Oliver arrived at Gluck's at his usual time, sat at his usual spot, and placed his usual order. As the waiter turned to get the coffee and roll, Oliver noticed him glancing furtively toward a group of men talking heatedly at the other end of the counter. Three were seated and one, in an overcoat was standing. Oliver's attention was drawn to them by the waiter's interest. He

13. Interview with Oneida Drouant Jackson, June 23, 1987.

14. New Orleans *Times-Picayune*, December 17, 1935, Sec. 1, pp. 3, 4, 6; New Orleans *Item*, December 16, 1935, Sec. 1, pp. 1, 6.

15. Jackson Transcripts, No. 9, p. 4, from which the details of the following incident are taken. *Soards' New Orleans City Directory*, 1933 lists the various Gluck Restaurant locations, 580.

looked down the counter and found himself staring at a .45 revolver. The man in the overcoat had drawn the gun. Two of the seated men jumped up and ran from the restaurant. The third man, at whom the gun was pointed, made an effort to reach inside his coat, but the man in the overcoat fired two quick shots. One bullet went wide; the other entered the seated man's left shoulder and penetrated his chest.

The counter attendant had dropped down to hide at the first shot. Oliver ran behind the counter to join him. After the shooting, Oliver picked up his newspaper package from the counter—it contained a clean shirt to be worn after work—and headed for the exit. As he walked out, the shooter put the gun back in his pocket and walked out too. He went through the center glass door while Oliver used the door alongside of it. The gunman glanced at Oliver briefly. His face showed no expression.

For a little while Oliver stood across the street watching the scene unfold. The man in the overcoat threw his gun into an automobile parked in front of the restaurant but made no attempt to get away. Employees and patrons from Gluck's gathered as a traffic policeman arrived in answer to a call from the restaurant. The counterman identified the gunman for the policeman. At this point, as more police showed up, Oliver decided he had better head for the ferry landing. He figured this was a grudge fight involving gamblers. He didn't want to be a witness in such a case. Gambling, although illegal, was rampant in New Orleans. High-stakes poker and crap games were easy to find, and roulette and keno houses were popular. Testifying in a case involving professional gamblers could bring retaliation down upon the witness from associates of the side that stood to lose by the testimony. Oliver had heard of such incidents. He wanted to avoid testifying if he could, but knew that the counterman was acquainted with him and would probably give his name to the police. He just had to wait and see if he would be called.

On the front page of the newspaper the next day, Oliver discovered the circumstances surrounding the shooting.[16] The victim—he had died—was John "Gene" Gallicio, thirty-two, who had served time in prison for extorting money from a gambler. The man who shot him was Clarence Williams, thirty-nine, a partner in a gambling establishment that had just opened. Williams told police that Gallicio had robbed him twice. The first time, five years earlier, Gallicio had been one of five men who robbed patrons, employees, and the house of $5,000 in a gambling club where Williams worked in St. Bernard Parish. A year or two later, "Gallicio and

16. New Orleans *Times-Picayune*, December 18, 1935, Sec. 1, pp. 1, 19; New Orleans *Item*, December 17, 1935, Sec. 1, pp. 1, 12.

another man jumped on the running board of his [Williams'] automobile and forced him to surrender about $2,500 in gambling winnings."[17]

Despite this history, Williams maintained that he was not gunning for Gallicio the morning of the shooting and that their meeting was accidental.[18] He claimed that he had come into the restaurant with his partner, their two female companions, and his partner's bodyguard to get coffee after winding up their first night in their gambling house. The couples sat together at one table, the bodyguard stationed at a table nearby. Williams had a sack with four hundred dollars in silver coins, which he placed on his table. The encounter with Gallicio came about when Williams went to the men's room. The counter section was not visible from the area where Williams' party was seated. It was only as he walked toward the rest rooms that he encountered Gallicio. Recognizing each other, he and Gallicio became highly agitated and began arguing. Williams claimed that Gallicio threw a cup at him and challenged him to "have it out." He responded by firing in what he called self-defense as Gallicio reached into his pocket.

Williams' partner, the women, and the bodyguard heard the shots but could see nothing from where they were sitting. Their waitress told them the sounds were "just fireworks." But the bodyguard knew better. He left the restaurant immediately to get his gun out of their car. Somehow, in the confusion that followed the realization that a fatal shooting had occurred, the sack with the four hundred dollars disappeared. It was never recovered.

On January 15, 1936, a grand jury indicted Williams for murder. He was given a preliminary hearing on January 31, 1936, in which he pleaded self-defense. He was told he would have to stand trial.[19] There is no evidence in the records of the Criminal District Court that he ever did. Both Oliver and the counterman were in a position to see the slain man reach inside his coat, an action that prompted Williams to shoot him. If they had been called upon to testify, their statements might have substantiated Williams' claim of self-defense. It is possible that the district attorney's office dropped the charges based on this self-defense plea.

Oliver was shaken by the violent drama he had witnessed in Gluck's. He quit stopping there for morning coffee. The horror of those few moments seemed to hang over the restaurant for him.

17. New Orleans *Times-Picayune*, December 18, 1935, Sec. 1, p. 19.

18. *Ibid.*, 1. The account of Williams' version of his activities at the scene of the shooting is from this issue of the New Orleans *Times-Picayune*.

19. New Orleans *Times-Picayune*, January 16, 1936, Sec. 1, p. 11, February 1, 1936, Sec. 1, p. 7.

Luckily, life for Oliver in the 1930s was not always as high-geared and hazardous as the sniper attack on the *Corona* or the murder in Gluck's. Most of his work aboard the Coyle tugs was routine harbor activity: helping ships to dock and undock, delivering coal to ships or businesses along the river, and moving barges back and forth. The job took him to the grain elevators, where grain dust hung relentlessly over the ships and tugs like a grimy cloud, and to the huge public cotton warehouse, built in 1915, which could load four ships at once and was the largest of its kind in the world, extending over thirty-three acres.[20] In a day's operations his tug might be occupied along the docks that handled molasses, coffee, sand, gravel, oil, lumber, or bananas.

Unloading bananas had changed drastically since Oliver worked as a longshoreman. Men no longer carried the heavy green bunches on their backs from the hold to the deck and down a ramp to the wharf. Conveyor belts now neatly transferred the fruit from ship to shore. On the wharves the longshoremen still had to do some manual hefting of the bananas, but the whole operation moved much more swiftly and efficiently than in the past. Alongside the sleek white fruit ships a number of small skiffs always idled under the conveyor belts, their occupants waiting for an occasional bunch of bananas to fall into the river. The skiff operator closest to it would quickly retrieve it. When their skiffs were filled with bananas, the boatmen would row off to various wharves along the river and unload their hauls. Later they would peddle the bananas on the city streets.[21]

Like other American cities in the depression era, New Orleans had homeless squatters who lived on the edge of dumps and in deserted houses. But also along its riverfront were unique shanty communities that predated the hard times of the 1930s. Tenacious river folk perched their makeshift dwellings on narrow strips of alluvial land the river had built up between the waterline and the levees—the batture. Since the earliest occupation of the city, residents had watched the river eat away some points along its banks and build up others, and batture land had been the object of bitter controversy as to its ownership and occupation. In the early nineteenth century, John Gravier had fenced off the batture in front of his property and claimed it as his own. His claim was contested but later upheld in court.[22] By the twentieth century, batture was recognized as federal land.

20. *New Orleans City Guide*, 276; *Fortieth Report of the Board of Commissioners of the Port of New Orleans* (New Orleans, 1936), 8.

21. "Port of New Orleans," *Fortune*, IV (November, 1931), 42–49, 133 has a review of the port's facilities in the early 1930s, with a photograph of banana scavengers waiting alongside fruit ships.

22. *Soards' New Orleans City Directory*, 1933, p. 14.

Its squatter dwellers could not claim legal title to the plots on which they lived. In the 1930s shanty homes occupied much of the batture. The occupants were a hardy breed who built their frail shacks near the brink of the Mississippi and remained unruffled when the high water in spring washed at their doorsteps. Some grew small vegetable gardens and kept chicken yards.

The point in the New Orleans harbor that had built up the most by the 1930s was at the foot of St. Joseph Street on the east bank. It had grown 1,800 feet in the 150 years its changes had been recorded.[23] Most of its built-up land had been incorporated into the city by extending the levee and was not batture anymore. Elsewhere on the east bank, there were quite a few batture residents living between Audubon Park and the Jefferson Parish line. Their settlement of shacks and houseboats was known as "Depression Colony." Others were located on the west bank just above Coyle's landing in Algiers. Smoke coming from a batture chimney or clothes hanging on a line behind a batture house was a familiar sight for Coyle's rivermen.

Compared with the primitive conditions in the batture shanties, Coyle's crews had comfortable accommodations aboard their tugs, which provided living quarters as well as working space. There were neat, clean bunks for men who had to sleep aboard, and a well-equipped galley with a cook. Breakfast and lunch on the tugs were always hearty and delicious. Coyle's cooks provided tasty, masculine meals from steaks to ham and biscuits to rich, strong coffee. Early in the morning or late at night, sitting at the galley table eating or directing the tug from the pilothouse, Oliver felt a sense of belonging to the fraternity of tugboatmen who worked at Coyle's.

Each tug in the New Orleans harbor had its own special whistle, such as two long blasts and three short, or long, short, long, short. Oliver and his fellow rivermen knew each tug by its whistle blasts. That was its signature. Some of the tugs had ship-to-shore telephones, others did not— the Corona did have one. A good tug was a snug, self-contained little world—even adorned by pinup girls' pictures on the bulkheads (Neda was amused to find a photograph of Ginger Rogers in black lace "undies" in the Corona's pilothouse when she was invited aboard one day for a visit).

Piloting the tug, Oliver always leaned against the open right window while guiding the wheel with his left hand. When he had to give orders to the deckhands he used a megaphone. Orders to the engineer to speed up or slow down the engine were given through a speaking tube that con-

23. Ibid.

nected the pilothouse to the engine room. When a ship had to be assisted to dock or undock, Oliver as captain of the *Corona* would go aboard to the ship's pilothouse, from which he could direct the actions to be taken. The small tug was secured to the ship by rope and cable. Oliver would call down to his crew on the *Corona* by megaphone what movements to make to guide the large vessel to or from the dock. Big ships' size and lack of maneuverability in close quarters made it hazardous, and in many cases impossible, for them to dock and undock on their own.

The perspective from the ship's pilothouse was very different from that on the *Corona.* Oliver had to learn to judge distances from this height and calculate how much power was needed for the tug to effectively handle the ship. He also had to know the currents at the various docks in the harbor. Poydras Street was one of the most hazardous, with a current that ran in circles.

The season of Carnival festivities, which concludes with the hectic all-day parades and masking of Mardi Gras, touches everything in New Orleans, and it extended to Coyle's tugboat yard on the day before Mardi Gras. The Alla Krewe, which paraded in Algiers on that day, sometimes used Coyle's dock as a place to end the water parade that preceded their float parade through the streets of Algiers. The river procession usually began at a spot upriver on the west bank, crossed over to a point on the east bank, and then ended at Coyle's or a landing nearby. Alla was one of the new krewes that drew their support from the middle- and working-class population of Algiers, rather than from society blue bloods; it had first paraded in 1932.

Richard Buras' son, Richard, Jr., always loved the Alla parade because some family members were allowed to go aboard Coyle tugs, which took part in it. He recalled riding with his father and enjoying the whistles and the graceful jets of water the Dock Board's fire tug sprayed into the river. Crowds lining the docks where the lead boat landed and departed on both sides of the river always enthusiastically waved and called out to the water procession.[24]

In 1936 a naval vessel acted as the lead boat for the king and his krewe. Coast Guard vessels, boats from the Southern Yacht Club, tugs from Bisso's and Coyle's, and a few other vessels all took part in the parade. They sailed from Todd-Johnson Dry Docks about 11:30 A.M. across to the Jackson Avenue ferry landing on the east bank and then back across the river to the Opelousas Avenue landing near Coyle's. The Washington Artil-

24. Interview with Richard Buras, Jr., September 26, 1987.

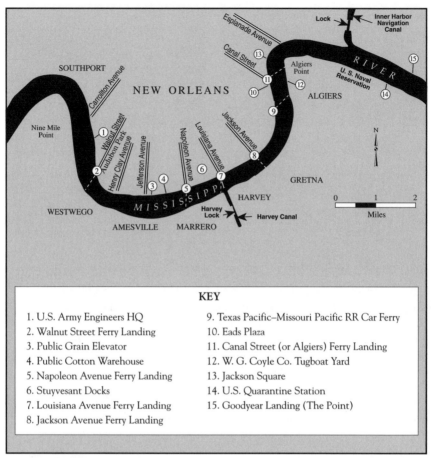

KEY

1. U.S. Army Engineers HQ
2. Walnut Street Ferry Landing
3. Public Grain Elevator
4. Public Cotton Warehouse
5. Napoleon Avenue Ferry Landing
6. Stuyvesant Docks
7. Louisiana Avenue Ferry Landing
8. Jackson Avenue Ferry Landing

9. Texas Pacific–Missouri Pacific RR Car Ferry
10. Eads Plaza
11. Canal Street (or Algiers) Ferry Landing
12. W. G. Coyle Co. Tugboat Yard
13. Jackson Square
14. U.S. Quarantine Station
15. Goodyear Landing (The Point)

New Orleans Harbor in the Mid-1930s.

lery fired a salute to King Alla, who disembarked and mounted his land float. There were five floats altogether in that year's parade, and four bands that accompanied them, along with marching Boy Scouts and other groups.[25] The Alla river parade was anticipated and enjoyed not only by the children and family members of Coyle's crews but by the men themselves, who loved having their workaday tugs participate in the Carnival festivities.

On his days off, Oliver did repair or touch-up work about the house. For amusement, the Jacksons went to movies downtown and then window-shopped on Canal Street. After they acquired their coupe, they took rides around the city on Sundays, went to City Park, where their daughter could play on the swings and ride the merry-go-round, and sometimes rode out Frenchmen Street, which from Gentilly Boulevard to the Lake became a graveled humpback road running through mostly undeveloped stretches of land covered by heavy underbrush.[26]

In its early stages of development in the 1930s, the Lakefront boasted newly constructed seawalls and swimming in Lake Pontchartrain, which had a shell bottom (Neda and Joy wore rubber bathing shoes to protect their feet). During the summer months after Joy reached five or six, her parents might let her stay up late and accompany them out to West End to eat boiled crabs served on picnic tables in the open with newspapers spread out to handle the cracked shells. For stay-at-home nights, they bought a radio and listened to such programs as the comedy shows of Jack Benny and Burns and Allen, Bing Crosby's *Kraft Music Hall,* dramas such as the *Lux Radio Theatre,* amateur competitors on *Major Bowes' Original Amateur Hour,* and the late-night thrillers *Lights Out* and *The Shadow.* Once or twice, Oliver took Neda dancing at a nightclub near the Lakefront in Little Woods.

In the spring of 1935, when Joy was six, she developed polio, which the doctor visiting her first diagnosed as a sore throat. On her third day in bed, when her fever rose and she could no longer move her right leg or feel pinpricks on the right foot or leg, the doctor left in dismay, promising to pray for her. Neda and Oliver were distraught. They turned to Neda's mother, who as a midwife had brought their daughter into the world. Mrs. Drouant called a friend who was a chiropractor, Dr. Stanford Beatty. He stayed all night with the Jacksons and Mrs. Drouant, using various treatments to break the fever of the ill child. By daylight Joy's fever had sub-

25. New Orleans *Times-Picayune,* February 24, 1936, Sec. 1, pp. 1–3, February 25, 1936, Sec. 2, p. 22.

26. The material in this and the next few paragraphs is from personal reminiscences of the author and of Oneida Jackson.

sided, and she fell into an exhausted sleep. Dr. Beatty treated her with massages, warm baths, a healthy diet, and selective exercises. He would always be special to the Jacksons because of his help with Joy's recovery and recuperation, and he remained a lifelong friend of the family. By the end of the summer when school opened, Joy was walking again and strong enough to take her place as a second grader.

Joy's bout with polio deeply frightened Oliver and Neda. It took Oliver back to his own illness in 1914. This time it was his daughter who was sick, and he felt more fearful for her than he ever felt for himself. But she survived, just as he had done twenty years earlier. For that, Oliver and Neda were thankful. Despite the worry surrounding Joy's condition, Oliver managed to continue the daily grind of his job. By year's end he had compiled a perfect safety record, not being responsible for a dime's worth of damage to tugs, barges, or wharves in the past twelve months. This was unusual and a record to be proud of. It qualified him for a full bonus of $450 at Christmas from Coyle Company.

Just as Oliver and Neda were deciding how they would spend the bonus money, they got a notice from the city: Venus Street was to be paved. Their share of the expenses would be $435. After sending a check for that amount to the City of New Orleans, Neda convinced Oliver to take the remaining $15 and buy a new overcoat—his was old, frayed, and shiny; even her talent in sewing could not revive it.

Oliver felt bitter. He had struggled to build the house, to keep it repaired and painted, and to make the monthly payments. Now it had even taken his whole year's bonus. He was ready to give up. He told Neda he wanted to sell. She was distressed but realized how discouraged he was. They put their house on the market early in 1936 and sold it in August.[27] After the sale the Jacksons moved in with Neda's parents for a few months until they could decide where they wanted to live. It was a short move, since the Drouants lived only about eight blocks away, on Piedmont Drive. Neda cried bitterly the day she moved. Parting with the Venus Street house was like losing a part of herself.

In the spring of 1937 the Jacksons moved to Algiers. Neda had tried to make the changes as congenial as she could by renting half of a double house next to the Buras family. Just as Richard Buras was one of Oliver's closest friends, his wife was a friend to Neda, and Joy became friends with Richard, Jr., who was a few years older than she.

27. Statement of Act of Sale of house and lot at 4631 Venus Street, New Orleans, Louisiana, Mr. and Mrs. O. D. Jackson to Miss Rosalie Kirn, August 26, 1936, in Oliver D. Jackson Papers.

Oliver had changed jobs at Coyle's shortly after the shooting in Gluck's. He had given up working in the harbor to become captain of one of the largest steamers Coyle sent along the Intracoastal Canal to Texas. The job meant a little more money, but it also meant long days of travel from New Orleans to Galveston and back again. He began traveling this intracoastal route about nineteen months after it was completed to Texas. He and his crew were among the early towboat crews who pioneered the run on this section of the canal during its first decade.

11

NEW DEPARTURES, OLD AMBITIONS
Canal Captain to River Pilot, 1935 – 1939

Traveling on the Intracoastal Canal as captain of Coyle's large canal steamer *Donie* was an entirely different experience from jockeying the spry little *Corona* around the New Orleans harbor. The *Donie* was a towboat, square-built and larger than the tugs Oliver was used to handling. It lumbered along pulling three or four barges, its progress steady and usually uneventful. The tricky currents of the river were missing in the canal. Oliver simply had to guide the boat and its tow straight, keeping to his side and watching the entrances and exits from the locks, small lakes, and bayous that were all part of the intricate chain of the Intracoastal Canal between New Orleans and Galveston. The port of Houston, the *Donie's* destination, was then reached by way of Galveston Bay and the Houston Ship Channel. Houston was 357 miles from New Orleans via the canal.[1] The Coyle steamer stopped at Galveston on its return trip. The entire journey over and back took six or seven days. The *Donie* traveled twenty-four hours a day, with its captain and first mate working six-hour alternating shifts. Other crew members worked the same type of alternating schedule. The cargo going to Texas usually consisted of general dry cargo in several barges. Return cargo was usually sulphur picked up at Galveston. Oliver began the Intracoastal Canal run as captain of the *Donie* in late December, 1935.[2]

The commerce along the Intracoastal between New Orleans and Texas ports had grown dramatically in just the year and a half since the route had been completed in 1934. W. G. Coyle Company boats carried 30,465 tons of cargo on the canal in 1934. This tonnage almost quadrupled in 1935, to 114,433. In 1936 the total rose to 188,347 tons. This trend was to continue and dramatically affect the course of Coyle's operations.[3]

1. Dufour, *Story of Coyle Lines*, 10.
2. O. D. Jackson to U.S. Local Inspectors, July 18, 1938, copy in Oliver D. Jackson Papers; Jackson Transcripts, No. 9, p. 5.
3. Dufour, *Story of Coyle Lines*, 13.

The Gulf Intracoastal Waterway—the canal's official name—had been proposed by government engineers and Texas and Louisiana businessmen since the late nineteenth century. The first federal appropriation to survey coastal areas in Texas and Louisiana as possible sites for canal construction was the Rivers and Harbors Act of 1873. It provided funds for three teams of surveyors to undertake surveying in these Gulf states. The report on this work was completed by Captain Charles W. Howell of the Corps of Engineers in 1875 and recommended a waterway from the Mississippi River at Donaldsonville, Louisiana, making use of Bayou Lafourche to move southwestward across Louisiana and connect with other waterways to reach Texas and cross that state to the Rio Grande.[4] In the 1870s only one major city was close enough to make use of such a canal—New Orleans. Digging through more than seven hundred miles of swamp and trembling prairie inhabited mainly by trappers, fishermen, and wildlife did not appeal to Congress or the country in general, still grappling with the last days of Reconstruction.

Some piecemeal progress was made in the 1890s when the federal government authorized dredging in West Galveston Bay to enlarge the ship channel there and purchased the privately owned Galveston and Brazos Navigation Canal connecting Galveston to the Brazos River. Another incentive to reconsider an intracoastal waterway came with the spectacular discovery of the Spindletop oil field south of Beaumont, Texas, in 1901. The birth of the oil industry in Texas brought strong support from petroleum investors for cheap water-transportation facilities. Their advocacy of a canal along the Texas-Louisiana Gulf Coast prompted action from Congress in a 1905 bill providing for another series of surveys. The assessment of these surveys by army engineer Major Edgar Jadwin called for connecting with the Mississippi River via Bayou Plaquemine, which was in the process of being improved with a lock to link it to the Mississippi. But this lock, completed in 1909, was a hundred miles above New Orleans.[5]

A group of army engineers working with a later (1909) set of surveys rejected Jadwin's suggestion and agreed that New Orleans definitely had to be the major eastern terminus for a Louisiana-Texas federally funded canal. They recommended the eventual site—the historic Harvey Canal on the west bank of the Mississippi across from uptown New Orleans. By 1910, various segments of what would be the Intracoastal Canal in Loui-

4. Lynn M. Alperin, *History of the Gulf Intracoastal Waterway*, National Waterways Study, Corps of Engineers, U.S. Army (Washington, D.C., 1938), 21–22.

5. *Ibid.*, 24–25; T. E. L. Lipsey, "The Intracoastal Canal in Louisiana and Methods of Dredging," *Professional Memoirs*, VIII (May–June, 1916), 267, 268, 272–75.

siana and Texas had been approved for funding in Congress. But no one plan or appropriation bill had been drawn up.[6]

In the early twentieth century a strong lobbying agency for the canal was the Intracoastal Canal Association of Louisiana and Texas. Its beginnings dated back to 1905, when it had begun as the Interstate Inland Waterway League in Texas. In 1923 the famous retired United States Army engineer Major General George W. Goethals, who had played an important part in building the Panama Canal, accepted a commission from the Intracoastal Canal Association to investigate the progress of the canal segments and make estimates of the commercial viability of the canal. In his report Goethals predicted a doubling of tonnage achieved on the isolated portions already completed once all segments of the canal were joined together as one continuous waterway. Goethals and the association also favored a nine-foot channel for the entire canal instead of the four-foot channel that had been dug in some of the completed canal stretches. In March of 1925, $9,000,000 was approved in Congress for a nine-foot-deep, one-hundred-foot-wide canal as far as Galveston. In 1927 the canal's length was extended to Corpus Christi, Texas. The Harvey Canal segment was the last to be completed, in 1934.[7]

Captain Horace H. Harvey of New Orleans attended the dedication ceremonies on March 28, 1934, when his family's canal was reopened after alteration to make it a part of the Intracoastal Canal. He spoke with pride of his heritage and of the Harvey Canal:

> My grandsire, Jean Baptist Destrehan, built the original Harvey canal, the first reach of artificial waterways to the west of New Orleans, between 1739 and 1741. . . . That canal was five and a third miles long, 34 feet wide, four and a half feet deep. Lafitte used it. It carried many thousands of tons of commerce, it and other extensions to the west, which served a country not well served even today by land transportation facilities. The old Harvey canal lock was finished in 1907—165 feet long, 29 feet and 11 inches wide, and seven feet deep. Transportation demanded larger facilities, now we have them.[8]

Captain Harvey was wearing a new suit for the dedication. It was payment of a bet he had made thirty years earlier when he was advocating the Intracoastal Canal to a scoffing friend. The friend bet him a suit of clothes

6. Alperin, *History of the Gulf Intracoastal Waterway*, 25.

7. *Ibid.*, 27–30; Department of War, *Annual Report of the Chief of Engineers, U.S. Army*, 1936 (2 vols.; Washington, D.C., 1936), I, 701–705.

8. Centennial Edition, New Orleans *Times-Picayune*, January 25, 1937, Sec. K, pp. 1, 14.

that he would never live to see such a canal completed. Harvey was proud to have proved him wrong and to be wearing his new suit.[9]

The first barges from the northeastern end of the Ohio River–Mississippi River–Intracoastal Canal chain reached Houston on August 17, 1934. The barges had been loaded with steel in Pittsburgh and had traveled downriver to New Orleans, where a local tug took over and guided them all the way to Houston. Sulphur was the return cargo shipped to Pittsburgh.[10]

Oliver had never visited southwest Louisiana and was not familiar with its sprawling prairielike terrain. At first there were houses along the banks of the Harvey Canal and later small farms with patches of corn and other vegetables. Occasionally little villages came into view, such as Larose and Lockport on Bayou Lafourche, and later the thriving town of Houma. But after bypassing Morgan City, the canal entered the primeval swampland of the Atchafalaya River and its connecting waterways—Little Wax Bayou, Possum Bayou, a cut through North Bend Plantation to Bayou Bartholomew, then on to Little Bay, a land cut skirting Cote Blanche Island and Weeks Island to the Vermilion River about twenty-four miles below Abbeville.[11]

The land seemed desolate to Oliver. Once in a while a trapper's cabin would grace the banks of the canal, skins of muskrats or other swamp animals stretched out to dry on frames set against the walls. From a nearby clothesline, the wash of the trapper's family waved a lackadaisical welcome to the passing boat and its crew. Sometimes half-clad or naked small children playing along the bank of the canal looked up and shouted enthusiastically at the passing boat in French. The men on the *Donie* felt sorry for the isolated children. They began throwing fruit or what candy they had aboard to the eager, wide-eyed youngsters. When Oliver returned from his first trip into the canal and told Henry F. DeBardeleben about the children, DeBardeleben ordered a barrel of candy for the *Donie's* next trip and supplied papers for wrapping small portions to be thrown from the Coyle boat.[12] After that the *Donie* always carried candy for the canal children and became a legend in canal folklore as the "candy boat." This custom was kept alive by other captains and crews long after Oliver had left the canal. Thirty years later he met a young man who as a child

9. *Ibid.*

10. New Orleans *Times-Picayune*, August 18, 1934, Sec. 1, p. 5.

11. Jackson Transcripts, No. 9, pp. 7, 10–12; *Annual Report of the Chief of Engineers, U.S. Army, 1936*, I, 701–702.

12. Jackson Transcripts, No. 9, pp. 8, 13.

had been thrown candy from the *Donie*. The man still treasured the "candy boat" as a special memory.

The canal followed the Vermilion River, the Schooner Bayou cutoff canal, and a land cut to the Mermentau River. There was a lock on the Vermilion River to prevent the intrusion of salt water from Vermilion Bay. From the Mermentau River, the canal route meandered northwestward above Lake Misere and Bayou Misere and on to Sweet Lake. Then the route went south and west of Sweet Lake and moved northwestward to Bayou Tete Bois, Black Bayou, and the Calcasieu River below Lake Charles, Louisiana. From the Calcasieu, a land cut ran westward for about twenty-two miles to the Sabine River just below Orange, Texas. From there the canal wound its way across the Texas lower coast to Galveston and its ample bay. A ship canal connected Houston to Galveston Bay.[13]

One of Oliver's watches aboard the *Donie* was from 6 P.M. to midnight. Traveling through the inky darkness of the prairie land that stretched for miles on each side of the canal with light from only the moon and faint stars overhead, he found companionship in listening to the radio. Most of the stations the crew could pick up played Texas cowboy music. But at 11 P.M., they usually were able to tune into Ted Lewis and his band broadcasting from a New York nightclub. Lewis' trademark question, "Is everybody happy?" would be followed by his theme song, "When My Baby Smiles at Me," and then a series of foxtrots and popular ballads.[14] Oliver would listen and imagine couples in evening clothes dancing to dinner music in the penthouse supper club of a fancy hotel overlooking big-city lights.

Coyle's allowed the captains and mates traveling to Texas on the Intracoastal Canal to take their wives on an occasional trip. Neda went with Oliver once in the spring of 1936. The wife of the mate also made that trip. The time on the canal seemed to pass a little faster for the men, who were eager to explain to their wives each segment of the canal as they passed it. Neda was delighted to learn more about her husband's work and to see the coastal plain of southwest Louisiana (Joy stayed home with her Drouant grandparents). During his time on the canal, Oliver got a job for his cousin Charles Vogt on the *Donie*. A young man who wanted to follow a river profession as his father, Captain Garrett Vogt, had done, Charlie had started work at Coyle's as a deckhand in 1935. He was the son of Ella Jackson Vogt, the sister of Oliver's father, Monroe.[15]

13. *Ibid.*, 9–10; *Annual Report of the Chief of Engineers, U.S. Army*, 1936, I, 701–702.
14. Jackson Transcripts, No. 9, pp. 12–13.
15. *Ibid.*, 7; O. D. Jackson to U.S. Local Inspectors, July 18, 1938.

Oliver worked the Intracoastal route for a little more than a year. In early March, 1937, he was transferred back to the *Corona* and sent to Baton Rouge to pick up oil barges at the Standard Oil Company for delivery upriver to a Standard Oil installation at Grand Lake, Arkansas. Coyle's had signed a contract with Standard Oil to provide this service.

Oliver had not worked this far upriver in about five years, but that trip had been memorable for a superb piece of river boatsmanship. In the early 1930s, a request had come into Coyle's office for one of their large tugs to pull several barges up to Vicksburg, Mississippi, for a company whose towboats were all engaged elsewhere. Oliver was chosen to do the job as captain of the oceangoing tug *H. T. DeBardeleben* (the same boat that sank off South Pass in 1934). He had to take along an extra pilot licensed for the river above Baton Rouge, which was as far as Oliver's license allowed him to pilot. When the tug got to Vicksburg, Oliver was faced with a problem that at first seemed unsolvable: the mast of the *H. T. De-Bardeleben* reached higher than a bridge under which the tug had to pass.

Oliver pondered the difficulty for a while before coming up with a solution. First he had the barges moved to the front of the tug, since it would be impossible to hold them securely to the sides of the boat under the maneuver he had in mind. Then he instructed the engineer to shift all of the tug's coal to one side. This caused the tug to list—and the mast to lean. Oliver had one of the crew climb the mast and watch carefully to make sure it was leaning enough to clear the bridge as the tug slowly approached. When the man called down that they were going to make it, Oliver kept the *H. T. DeBardeleben* steady and proceeded under the bridge without incident—although it must have looked strange to anyone watching from the riverbank. After dropping off the barges, Oliver started back downriver with the *H. T. DeBardeleben* still alist. Fearing that with the high river current the tug might roll to a more upright position if he tried to guide it downstream with the engine running, he shifted the tug around when he reached the bridge, turned off the engine, and drifted backward under the structure. Safely past the obstacle once again, he called for full power from the engine room, turned the tug around, distributed the coal properly, and headed for New Orleans.[16]

Between March and June of 1937, Oliver made twelve trips back and forth conveying barges for Standard Oil between Baton Rouge and Grand Lake.[17] (Since he still did not have a license for this stretch of the river,

---

16. Jackson Transcripts, No. 10, June 7, 1982, pp. 12–16.

17. H. F. DeBardeleben to U.S. Local Inspectors, December 31, 1937, copy in Oliver D. Jackson Papers; Jackson Transcripts, No. 9, pp. 18–20.

Coyle's contracted with two pilots who had the appropriate licenses. Oliver later passed the test to get a license covering this section of the Mississippi, but by that time he was not making this run anymore.) In the course of these trips, Oliver got to know the men who worked on tugs and the docks at the Standard Oil's plant in north Baton Rouge. In the summer of 1937, he learned that a pilot on the large Standard Oil tug *Istrouma* was leaving. He decided to apply for the vacant position. Working for Standard Oil would mean a higher salary, a paid vacation, and a pension when he retired—benefits that Coyle's did not offer at that time.

Working at Coyle's was more than just a job to Oliver, however. It had been a great learning experience, a haven during the dark years of the depression, and a second home where he had made lifelong friendships. Working for Henry F. DeBardeleben, a man of vision and compassion, had been a privilege. DeBardeleben had shown trust in Oliver's judgment by hiring his brother Eric and his cousin Charlie, and he had always treated Oliver with fairness. His reaction when Oliver told him of his decision to seek a position at Standard Oil was typical of his generous nature. He told Oliver that although he was sorry to lose him, he would speak to the Standard Oil officials for him. Later, in writing instructions to Oliver concerning one of his trips to Grand Lake, DeBardeleben added:

> I talked with Mr. Reynaud [superintendent of the Lighterage Department at Standard Oil Company] this morning, explaining to him you had been with us for over fifteen years and that your reputation and habits were good, your services with W. G. Coyle & Co., Inc., entirely satisfactory, and although I hated to see you leave our company, I did not want to stand in the way of your advancement, and if the job was available, I would be very glad indeed if he would give you every consideration. I also asked Mr. Reynaud should he decide to place you on the Tug *Istrouma,* to please give me ample notice so that we could select another Master to assume command of the work between Baton Rouge and Grand Lake.[18]

The day Oliver went to Baton Rouge to be interviewed for the job, Neda and Joy drove up with him. They sat in the family car outside the Standard Oil gates while Oliver went inside to see the proper officials in the Lighterage Department. After several hours, he came out with good news: he had the job. He went to work aboard the *Istrouma* in mid-July, 1937.[19]

Although the Jacksons had moved about quite a lot during their married life, the move to Baton Rouge was their first out of the city. They

18. H. F. DeBardeleben to O. D. Jackson, July 8, 1937, original in Oliver D. Jackson Papers.

19. Jackson Transcripts, No. 9, pp. 22–23; Jackson Notebook, No. 6, n.p. (pages unnumbered).

managed to find a rental house on Madison Avenue, and after a few months purchased a house that had just been built on Adams Avenue, one street over from Madison.[20] Neda loved Baton Rouge and her new home. Joy liked to play on the large empty lots on Adams and to ride the new bicycle her parents had bought her. The school she attended, Fairfield, was within walking distance, and the children were friendly.

Oliver's work at Standard Oil was pleasant and uneventful. He was one of two masters assigned to the *Istrouma*. One came on when the other got off. Since the other man, Harold Davidson, was a Standard Oil employee of long standing, he held the title of captain of the *Istrouma*. Oliver filled the position of pilot. But actually they alternated the command of the tug. Each worked a twelve-hour shift, one week on the day shift and one at night. The job mainly involved shifting barges—moving them from tows on the river to berths alongside the dock to unload or load, or taking empties to the dock reserved for washing and steaming their insides to remove all traces of gas and oil.[21] The *Istrouma* was considered to be the largest tugboat on the lower Mississippi when Standard Oil acquired it in the 1920s from the Cornell Steamboat Company of New York City. In addition to its barge-handling capabilities, it was a fireboat, equipped with pumps for delivery of twenty-one two-inch streams of water.[22]

The Standard Oil plant at Baton Rouge was a massive, complicated operation employing thousands of persons. It boasted numerous buildings and storage tanks. Operations went on twenty-four hours a day to receive oil, refine it into gasoline and many other petroleum products, store these products, and then ship them by barge, tanker, pipeline, or railroad tank car. In the Lighterage Department, in addition to the harbor-bound *Istrouma*, Standard Oil owned and operated the largest stern-wheel towboat in the world, the *Sprague*. During one four-month period, it had handled 1,500,000 barrels of oil in its tows. On one trip alone in the 1920s, it had carried a cargo of 225,000 barrels of oil loaded in nineteen barges. This historic tow was 260 feet wide and 1,123 feet long.[23] The *Sprague* was affectionately called "Big Mama" by the rivermen who worked for Standard Oil.[24]

20. Jackson Transcripts, No. 9, p. 23.

21. *Ibid.*, 24.

22. "The *Istrouma*," *Waterways Journal*, April 11, 1925, p. 7. A photograph of the *Istrouma* and its crew was printed in this issue with a small story. One of the crew was J. P. T. Roberts, later a New Orleans–Baton Rouge Steamship pilot.

23. "Towboat *Sprague*," and "Towboat *Sprague* Bought Tuesday by Standard Oil Company," *Waterways Journal*, May 23, 1925, p. 9; "A Record Tow," *ibid.*, March 27, 1926, p. 5.

24. *Fifty Years, Baton Rouge Refinery, 1909–1959* (Baton Rouge, 1959), n.p.

The Standard Oil Refinery had been responsible for making Baton Rouge a deep-sea port—the inlandmost port of entry in the entire country. The Standard Oil docks are approximately 253 river miles inland from the Gulf of Mexico.[25] Standard Oil of New Jersey officials had chosen this site for several reasons in 1909 when they decided to set up an affiliate in Louisiana. It was the last high ground above flood stage as one traveled downstream. Baton Rouge was also the lower terminus of the twelve-foot channel for shallow-draft vessels, such as tugs and tows, journeying downriver and the beginning of the deep-draft channel for oceangoing vessels that needed thirty to thirty-five feet clearance. New Orleans had been considered—it would seem to have been a more obvious choice, since it was already an established port and much closer to the Gulf than Baton Rouge. But Standard Oil officials wanted security against flooding and a location closer to the oil fields of north Louisiana and Oklahoma—they intended to lay a pipeline connecting these fields with the refinery.[26] For all of these reasons, Standard purchased 213 acres of land on the river in north Baton Rouge in March, 1909.[27]

On April 13, 1909, the legal existence of Standard Oil of Louisiana began with the filing of its charter in the East Baton Rouge Parish Courthouse and publication in local newspapers. The charter defined the intentions of the company as follows:

> To prospect and bore for, mine, market and sell petroleum and gas; to purchase, transport, sell, produce, refine and export petroleum and its products therefrom arising; to buy and sell naval stores; to lease or construct, maintain and operate pipe lines, with proper pumping stations and storage tanks for the distribution and storage of petroleum or gas, and, in connection therewith to erect, maintain and operate a telegraph or telephone line or lines; to charter, own, and operate ships, tugs, barges and other vessels for the transportation of petroleum and its products, and to lease or own wharves and docks, tanks, cars and other equipment necessary for the transportation of petroleum and its by-products by land or water and generally to have, hold and exercise all such incidental powers as relate to the object herewith above set forth.[28]

A prominent New Orleans attorney, Hunter C. Leake, who had acted as an intermediary between the Standard Oil and Baton Rouge officials

25. Jackson Notebooks, Nos. 2, 6, n.p. for either.
26. *Fifty Years*, n.p.; "Seventy-Fifth Anniversary of Jersey Standard, Standard Oil Company, 1882–1957," *Lamp* (1957), 3, 17; New Orleans *Daily Picayune*, April 15, 1909, Sec. 1, p. 16.
27. Jackson Notebook, No. 6, n.p.; New Orleans *Daily Picayune*, April 15, 1909, Sec. 1, p. 16.
28. New Orleans *Daily Picayune*, April 14, 1909, Sec. 1, p. 4.

and businessmen in choosing Baton Rouge for the site of the plant, filed the charter. As the legal representative of Standard Oil in Louisiana, he had drafted these articles of incorporation.[29] On the next day, April 14, a ground-breaking ceremony took place in what had formerly been a cotton patch.[30] The work of building the plant began immediately. The president of the new company was E. W. Weller of New York. He announced to the press that the plant's construction would employ at least 1,200 men, most of whom would be skilled masons and steelworkers. Within a year, Standard hoped to have the plant fully operational with 500 to 750 employees.[31]

This assessment seems to have been accurate. Refining at the plant began on a limited scale before the year was over. The first still was fired in November, 1909, primarily to produce kerosene, with gasoline and heavy fuel oil as by-products of the skimming process used. Two thousand barrels of crude oil a day were processed.[32] By February, 1910, the plant was running almost at full capacity. The pipeline had been laid as far as the state line of Oklahoma, but would take about two more months to complete. Until then, crude oil from the Oklahoma fields was brought to the plant by rail.[33]

The first fuel oil produced at the Baton Rouge refinery was delivered to sugar plantations along the Mississippi and Bayous Lafourche and Teche for use in sugarcane mills' machinery. As the company expanded, it added a steel-hulled stern-wheeler, the *Standard,* to its fleet of smaller boats in 1916 to deliver refinery products by barge to cities upriver on the Mississippi and along the Ohio. In 1917 the first barge made completely of steel was added to the Lighterage Department. For transporting oil and its by-products to and from Texas or East Coast ports, Standard Oil developed a fleet of tankers. Foreign companies also were welcomed to call at Baton Rouge after it was declared a port of entry for foreign ships through an act of Congress in 1910.[34]

When oceangoing ships began to come to Baton Rouge, the Standard Oil Company had to arrange for pilots to guide them upriver from New Orleans. Between 1911 and 1916, an upriver pilots' organization, the New Orleans–Baton Rouge Steamship Pilots Association, was formed.[35] Be-

29. *Ibid.,* 16.

30. Jackson Notebook, No. 6, n.p.

31. New Orleans *Daily Picayune,* April 14, 1909, Sec. 1, p. 16.

32. *Fifty Years,* n.p.

33. New Orleans *Daily Picayune,* February 11, 1910, Sec. 1, p. 16.

34. *Fifty Years,* n.p.; New Orleans *Daily Picayune,* April 28, 1910, Sec. 1, p. 16, May 5, 1910, Sec. 1, p. 14.

35. The date 1911 is established from a letter written in 1931 by Captain Harry Koch in

cause the Standard Oil refinery was the destination of almost all of the ships that called at Baton Rouge in the early twentieth century, the company naturally had an influence on the association's affairs. President Weller expected to be given the right of approval of all pilots entering its ranks.[36] Although several other oil companies had installations along the river between New Orleans and Baton Rouge and used the upriver pilots to handle their ships, their business contributed only minimally to the pilots' total income.

In 1931, when the depression was hurting even a giant like Standard Oil, the manager of the pilots' association, Captain Harry Koch, agreed to cuts in pilotage fees, as requested by Standard Oil officials. The cuts affected ships traveling upriver as far as Norco and Destrehan, but did not apply to the run to Baton Rouge.[37] In 1936 Koch wrote to Standard Oil and the other companies using the upriver pilots' services to announce that his association felt the depression was coming to an end and the former fees should be restored.[38] Business was good enough for Standard Oil to agree to this. Even so, when Oliver came to work for the Baton Rouge refinery in 1937, the New Orleans–Baton Rouge Steamship Pilots Association had only eight members, and their small numbers and dependence on Standard Oil for most of their business put them at a disadvantage in bargaining with this large corporation.[39]

---

which he states, "We are an association of Pilots that have piloted on the upper river since the commencement of navigation for ships some 20 years." Captain Harry Koch to G. S. Phelps, president of Kellogg Steamship Corporation, November 16, 1931, copy in Oliver D. Jackson Papers. By 1916 the pilots' organization had definitely come into formal existence, since Charles Jackson entered the association that year.

36. E. F. Wieck, superintendent of Lighterage Department, Standard Oil Company, Baton Rouge, to Captain S. T. Wadlington, manager of New Orleans–Baton Rouge Steamship Pilots Association, October 1, 1921; Wieck to Wadlington, October 14, 1921; Wadlington to Wieck, October 24, 1921; copies of all in Oliver D. Jackson Papers.

37. Captain Harry Koch to E. S. Binnings, manager, Texas Transport and Terminal Company, November 16, 1931; Koch to D. Federoff, general manager, Trosdale, Plant, and Lafonte, November 16, 1931; Koch to P. N. Ellis, marine superintendent, Pan American Petroleum and Transport Company, November 16, 1931; Koch to Captain J. E. Hart, port captain, Mississippi Shipping Company, November 17, 1931; Koch to Pure Oil Company, November 18, 1931; Koch to Strachan Shipping Company, November 25, 1931; Koch to M. T. Ball, president, Sabine Towing Company, November 25, 1931; Koch to Captain W. J. Ryan, port captain, Standard Oil Company, Baton Rouge, December 21, 1931; Koch to C. Storey, Cities Service Transport Company, December 21, 1931; Koch to Ross and Heyn, Inc., December 21, 1931; copies of all in Oliver D. Jackson Papers.

38. Captain Harry Koch to Captain W. J. Ryan, December 8, 1936, copy in Oliver D. Jackson Papers.

39. Jackson Notebook, No. 6, n.p.

Since the New Orleans–Baton Rouge pilots brought ships up to Standard's docks and then had to wait until they were loaded or unloaded before guiding them back down the river, they needed quarters in which to sleep, wash up, and relax. Sometimes a ship might be ready to leave in the middle of the night, and taxi transportation from downtown Baton Rouge after midnight was difficult, if not impossible, to find in the 1930s. The Standard Oil Lighterage Department provided accommodations in an old pumphouse near the docks. Called simply "the pilots' shack," it had beds, tables, chairs, and bathroom facilities.

While Oliver was operating the *Istrouma* he met several of the New Orleans–Baton Rouge pilots. Captain James P. T. Roberts had been a pilot on the *Istrouma* himself before becoming a member of the upriver pilots' association. Another pilot, Captain Guy Mallory, had been a captain on one of the Standard Oil tankers. Men like these enjoyed coming aboard and talking to others who were old friends while waiting for ships. Captain Koch, who had joined the pilots in 1929, liked to drop in for a cup of coffee with Oliver when the tug was idle and awaiting orders.[40] He knew Oliver from his days at Coyle's, and he realized that his friend's years of experience and skill in tugboat work in the New Orleans harbor were wasted on shifting barges at the Standard Oil refinery. "O. D., why don't you put your application in with us," he suggested one day, "and the next time we make a pilot we will try and elect you in our association."[41] Oliver was flattered, but he thought that he had finally found his niche and would stay at Standard Oil until he retired and received his pension.

Oliver and Neda were so satisfied in Baton Rouge that they decided to build a house there, out on Plank Road. They purchased a tract of five acres and began planning for the day when they would have the lot paid for and could begin to build.[42] The house would be a Dutch colonial— they found the blueprint they wanted in a book of new-house plans. Then, on November 11, 1938, a little over a year since they had moved to Baton Rouge, Captain William L. Heuer, a member of the New Orleans–Baton Rouge Pilots Association, died.[43] This was the same man who had been a

---

40. "The *Istrouma*," p. 7; Wieck to Wadlington, October 1, 1921; Jackson Transcripts, No. 10, p. 18.

41. O. D. Jackson, "History of the New Orleans Pilots," n.p. (handwritten manuscript in Oliver D. Jackson Papers).

42. Sale with Mortgage, Napoleon M. Hughes *et al.* to Oliver D. Jackson, Conveyance Book 214, fol. 482, East Baton Rouge Courthouse, Baton Rouge, Louisiana, copy in Oliver D. Jackson Papers.

43. New Orleans *Times-Picayune*, November 12, 1938, Sec. 1, p. 2; Jackson Notebook, No. 6, n.p.

captain at Coyle's when Oliver was a small boy, and who had made trips to Port Eads to deliver coal. He had been responsible for convincing Oliver's parents to move to Algiers and open their oyster shop. Now Oliver had to decide whether he wanted to try to take Captain Heuer's place. He had put in an application with the Crescent River Port Pilots in 1928, but nothing had come of that after his uncle John's death. Was it worth trying again?

Oliver decided to apply. He wrote out his application in longhand and got Harold Davidson, the captain of the *Istrouma,* who had offered to do it, to type the letter for him.[44] It read as follows:

Baton Rouge, La.
November 17, 1938

Baton Rouge & New Orleans S.S. Pilots
New Orleans, Louisiana
Gentlemen:

For your information, I herewith state the status of my past experience.

I served as apprentice from 1914 to 1919 with Associated Branch Bar Pilots at Port Eads, Louisiana. From 1919 through 1922 acted as 2nd and 3rd mate on various Steamships for Sinclair Navigation Company and Texas Oil Company. From January 1923 through July 1937 was employed mainly by W. G. Coyle Company as Master and Pilot aboard their tugs in and out of the New Orleans Harbor. Since July 1937 have been pilot on tug *Istrouma* for the Standard Oil Company. I hold license as Master of Lake, Bay and Sound; First Class Pilot on Mississippi River from Grand Lake, Arkansas to sea via both passes; Pilot for Houston, Texas Ship Channel, Texas City and Galveston, Texas on Intracoastal Canal from Harvey Canal to Galveston and all connecting ship channels; also 2nd mate of ocean going vessels of any gross tonnage.

For reference to my character, ability and etc., I refer you to Mr. F. W. Sadler, Assistant Boiler Inspector of New Orleans. Also Mr. H. F. DeBardeleben of W. G. Coyle Company.

Yours truly,
Capt. O. D. Jackson[45]

Captain Koch explained to Oliver that he had a good chance of getting into the association, but that another man, a captain on one of Standard's tankers who had applied years earlier, first had to be considered. The New Orleans–Baton Rouge pilots met and voted to pursue the following course of action: they would offer the position to the tanker captain because of his long-standing application; if he did not accept the position (which they had heard would be the case), they would offer it to O. D. Jackson.

44. Jackson, "History of the New Orleans Pilots," n.p.

45. Captain O. D. Jackson to Baton Rouge and New Orleans Steamship Pilots Association, November 17, 1938, copy in Oliver D. Jackson Papers.

The tanker man turned down the affiliation—he preferred to remain a seagoing captain. The offer went then to Oliver—and he accepted.[46] His life's ambition—to be a river pilot—had finally come true. It was ironic. He had hoped and strived to be a pilot for a long time—during the early learning years with Captain Albro Michell and the bar pilots, and through all the years in the harbor of New Orleans aboard the *Corona,* hoping that the Crescent River Port pilots would elect him. Finally, when he had given up, the dream became reality.

This turn of events meant that Oliver had to quit his job at Standard Oil, sell his house in Baton Rouge and the acreage on Plank Road, and move back to New Orleans. Neda, who had always wanted what was best for her husband and loved being near her family in New Orleans, was satisfied with the change. They rented half a double house on St. Claude Avenue downtown near "the Point," the location on the river where Oliver would be boarding ships going upstream to Baton Rouge.

A new "cub" pilot coming into the association paid an entrance fee, which at the time was $350. The members already in the association divided this sum. Then the cub worked at least three months for nothing to learn the routine of piloting. Captain Mallory, the manager of the pilots in 1938, told Oliver that the group had agreed to allow him to work only one month without pay, since he was such an experienced ship handler, in return for his paying an entrance fee double the normal amount—$700. Oliver decided to take advantage of this offer. It would put him on the payroll much faster, and he believed he could make up the additional money paid out in a short time. In a generous gesture, Harry Koch returned to Oliver half of his share of the $700. Koch said he wanted only the original $50 to which he was entitled and did not want to penalize Oliver by making him pay double.[47]

Oliver's month as a cub pilot began on December 1, 1938. As a cub, he always boarded a ship with another pilot and stood by to observe or offer whatever assistance was requested. Although the average ship made the trip upstream to Baton Rouge in ten to twelve hours, when the river was high or the ship heavily loaded or mechanically slower than average, the trip could take fifteen to sixteen hours. The pilot was obligated to remain on the bridge or in the pilothouse during the entire journey. In order to divide their work fairly, the pilots simply took turns. Whoever was first on turn in New Orleans would be the first one called when a ship needed a pilot to go upriver.

Because the pilots had a small membership, they shared the office of

46. Jackson, "History of the New Orleans Pilots," n.p.
47. Jackson Transcripts, No. 10, pp. 18–20.

the Crescent River Port Pilots Assocation in New Orleans. In 1920 they had signed a contract with one of the lower-river pilots' office staff, Julius Prinz, to act as their agent and office manager in addition to his work for the Crescent River Port pilots.[48] Prinz kept a record of who was on turn and called the men as their turns came up. He also kept their books, collected their fees from shipping companies, and paid their bills and salaries. Salaries consisted of the total income after all bills and expenses had been paid. The pilots divided their combined income equally, subtracting only if a man had taken time off.

Although the New Orleans–Baton Rouge pilots did not handle ships strictly within the harbor of New Orleans—these being the responsibility of the Crescent River Port pilots—they were allowed to board ships in New Orleans that were going upriver above the city or all the way to Baton Rouge. If a ship coming up the river was going straight to Baton Rouge and would not stop off in the New Orleans harbor, an upriver pilot could board it at the Point, the old Dolly Goodyear Landing on the east bank across the river from the Quarantine Station.[49] This location was in St. Bernard Parish just below the St. Bernard–Orleans Parish line. There was a port ship service located there with a motor launch that took pilots and seamen to and from ships twenty-four hours a day. The "point" referred to was Algiers Point. The landing was actually well below Algiers Point, but it was the closest spot to that landmark at which a port service could feasibly be located and pilot exchanges could safely take place. It also served ships at anchor that were being detained by quarantine or immigration inspectors across the river in Orleans Parish.

After his month of apprenticeship, Oliver was ready to "go on the books," as the pilots called it, at the end of December, 1938. On New Year's Eve he waited restlessly for the call that would send him on his first trip as a full-fledged pilot. To celebrate the New Year and his new job, the Jacksons had invited members of Neda's family to their house to toast the occasion. As Oliver mingled and exchanged best wishes for the New Year with his in-laws, the phone rang. It was Julius Prinz. A Norwegian ship, the *Haakon Hauan*, was coming up the river bound for Baton Rouge.[50] It

48. Jackson Notebook, No. 6, n.p.; "An Agreement made this 26th day of September, 1920, by and between the New Orleans-Baton Rouge Steamship Pilots . . . and Julius Prinz," original in office of New Orleans–Baton Rouge Steamship Pilots Association, Kenner, Louisiana.

49. Jackson Transcripts, No. 11, August 10, 1982, pp. 2, 7. For the location of the Dolly Goodyear landing, see *Sanborn Insurance Map of New Orleans, 1937*, IX, 1206.

50. The *Haakon Hauan*'s passage up and down the river was recorded in Ledger Listing Ships Handled by New Orleans–Baton Rouge Steamship Pilots Association, 1939–1941, on

needed a pilot for approximately midnight. Since Oliver would be on the books at midnight as a full pilot, no one would accompany him. This was to be his first solo trip.

The Jacksons' house was less than five minutes from the Point. But Oliver did not want to be late for this assignment. A little after 11 P.M. Neda, accompanied by her sister Nora, drove Oliver down to the landing while the others stayed at the house.[51] Oliver kissed Neda and Nora and wished them "Happy New Year." Then, carrying a small valise with his razor and a change of clothes, he climbed over the levee and walked down to the port ship service. After a brief wait, the *Haakon Hauan* came into view and the ship-service launch, with Oliver aboard, roared out to meet it. The ship slowed, but did not stop; halting and restarting a large vessel wastes time and fuel, and then as now, pilots often changed "on the fly." As the launch swung alongside, deckhands on the *Haakon Hauan* lowered a rope ladder. The Crescent River Port pilot who had guided the ship from Pilottown descended, and Oliver climbed to the ship's deck; his valise was lifted via a line tossed to the launch.

Once aboard, Oliver climbed to the bridge and entered the pilothouse to meet the captain. The night was cold but clear, and the lights of the city seemed brighter than ever. New Year's Eve had called out special illumination in the heart of the city. As the ship passed between Canal Street on the east bank and Coyle's landing on the west, the New Year 1939 arrived in an outburst of fireworks, loud whistles, and car horns. The impact upon the new pilot was exhilarating. Watching the bright patterns of fireworks light up the sky and listening to the harsh, joyous sounds of revelry all over the city, he laughed to himself: What a moment to begin the career he had wanted for so long.

January 2, 1939, p. 7. This is a handwritten contemporary record in the Oliver D. Jackson Papers.

51. Descriptions of Oliver's first trip as a pilot are in Jackson, "History of the New Orleans Pilots," n.p.; and Jackson Notebook, No. 12, pp. 5–6.

12

EARLY PILOT DAYS
AND WINNING THE CHARTER
1939 – 1943

Oliver fitted into the new position of New Orleans–Baton Rouge pilot with enthusiasm. His wife and daughter easily resumed life in New Orleans. Neda renewed her close contacts with family and friends, and Joy's school, McDonogh No. 19, was located across the street from their rented house. Even after the Jacksons moved to a new house they purchased on the corner of Marigny and Sere streets in 1941, Joy liked her Ninth Ward school so much that she continued to attend it until she graduated from grammar school in 1942.

Upriver piloting was no nine-to-five job with weekends off. Although the bar pilots had a schedule of working two weeks at the mouth of the river and then taking two weeks off, which they spent with their families in New Orleans, the New Orleans–Baton Rouge pilots had no such arrangement. Each man's name was placed on a list, and he was assigned a ship when his name reached the top. He would be called several hours ahead of time and given his "turn." His job was a seven-days-a-week affair. He was subject to call any hour of the day or night, in good weather or bad. He might get a long turn taking a ship from New Orleans to Baton Rouge or the other way around, or a short turn between New Orleans and refinery locations just upriver at St. Rose, Destrehan, Good Hope, or Norco, or between one of these refineries and another. Sometimes a short turn involved nothing more than shifting a ship from a dock to anchorage out in the river or vice versa. Such jobs took from a few hours' to eight or nine hours' work, but that did not include transportation, which had to be provided by the pilot himself. In 1939 Oliver's association had not yet hired a driver to take pilots to and from ships. Family members usually dropped off and picked up the pilot, or he might drive himself if the job involved only shifting. Neda drove Oliver to Goodyear's Landing, just below the Orleans Parish line, to wharves in the city, and to the upriver landings. If a turn to an upriver refinery came early in the evening, Joy accompanied her parents. While Oliver shifted a ship, Neda and Joy would often sit on the levee on a balmy spring or summer night and watch the brilliant display of fireflies compete with the flickering lights of the local refinery. An occasional fresh breeze from the river chased away the mosquitoes and counteracted the pungent smell of oil from the plant.

Captain Roberts, a vigorous, energetic pilot, always tied a pirogue to the top of his car when he had a short turn to shift a ship or move a ship from one refinery to another nearby. He would paddle out to the ship and have the pirogue secured to it. After he completed his job, he would climb down the rope ladder, jump into the pirogue, and paddle back to the landing where he had parked his automobile. It was a cypress pirogue, but so light that he could carry it on his back easily.[1]

On long turns from New Orleans to Baton Rouge, a pilot had to stay constantly alert and remain most of the time on his feet, guiding the vessel for sometimes as long as fifteen hours. When a pilot stepped aboard, however, he did not take command. The captain remained master of his ship. The pilot's job was to give instructions to the helmsman for steering in the ship channel, where the river was the deepest and safest for large seagoing vessels such as oil tankers, which were the major ships making the trip between New Orleans and Baton Rouge. Because of the river's many turns and twists and other idiosyncrasies, the channel has never carved its way strictly down the center. It runs with the winding river from side to side, coming closer to one side than the other, then crossing the river to run for a while along the opposite bank. It has always been the river pilot's job to know the channel and be aware of any changes high or low water brings.[2] The Corps of Engineers also sent each pilot in the three associations working between the Gulf and Baton Rouge frequent updated reports on their dredging and levee-building activities and on any cables or special bulky equipment they were using at certain locations along the lower Mississippi.

To help pilots hold to the channel at night, lights have been placed at strategic points for decades. In years past, the lights usually were named for communities or plantations in their vicinity, such as Waggaman, Taft, White Castle, Uncle Sam, St. Louis Plantation, and Longwood Plantation. In recent times, industries along the river have given their names to new lights. Occasionally a light will have a colorful name like Red Eye Crossing, below Baton Rouge on the west bank. Two men who were New Orleans–Baton Rouge pilots in 1939 later had lights named for them.

1. Jackson Transcripts, No. 11, pp. 23–24.

2. Directions for following the ship channel on the Mississippi between New Orleans and Baton Rouge in the 1950s may be found in *Advisory Information on Normal Sailing Route for Ships on Mississippi River Between Baton Rouge Harbor and Huey P. Long Bridge*, published by American Waterways Operations, Inc. (Washington, D.C., n.d.), 1–7.

Charles Lauterbach's name was given to a light near Geismar, and Guy Mallory's to one in Kenner.[3]

In the harbor of New Orleans, seasonal traffic lights were set up near Algiers Point, one of the most dangerous points to pass on the lower river. One was located on the east bank at the Barracks Street wharf to alert vessels coming upriver. The other, for downriver traffic, was on the west bank on the levee near the Southern Pacific Railroad in Gretna. The lights were manually operated by towermen who were experienced pilots and who kept watch over ships coming up or down the river and instructed them on safely passing each other through the use of red or green lights. Pilots might signal the traffic light towermen by telephone before leaving a city dock or through whistle signals. The traffic lights were used only during the high-water season in the spring.[4]

In addition to the lights on shore, the rivercraft themselves had a system of lights that aided in their navigation and is still used today. When Oliver became a pilot in 1939, radar had not yet come into use. Ships did have ship-to-shore phones, but communication between ships on the river was mainly by whistles and lights. At night vessels traveled with a green light on the starboard side, a red light to port, and a white masthead light with a white range light at least fifteen feet above and behind it so that the alignment of the two allowed a distant viewer to judge the ship's course.[5] Whistle blasts were used by a pilot on one ship to signal another vessel of his intentions. Two sets of rules of the road cover the use of whistles in United States water—the International, or Inland, Rules and the Western Rivers Rules. The Inland Rules apply up to the Huey P. Long Bridge, where the Western Rivers Rules take over and apply all the way up the Mississippi.[6] The New Orleans–Baton Rouge pilots, therefore, work in the jurisdiction of both of these sets of rules, although in many instances the rules are the same. One whistle blast generally means that a pilot wishes to pass another vessel coming in the opposite direction port to port or, if the two vessels are going in the same direction, that he wishes

3. For the Lauterbach and Mallory lights, see Department of War, Corps of Engineers, U.S. Army, *Flood Control and Navigation Maps of the Mississippi River, Cairo, Illinois to the Gulf of Mexico*, prepared in the office of the president, Mississippi River Commission (Vicksburg, 1961), maps 48 and 51.

4. For location of traffic lights and methods used to communicate between vessels and towermen, see *Port of New Orleans*, 184. In spring, 1939, the traffic lights were operated for three months. See Department of War, *Annual Report of the Chief of Engineers, U.S. Army, 1939*, (Washington, D.C., 1939), 854.

5. Department of the Treasury, U.S. Coast Guard, *Rules of the Road, International-Inland* (Washington, D.C., 1959), 6–21.

6. *Ibid.*, 60.

to pass on his own port side. If the other ship's pilot agrees, he answers with one blast. Two blasts mean that a pilot wishes to pass an oncoming vessel starboard to starboard or to pass on his own starboard side a ship going in the same direction. This signal has to be answered by two blasts before the action may be taken. If at any time a pilot feels that a dangerous situation is arising between his vessel and another, he blows the danger signal of four or more short, rapid blasts. In fog, intermittent whistle or horn blasts were used before radar to alert craft to one another's positions. Sometimes, too, a pilot blew a long whistle as he approached a bend. If it was answered, he knew to watch out for another vessel at the crossing. The pilot would then communicate with one or two blasts as to how they would pass each other.[7]

Oliver loved the variety of the sights and sounds along the river between New Orleans and Baton Rouge.[8] The harbor of New Orleans, of course, was an old familiar scene to him. Getting on a ship at Goodyear's Landing, at the lower end of the city's riverfront, he had to pass the United States Quarantine Station, Immigration Station, and Naval Station wharves on the left going upriver. On his right, the Inner Harbor Navigation Canal (called simply the "Industrial Canal") came into view next. Beyond it stretched a line of east-bank wharves up to Eads Plaza at the foot of Canal Street. On the west bank, the Southern Pacific wharves and Todd-Johnson Dry Docks stretched around Algiers Point to the Algiers ferry landing.

On the west bank a few blocks beyond Algiers Point was Oliver's former place of employment, W. G. Coyle Company, with its mooring. The river made a wide curve here called Gouldsboro Bend past McDonoghville and Gretna on the west bank with the Texas Pacific–Missouri Pacific Railroad terminal, the Southern Pacific Railroad wharves, the wharves of the Gulf Oil Refining Company, and the Southern Cotton Oil Company. On the east bank going upriver from Eads Plaza, one would see a continuous line of docks broken occasionally by ferry landings.

Above Gretna lay Harvey on the west bank where the Harvey Canal, the link with the Intracoastal Canal, entered the Mississippi River. From the east bank at this point, the Louisiana Avenue Ferry ran across to the opposite side below the canal entrance. Above Louisiana Avenue a number of important terminals were located on the east bank—the Stuyvesant

7. *Ibid.*, 36–40.

8. The places mentioned along the riverfront in the next four paragraphs may be found in the foldout map "Port Facilities at New Orleans, La., 1938," in Department of War, Corps of Engineers, U.S. Army, United States Maritime Commission, Port Series No. 5, *The Port of New Orleans, Louisiana* (Washington, D.C.), n.p. for map, but the map key is on 177–78.

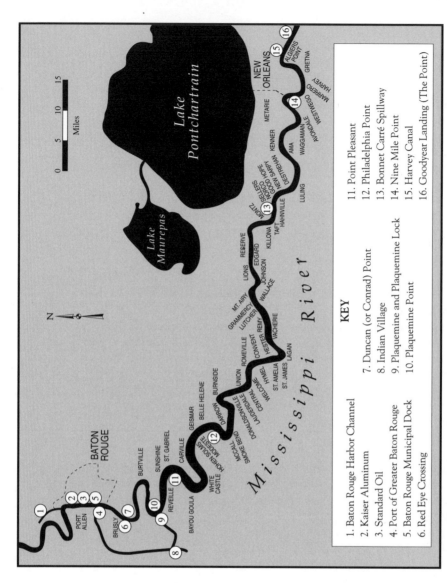

KEY

1. Baton Rouge Harbor Channel
2. Kaiser Aluminum
3. Standard Oil
4. Port of Greater Baton Rouge
5. Baton Rouge Municipal Dock
6. Red Eye Crossing

7. Duncan (or Conrad) Point
8. Indian Village
9. Plaquemine and Plaquemine Lock
10. Plaquemine Point

11. Point Pleasant
12. Philadelphia Point
13. Bonnet Carré Spillway
14. Nine Mile Point
15. Harvey Canal
16. Goodyear Landing (The Point)

The River Route from New Orleans to Baton Rouge.

docks of the Illinois Central Railroad, the public grain elevator, the public bulk-commodity-handling plant's wharf, and the Corps of Engineers depot at Prytania Street. On the west bank going upstream from Harvey were a number of industrial and oil handling wharves through Marrero. Farther up, in Greenville Bend, lay Westwego on the west bank with another cluster of commercial docks, mainly operated by the Texas Pacific–Missouri Pacific Railroad.

Going through New Orleans harbor in 1939, Oliver had to pass five public ferry landings—at Canal Street, Jackson Avenue, Louisiana Avenue, Napoleon Avenue, and Walnut Street—and one used by the Texas Pacific–Missouri Pacific to transport rail cars across the river between Algiers and the east bank. The wharves, docks, and piers within the Crescent City port numbered one hundred, and most paralleled the riverfront. Of the seven miles of publicly owned wharves, five and a half miles had one-story steel sheds for cargo storage. The port's facilities also included one public and four private cotton warehouses and three tropical-fruit wharves which were provided with mechanical installations to unload bananas.

The Corps of Engineers issued a report on the port of New Orleans in 1938–1939 based on statistics from 1927 through 1936. The report showed that the average total commerce of the port was 13,688,586 tons per year. Foreign commerce amounted to 44.4 percent of that. The number-one import and export was petroleum and its allied products. The total foreign and coastwise commerce for petroleum reached an average of 5,698,191 tons during the ten-year period studied. Other important imports/exports in this same period included grain, sugar, lumber, syrup and molasses, bananas, cotton, bauxite ore, iron and steel, and fertilizer and fertilizer materials.[9] Oil had become king on the lower river instead of cotton, a meaningful change of the twentieth century.

Oliver's occupation as an upriver pilot was predicated on the supremacy of oil and petroleum products. The overwhelming number of New Orleans–Baton Rouge clients were oil companies with refineries or holding tanks on the river between New Orleans and Baton Rouge. Dominant among them, of course, was the mammoth Standard Oil Company refinery at Baton Rouge. As a man who had begun his piloting career on the coal-burning *Underwriter* of the bar pilots, Oliver's could personally testify to the change in energy sources on the river. He was now piloting huge tankers that themselves operated on oil products.

Passing under the Huey P. Long Bridge was always like going through

9. *Port of New Orleans,* 153–54.

an archway leading out of the port of New Orleans. Upstream lay 132 miles of river before reaching Baton Rouge. The life-style that could be seen on this run was on the verge of changing dramatically over the next twenty years as industry flooded into the river parishes. But in 1939 it was still a placid, rustic world.[10] Along the river's banks were open countryside, flat green farmfields, and clumps of willow trees hugging the water. Every few miles a plantation house came into view, set back from the winding, narrow river road. The river roads on both sides of the Mississippi between New Orleans and Baton Rouge wound past some of the most beautiful and legendary plantations in the entire South. Oak Alley, Destrehan Plantation, Houmas House, San Francisco—seeing them from the river has always been a feast for the eyes. Among them now and then appeared a trim, quiet small town hugging a bend or nestling on a point. Here and there fishermen sat patiently waiting for catfish to take their bait. Youngsters riding horses on the levee waved to the passing ship and its crew. Down on the river road, a man might be urging a tired mule to pull his dilapidated wagon up the levee loaded with driftwood collected from the riverbank. Once in a while the view from the vantage point of the pilothouse of a tanker revealed a small country store with a wooden bench on its front porch. There were always several men seated on the bench engaged in leisurely conversation. On the west bank below Baton Rouge, where a few small churches with black congregations were located, baptizing in the river still took place on warm Sunday mornings.

One of the places Oliver passed on his long turns to and from Baton Rouge was Edgard—the community near which his earliest ancestors in Louisiana had first settled in 1719. Ironically, he knew little or nothing about them at that time. The Frederics and Haydels (originally Heidel) were two German families who migrated to Louisiana as a result of the recruitment campaign in German states along the Rhine by John Law's agents. Sebastian Frederic and Regina Haydel, who married in Louisiana, were the parents of Marguerite Frederic, later the wife of Jean Pierre Burat. Both the Frederics and the Burats had moved permanently downriver to Plaquemines Parish by the 1760s.

On the other side of the river at Destrehan was the site of the Little Red Church of the early German Coast. It had been a nineteenth-century landmark for passing steamboats, but had to be razed in 1930. By the end of the fourth decade of the twentieth century, refineries began to increase

10. The description of the river roads on both sides of the river from Huey P. Long Bridge up to Baton Rouge is from personal recollections of the author in the 1940s and 1950s. See also [Joy Jackson], "Riding the River Road," *Dixie Roto Magazine*, New Orleans *Times-Picayune*, June 27, 1954.

in number while plantations such as the magnificent Uncle Sam were on the verge of demolition and old edifices such as the Little Red Church had already disappeared.

St. Rose was the depot for Cities Service Export Oil Company.[11] The Pan-American Oil Company had its plant at Destrehan.[12] Several miles above Destrehan was Good Hope Refinery, and farther upriver, the town of Norco, a company town of a subsidiary of the Shell Petroleum Company. Its very name reveals its origins, drawn from the first letters of its founder—New Orleans Refinery Company.[13] Other sights of interest along the New Orleans to Baton Rouge journey by river included Manresa House, the regal Jesuit retreat for laymen that was formerly Jefferson College, and Carville, the sanitorium for victims of Hansen's disease—leprosy.

Baton Rouge itself had only modest harbor installations in 1939. Modern port facilities dated from 1926. There was a reinforced-concrete dock 308 feet long with a covered shed area of twenty thousand square feet. This dock had a twelve-ton locomotive crane, and attached to the main wharf's downstream end was a floating wharf. The dock was served by a transfer boat and municipal terminal with a capacity of forty cars.[14] Two miles above Baton Rouge were the Standard Oil Company docks where a New Orleans–Baton Rouge pilot's job usually ended or began. These docks had facilities to transfer petroleum and other oil products to and from vessels. This was the highest point on the river for the travel of ocean-going vessels.

Throughout the port of New Orleans and up to Baton Rouge, the Corps of Engineers labored to keep the river's channel at least 35 feet deep. This was no problem in the Crescent City, where the average depth of the channel was 110 feet, but upstream there were places where sandbars built up, and these had to be periodically dredged. In 1939, for example, the Corps was engaged in such operations in the vicinity of Red Eye Crossing. The width of the channel within the port of New Orleans was estimated by the Corps of Engineers to range between 1,600 and 2,400 feet. Between New Orleans and Baton Rouge, the Corps endeavored to keep a minimum width of 1,500 feet in the channel. The average was 2,900 feet.[15]

Oliver's first year of piloting was a memorable working experience. He met captains from all over the world on the ships he handled, and he enjoyed the foreign cuisine they offered aboard ship. Greek and Norwe-

11. Hansen, *Louisiana: A Guide*, 540.
12. *Ibid.*, 539.
13. *Ibid.*, 538.
14. *Annual Report of the Chief of Engineers, U.S. Army*, 1939, p. 845.
15. *Ibid.*, 854–55.

gian foods were two of his favorites: he loved to eat fish for breakfast, Norwegian style, and savored a spinach-and-olive-oil dish that was served on certain Greek ships. He got accustomed to the bunk beds of the pilots' shack on the Standard Oil docks and to being called after a few hours' sleep in Baton Rouge to be told to catch the first bus to New Orleans because a ship would be arriving at the Point in a few hours and everyone else was occupied with other jobs. For turns that got him out of bed at three o'clock on winter mornings when the temperature was near freezing, he had a heavy overcoat, muffler, gloves, and woolen cap. In wet weather when he might have to stand out in the open on the bridge, he wore heavy rain gear. But winter weather on the river was numbing and brutal anyway; even hot coffee in the pilothouse could not take the bite out of it. Despite it all, getting underway and setting course gave him a sense of peace and satisfaction. He felt he was where he belonged.

Oliver liked and respected the other pilots in his association. They were experienced, capable, hard-working men. The elder statesman of the group was another Captain Jackson—Charles Murray Jackson, who had joined the New Orleans–Baton Rouge pilots in 1916. A native of Rising Sun, Indiana, he was the son and grandson of river pilots. He had received his pilot's license in 1885 at twenty-one years of age and had piloted side-wheeler and stern-wheeler steamboats, tugs, and other craft before coming into the pilot organization. A quiet man who kept a meticulous log of all of his ships, Captain Charles Jackson was in physical appearance and gestures surprisingly similar to Oliver. Others often made the mistake of thinking the two Jacksons were father and son.[16]

P. Alexander Chotin, called Alex, was a native of Berwick, Louisiana, and one of several brothers involved in careers on the Mississippi River. A skillful pilot who had worked on tugs and towboats, he had joined the association in 1921. His brother Richard Bernard ("Bon") Chotin became a member in 1936.[17] A third Chotin brother, Joe, operated his own towing company on the river.[18]

Captain James Guy Mallory, who was manager of the pilots association in 1939, during Oliver's first year as a pilot, was from Racine, Ohio. He had served as a captain on Standard Oil tankers before coming into the

16. Captain Charles Jackson's career as a pilot is discussed in a story on his retirement in the New Orleans *Item*, December 22, 1947, Sec. 1, p. 8.

17. *New Orleans Baton Rouge Steamship Pilots, Louisiana State Charter and Roster of State Commissioned Pilots and Members* (New Orleans, 1980), 2 (hereinafter cited as *NOBR Charter and Roster*); Jackson Notebooks, Nos. 6, 8, n.p.

18. See *Chotin: Of Men and Water and the Movement of Cargo* (New Orleans, n.d.), which discusses the career and business of Joseph Chotin.

pilots association in 1921.[19] Captain James P. T. Roberts had been pilot on the *Istrouma* and had years of experience piloting before he joined the association in 1927. He was the only one of the pilots who made his home in Baton Rouge. All of the others lived in New Orleans.[20]

Captain Harry Koch, who became a close friend of Oliver's during his first year in the association, had a background of service aboard seagoing vessels as well as of piloting rivercraft. He had joined the pilots' association in 1929.[21] Interested in river traffic in all its forms, Captain Koch invested in tugboats and barges and in a new shipbuilding firm, Avondale Marine Ways, founded in 1938, that was destined to make him a millionaire. By 1939 he was beginning to suffer from arthritis—climbing ship ladders caused him a great deal of pain—and was seriously considering retiring even though he was still in his prime as a pilot and highly respected as a leader by the others.

Captain Charles Lauterbach, a native New Orleanian, was the last pilot elected to the association before Oliver, having joined in April, 1938.[22]

During his time as a cub and his early months as a full pilot, Oliver found that the other pilots were more than willing to talk about problems of piloting with him and share their views on the profession and its fine points. He listened eagerly and contributed ideas and reactions of his own. In November, as his first year in the association drew to a close, Oliver was approached by Captain Koch one day with a startling proposition. Koch told him, "We are going to put you in charge and make you manager of the association next year." Oliver could hardly believe it. He was the newcomer. But the older pilots had discussed it and agreed that if he would accept the position, they would elect him.[23] Captain Mallory, who had been their manager, was gravely ill. He passed away on January 13, 1940.[24] Oliver was duly elected manager for 1940.

The pilots had to elect a new member to replace Captain Mallory. Charles Jackson had a candidate he wished to nominate, Eugene Higbee, whose grandfather had helped Captain Jackson get started as a crew member on a steamboat many years earlier. Jackson drew up a petition, and it was signed by himself and four other pilots; one was Oliver, who had been

19. NOBR *Charter and Roster*, 2; Jackson Notebooks, Nos. 6, 8, n.p.

20. NOBR *Charter and Roster*, 2; Jackson Notebooks, Nos. 6, 8, n.p.

21. NOBR *Charter and Roster*, 2; Jackson Notebooks, Nos. 6, 8, n.p.

22. The date of Lauterbach's entry into the pilots is listed *ibid.*, 2, and in Jackson Notebook No. 8, n.p.

23. Jackson Transcripts, No. 10, pp. 22–23.

24. Guy Mallory obituary in New Orleans *Times-Picayune*, January 14, 1940, Sec. 1, p. 6, January 15, 1940, Sec. 1, p. 2.

asked by Koch to sign.[25] Five signatures among eight pilots were enough to declare Higbee a member.

After signing the petition for Higbee, Oliver turned to Koch and said, "I sure wish I could make Captain A. P. Schwalb a pilot."[26]

Harry Koch thought awhile before he answered, "You want to make Schwalb? Let's put up a petition to make him; then I'll retire."

Oliver quickly objected, "Oh, Harry, no. I don't want to make him that way. I don't want you to retire to make Schwalb."

"Jack," Koch replied, using the nickname Oliver's in-laws favored, "I am going to retire anyway in a few months." He explained that his arthritis would not permit him to keep piloting ships.

Koch sat down immediately and wrote out a petition to make Captain Schwalb. A few months earlier Oliver had talked to Adolph about the association and asked if he might someday be interested in becoming a member. Adolph had answered emphatically in the affirmative. He subsequently wrote an application letter to the association's manager. But neither he nor Oliver had expected that an opportunity would come up for several years for him to realize his ambition. Schwalb's petition received the necessary signatures when other pilots were told of Koch's decision to retire. Schwalb, like Oliver, was well known as a skilled and reliable pilot. His years of working at Coyle's made him an excellent choice as an upriver pilot.

In January, 1940, Captain Higbee and Captain Schwalb began their cub apprenticeships, and Oliver became manager of the New Orleans–Baton Rouge Steamship Pilots Association. Captain Koch retired, but his name was kept on the pilots' roster as inactive during 1940. Oliver felt that he was going to need Harry Koch's help in a major project he was about to undertake. Harry had indicated his willingness to offer advice and counsel and lend the prestige of his name to its accomplishment.

Shortly after he took over as manager, Oliver called a meeting of the association. The purpose was to discuss the possibility of going to the Louisiana Legislature in the spring of 1940 to seek state commissions and the right to draft a state charter for the association.[27] Oliver, Harry, and a few other pilots had discussed this subject a number of times during 1939. Their association was the only group of pilots in the United States handling oceangoing vessels on an inland waterway without commissions and a state charter covering their territory. The bar pilots had received their state commissions and charter in 1879. The Crescent River Port pilots got

25. Jackson Transcripts, No. 10, p. 23.
26. *Ibid.*, 23–24, for this and the next five paragraphs.
27. *Ibid.*, 24–25.

theirs in 1908. A charter would define the association's territory, the fees it could charge, and the ships it would handle exclusively. All foreign ships traveling between New Orleans and Baton Rouge would have to take a state pilot. This stipulation was standard for all other harbor pilots in the United States. The two other associations of pilots on the Mississippi were both protected by such a clause.

Members were not in complete agreement at first about Oliver's proposal. Some openly opposed it, claiming that the Standard Oil Company would resist a charter and that to try to acquire one would alienate this giant customer. Oliver offered to discuss the matter with the port captain for Standard Oil at Baton Rouge. With this promise he got the majority of the members to approve the pursuit of a charter for the association.[28]

Oliver's interview with W. J. Ryan, the Standard Oil port captain, was cordial and positive. Captain Ryan stated that he had no objections to the pilots' attempt to get a state charter and wished Oliver good luck with the project. A charter would protect and upgrade the pilot association and set standards by which to operate that could only prove beneficial to its customers, including Standard Oil. With that hurdle behind him, Oliver engaged Harry Koch's attorney, Harry F. Styles, to write the pilots' bill and to help in finding legislators to introduce it and aid in its passage.[29]

The Louisiana Legislature convened in the spring, and Oliver, Koch, and Styles made innumerable trips to Baton Rouge to lobby for the bill. During the time that he was attempting to get the bill passed, Oliver never took time off from work or paid his expenses out of association funds. He did his lobbying on his own time and money. Friends he had made as a young man working for the bar pilots now helped him by introducing him to legislators.

Opposition came from two fronts—from a hostile oil firm below Baton Rouge that used several independent pilots who worked cheaper than the New Orleans–Baton Rouge pilots, and from the Crescent River Port pilots, who feared that the bill might allow the upper-river pilots to take business away from them in the harbor of New Orleans. This latter opposition was a total surprise to Oliver and Harry. No one in the New Orleans–Baton Rouge Steamship Pilots Association had ever considered trying to encroach on the territory of the Crescent River Port pilots, or wanted to do so. The two groups had always had cordial relations and even shared a New Orleans office. The misunderstanding stemmed from the vagueness with which the proposed New Orleans–Baton Rouge pilots' bill had been written. The president of the Crescent River Port group was

28. *Ibid.*, 25.
29. *Ibid.*, 25–26, for this and the next three paragraphs.

worried that it might imply that the upper-river pilots had the right to shift ships in the New Orleans harbor. Oliver assured him that no such action had ever been considered. They settled this difficulty by a letter addressed to the Crescent River Port pilots, signed by Oliver as manager of the New Orleans–Baton Rouge pilots and stating that the upper-river pilots would continue to take ships to the Point or pick them up there, but would do no shifting in the harbor.

The bill passed the state house of representatives and senate, but Governor Sam Jones vetoed it on advice from an associate who was connected to the oil firm that opposed it. After this crushing defeat, several pilots in the association, along with the legislators and lawyer who had handled the bill, contacted the governor to explain how mistaken they felt he had been. All the upper-river pilots were asking for was the same state protection and regulation already given to the bar pilots and the lower-river pilots. After listening to their side of the story, Governor Jones had an aide contact Oliver. This man explained that the governor had been misinformed concerning the pilots' bill and promised that he would give it full consideration if it were brought up again at the next legislative session. Unfortunately, the Louisiana Legislature at that time met only every two years. So Oliver had to wait until 1942 before he could try again (he was reelected manager of the association in 1941 and 1942). Early that year he began a second campaign to win the state charter for his association. This time the bill went through without opposition.[30]

There was even an amiable arrangement with the Crescent River Port pilots. They had put a bill before the legislature to delineate their territory more clearly. In their 1908 charter, their domain had been defined as extending from Pilottown to New Orleans. Now they wanted to identify it precisely as reaching from Pilottown to Southport, the upper boundary of the New Orleans harbor. This would give them the exclusive right to shifting throughout the harbor. New Orleans–Baton Rouge pilots could board a ship within the harbor if it was going above Southport. They also were permitted to board ships at Goodyear Landing or the Point to pilot them up the river to points above Southport. Finally, the upper-river pilots could take ships coming from upriver to the Point if the ships were headed downstream below New Orleans. But they were not to shift ships within the New Orleans harbor itself.[31]

When both of the pilot bills reached the senate, the senator who was

30. Ibid., 26–27.

31. The act defining the Crescent River Port pilots' territory is in Acts Passed by the Legislature of the State of Louisiana, Regular Session, 1942 (Baton Rouge, 1942), Act No. 134, pp. 429–30.

handling the Crescent River Port pilots' bill asked Oliver to let him attach it as a rider to the upper-river pilots' bill, which he knew was going
through without a hitch. Oliver agreed. The two bills thus passed together. As soon as they did, Oliver and Adolph Schwalb, who had been
present in the senate gallery, phoned the president of the Crescent River
Port Pilots Association to let him know that both bills had passed by a big
majority.[32]

The upper-river pilots' bill became Act 291 of the 1942 legislative session. The governor signed it on July 13, 1942. Its preamble lists its purposes: "To regulate the system of river port pilotage between the ports of
New Orleans and Baton Rouge and any intermediate ports; providing for
a Board of New Orleans and Baton Rouge Steamship Pilot Commissioners
and defining its duties; providing the qualifications of New Orleans and
Baton Rouge Pilots and fixing their charges; providing penalties for vio-
lations of this act."[33] The act also provided for the adoption of a charter
by the pilots. The charter took eight months to draft. Before the charter
went into effect, however, each of the nine pilots in the association received his state commission from the governor, dated September 21,
1942. The board of commissioners for the New Orleans–Baton Rouge
pilots, which was composed of three pilots in the association, received
their commissions from the governor on October 3, 1942.[34] Oliver was
one of these first commissioners, whose job was to pass on the credentials
of new pilots and investigate maritime accidents or misconduct involving
members, recommending remedial action if necessary. The charter was
officially filed with a notary on March 30, 1943.[35]

The charter incorporated the association with its domicile in New Orleans. It provided for a president, vice-president, and secretary-treasurer.
Since Oliver had been manager for three years straight and wished to
get a little rest from association duties now that the charter had been
achieved, he stepped down from the top slot. Captain Alex Chotin was
chosen as the first president of the new incorporated association. Oliver

32. Jackson Transcripts, No. 10, p. 30.

33. *Acts Passed by the Legislature of the State of Louisiana, Regular Session, 1942*, Act. No.
291, pp. 969–72.

34. New Orleans *Times-Picayune*, September 26, 1942, Sec. 1, p. 5; State Pilot Commission issued to Oliver D. Jackson by Governor Sam Jones, September 21, 1942, Appointment to the Board of Commissioners for the New Orleans–Baton Rouge Steamship Pilots
Association, granted to Oliver D. Jackson by Governor Sam Jones, October 3, 1942, both
in Oliver D. Jackson Papers.

35. Copy of Charter of New Orleans and Baton Rouge Steamship Pilots Association
filed with notary, James J. Morrison, on March 30, 1943, by O. D. Jackson and Eugene F.
Higbee, in Oliver D. Jackson Papers.

served as vice-president, and Charles Lauterbach was selected to be the first secretary-treasurer. Together, the three officers also constituted the board of directors who handled the business affairs of the association.[36]

The charter stated the purposes of the organization as follows: "To carry on the business of piloting sea-going and other vessels on the Mississippi River, between the Mississippi River ports of New Orleans and Baton Rouge and return, for fees, and to shift vessels in the harbors of Harahan, Avondale, St. Rose, Destrehan, Good Hope, Norco, Reserve, and other harbors to and including Baton Rouge, Louisiana, of 1942; and to inculcate, secure and maintain skill, discipline, merit and efficiency in the pilots engaged in this business, and to thereby promote and assist the commerce and prosperity of the said ports and intermediate ports."[37] Capital stock was fixed at nine thousand dollars, divided into nine shares of one thousand dollars for each of the nine pilots. Any future pilot elected into the association would have to be a citizen of the state, not over forty years of age, of moral character, and a holder of a First Class Pilot License issued by the United States Bureau of Marine Inspection and Navigation. He would also have to serve a six-month apprenticeship.[38]

Provisions were included regarding retirement at or after age sixty-five and the payment of a pension. Oliver had struggled and succeeded in getting the pilots to start a modest pension plan in the early 1940s. The charter also set a mandatory retirement age of seventy. There was an exception clause, meant to protect Captain Charles Jackson, exempting "members already over such age limit." Remarkably alert and physically agile, Captain Jackson continued to pilot ships until he was eighty-three years old in 1947.[39]

Other items provided for in the charter were the duties of the officers and the procedure to be followed in choosing new member pilots. Finally, the charter empowered the board of directors to draw up by-laws, rules, and regulations to govern the association's business.[40] The charter was signed by the nine pilots (in later years Oliver would refer to them fondly as the "Big Nine"). Oliver and Eugene Higbee were authorized to take the charter to a notary and act as official witnesses to it. A new era had begun for the upper-river pilots, and Oliver had played a meaningful role in launching it.

36. *Ibid.*, Article IX, 7.
37. *Ibid.*, Article III, 2.
38. *Ibid.*, Article IV, 3.
39. *Ibid.*, Article VII, 5.
40. *Ibid.*, Article IV, 3, Article X, 7–8, Article XVI, 10.

13

WORLD WAR II ON THE RIVER
The Embattled Homefront

Between the first attempt to get the New Orleans–Baton Rouge Steamship Pilots Association approved as state-licensed pilots in 1940 and the passage of the legislative act in 1942, the United States entered World War II. Wartime brought grave changes to commerce on the Mississippi River.

By the time that the pilots had their charter written and notarized in March, 1943, only four of the nine members listed in the charter were actually working full-time as pilots of the association. One, Captain Koch, had retired and was busily engaged as vice-president of Avondale Marine Ways in the feverish occupation of shipbuilding for the war effort. Four, including Oliver, had taken leave to fill river jobs on tows upriver or tugs in the New Orleans harbor. Oliver and Adolph Schwalb had returned to Coyle's. Oliver worked there for four months, from March 25, 1943, until July 23, 1943.[1]

Changing ship-traffic routes brought on by military demands for fuel and the toll of German submarine warfare had drastically reduced the oil-tanker traffic into the Mississippi River, decimating the commerce between New Orleans and Baton Rouge. Upriver refineries waited anxiously for the fortunate few ships that could slip past the U-boats. Some of the pilots frankly wondered, at the very time that their new charter went into effect, whether their association would be able to survive.

In the last two full years before the United States entered the war, 1939 and 1940, Japanese merchant ships had been fairly common on the New Orleans to Baton Rouge run. Bearing such names as *Asakasan Maru, Nosiro Maru, Sagami Maru, Kano Maru,* and *Takaoka Maru,* the Japanese vessels came up the Mississippi River above New Orleans to take on fuel at the smaller refineries. Sometimes they loaded grain or scrap metal. Their captains were always impeccably polite and dressed in the formal

---

1. Jackson Notebook, No. 8, p. 1; Ledger Listing Ships Handled by New Orleans–Baton Rouge Steamship Pilots, 1939–1943, p. 110.

uniforms of their companies. The crews were efficient and quick to comprehend communication in signs and gestures from the pilots. Meals served aboard ship to pilots were of good quality and always piping hot. In 1940, twenty-four Japanese ships made the trip to river ports above New Orleans, an average of two a month.[2] Many others called at New Orleans but had no occasion to come upriver.

In 1941, as relations between the United States and Japan deteriorated and the Japanese secretly completed their plans for the attack on Pearl Harbor, only eight Japanese ships made the journey up the Mississippi under the guidance of New Orleans–Baton Rouge pilots. The last to do so was the *Kirisima Maru* on July 11, 1941.[3]

Oliver had been called to take a Japanese ship upriver earlier that year.[4] When he boarded, the ship was not yet ready to sail and he was asked to wait for an hour or so until the ship finished loading. The pilots' association would be paid for the time. He was escorted into a large cabin that seemed to serve as a reading room, with comfortable chairs and books and magazines on small tables. Then the Japanese sailor who had shown him into the room withdrew, leaving him alone. Oliver sat down and picked up one of the magazines. It was printed in Japanese, but the photographs captured his attention. The magazine was filled with pictures of Japanese military officers posing with German military officials, and even of Hitler talking with Japanese diplomats. The entire magazine was devoted to Japanese-German relations. Although Oliver had read stories in the press about the close ties of the Japanese and the Germans, seeing these pictures alarmed him. As he turned the pages, he sensed the presence of others: several Japanese sailors who were peering at him from the open doorway. As his eyes moved from one to the other, they disappeared like frightened or guilty children.[5] Oliver felt uneasy, as if he were already on an enemy ship.

On Sunday, December 7, 1941, Oliver was spending a rare weekend at home. He was at the end of the list of pilots waiting for turns. Despite the luxury of having slept all night in his own bed, he rose very early (a habit he had acquired in St. Joseph orphanage and kept all of his life) and made strong coffee and chicory. Neda slept till about seven. Joy was recuperating from the flu and stayed in bed that day. Oliver and Neda remained at

2. Japanese ships handled in 1939 and 1940 are in Ledger Listing Ships Handled by New Orleans–Baton Rouge Steamship Pilots, 1939–1943, pp. 80–95.

3. *Ibid.*, 100.

4. Although Oliver did not remember the exact date of this ship, it was probably handled in late January or February. A Japanese ship on January 31 and two on February 12, 1941, which paid detention for one to two hours, are listed *ibid.*, 97.

5. Jackson Transcripts, No. 10, p. 40.

home all day, reading the newspapers and catching up on several household repairs they had been planning. They kept busy enough not to listen to the radio. Late that afternoon, a girl friend of Joy's came by. Shirley Breaux and her father had been to a movie and were on their way home when they decided to visit the Jacksons. Mr. Breaux broke the news about the attack on Pearl Harbor. The Jacksons immediately turned on their radio to try to get more information. Since the bombing had taken place only a few hours earlier, not many details were available.[6]

At first, life and work did not change for Oliver and his fellow pilots. During the early months of the war, from December, 1941, through June, 1942, Oliver was involved with the second bid to get his pilots' association bill through the legislature. But by the time the bill passed, the pilots were beginning to have a problem—the falling-off of their steady list of ships to handle.

A total reorganization of shipping had come about as a result of the war. In February, 1942, the War Shipping Administration was set up to act as the federal agency that would control the nation's ships. All United States flag tankers over three thousand gross tons, such as those operated by Standard Oil of New Jersey and its affiliates, were requisitioned by the WSA. The agency also took over Panamanian ships, with the consent of Panama. A Tanker Division of the WSA assigned tankers to military use or to commercial users. The building of new tankers came under its direction, as did the licensing of companies as agents of the WSA to operate tankers.[7]

Standard Oil of New Jersey and its affiliate Panama Transport operated their requisitioned fleets under the direction of the Marine Department of New York, an agent of the WSA. Traffic routes for vessels were changed to meet the military needs of the Allies. Coastwise traffic between the Gulf of Mexico ports and the East Coast was reduced. At the beginning of the war, Standard Oil of New Jersey and its various affiliates had 193 oil tankers in operation worldwide. Fifty-nine of these vessels were directly owned by Standard Oil of New Jersey, which was the major source of tankers sent to the Baton Rouge Standard Oil refinery. In 1942 alone, 17 of these Standard Oil of New Jersey tankers were lost to submarine assaults or other enemy attacks.[8] The New Orleans–Baton Rouge pilots

6. The attack on Pearl Harbor occurred at 7:35 A.M. in Hawaii, which was 12:05 P.M., Central Standard Time, in New Orleans.

7. Henrietta M. Larson, Evelyn H. Knowlton, and Charles S. Popple, *New Horizons 1927–1950* (New York, 1971), 522, Vol. III of N. S. B. Gras and Henrietta M. Larson, eds., *History of Standard Oil Company (New Jersey)*, 3 vols.

8. *Ibid.*, 421–529.

felt keenly the change in the coastwise traffic of Standard Oil ships (known more commonly then as Esso tankers) and their sinking by German U-boats.

One of the top priorities of the German navy in the first year after United States entry into the war was to attack all types of merchant ships sailing from the United States to Great Britain. The loss of ships to carry military weapons and supplies, grain, and other vitally needed items to the British would greatly damage the Allied war effort. With this in mind, the German military high command set into motion an operation called *Paukenschlag*, meaning "drumroll" or "drumbeat." This operation called for the massive use of German submarines in the western Atlantic.[9] In the battle of Norway, the Germans had lost one pocket battleship, three cruisers, and half of their destroyers. In May, 1941, the German battleship *Bismarck* was also sunk. With these losses, Germany could no longer compete with the Allies in surface naval operations.[10] German vice-admiral Karl Doenitz, commander of submarines, therefore unleashed his elite submarine crews upon shipping between America and Britain with greater intensity than ever before.

German submarines sailed from ports along the west coast of France. They rendezvoused in mid-Atlantic, in a three-hundred-mile-wide area known as the Greenland Gap, with submarine tankers that carried the fuel, weapons, and other supplies they needed to stay at sea. The diesel-oil capacity of these tankers, called "sea cows," was 432 tons. The sea cows replenished their fuel stocks from commercial tankers sent to the Canary Islands. This system allowed German submarines to take on enough fuel to last them from two to six weeks.[11] The term *Greenland Gap* derived from the range of Allied land bombers, which could fly only a certain distance out to sea before they had to turn around if they wanted to reach land without running out of fuel. A three-hundred-mile stretch of ocean down the middle of the Atlantic, approximately at the longitude of Greenland, was beyond the reach of either American or British bombers. There the German submarines could surface and refuel.[12]

9. Samuel Eliot Morison, *The Battle of the Atlantic, September 1939–May 1943* (Boston, 1961), 126, Vol. I of Morison, *History of United States Naval Operations in World War II*, 15 vols.; Carole F. Corkern, "U-Boats in the Gulf of Mexico, World War II," *Southeast Louisiana Historical Association Papers*, V (1978), 31.

10. Clayton Roberts and David Roberts, *A History of England, 1688 to the Present* (2 vols.; Englewood Cliffs, 1985), II, 766.

11. Morison, *Battle of the Atlantic*, 129; Corkern, "U-Boats in the Gulf of Mexico, World War II," 31–32.

12. Roberts and Roberts, *History of England*, II, 767.

The German U-boats operated sometimes in wolf packs attacking convoys, sometimes as lone hunters stalking individual ships. Either way, they took a devastating toll in 1942. During that year the Germans, through combined submarine and bomber attacks, sank more than 650,000 tons of shipping per *month* in the Atlantic.[13] In the first months of the war, the United States was hard pressed to meet this threat to its shipping. United States naval operations in the Pacific required that all vessels in that area remain and be reinforced as quickly as possible to fight the Japanese. Along the Atlantic coast, the United States armed forces had to make do with what they had or could hurriedly acquire for coastal defenses.

The first Standard Oil of New Jersey tanker to be sunk by torpedoes from a German submarine was the *Allan Jackson,* a ship the New Orleans–Baton Rouge Steamship pilots had handled often on trips to the Baton Rouge Standard Oil refinery. They had brought it down the river from the Baton Rouge refinery on what turned out to be its last trip, only three weeks before it was sunk.[14] It was traveling in the Atlantic close to the Eastern Seaboard in the early hours of January 18, 1942, when two torpedoes tore into it and set its cargo of crude oil ablaze. The *Allan Jackson* was destroyed in ten minutes. Thirteen men survived out of a crew of thirty-five.[15]

Attacks on ships close to shore decreased later in the year as military resources strengthened through the addition of small ships, planes, and blimps along the Atlantic coastline. U-boats found it more difficult to come in close to land, to surface in daylight, and to find their quarry by night near the mainland than during the first months of the war. Between April and May, 1942, the Germans shifted their attack from along the Eastern Seaboard to two spots they considered primarily undefended and vulnerable—the entrance to the St. Lawrence River and the Gulf of Mexico.[16] The attacks in the Gulf appear to have begun on a regular basis in early May of 1942.[17]

The German submarines followed a bold pattern in pursuing their prey in the Gulf. They lay in wait in the shipping lanes at approximately peri-

13. *Ibid.*

14. The *Allan Jackson* was last handled by a New Orleans–Baton Rouge pilot on December 26, 1941, according to Ledger Listing Ships Handled by New Orleans–Baton Rouge Steamship Pilots, 1939–1943, p. 36.

15. *Ships of the Esso Fleet in World War II* (New Jersey, 1946), 76–80; Larson, Knowlton, and Popple, *New Horizons,* 524.

16. New Orleans *Times-Picayune,* May 17, 1942, Sec. 1, p. 17.

17. Morison, *Battle of the Atlantic,* 142; Allen Cronenberg, "U-Boats in the Gulf: The Undersea War in 1942," *Gulf Coast Historical Review,* V (Spring, 1990), 163.

scope depth and, after dark, fired torpedoes upon a passing ship, sometimes using shore lights to silhouette the vessel. The average submarine had fourteen torpedoes. The subs were also armed with deck guns, which could be used to finish off any ship merely crippled by the torpedoing. After the initial attack, the submarine would surface as the ship's crew evacuated their burning vessel. German officers frequently called out to the victims, requesting their ship's name and cargo. Sometimes they offered food or cigarettes to the lifeboat survivors.[18]

One German submarine commander, after torpedoing an American vessel in the Caribbean and surfacing to survey the sinking ship, even saved an American seaman whose injured shoulder was hindering his attempt to swim to a lifeboat. The officer gave orders to his men to lower the prow of the submarine under the seaman and pick him up with it. With this maneuver accomplished, the commander called in English to a nearby lifeboat to come and rescue the injured sailor.[19] Not all victims of the German submarine attacks were as gallantly treated. After a direct hit from a German torpedo on their ship in the Gulf, an American captain and at least twenty-one of his crew were lowering a lifeboat from the burning vessel when the lifeboat itself was hit by a second torpedo from the submarine, which had surfaced. All the men in the lifeboat were killed. The submarine's captain had inquired of men in a lifeboat already in the water whether everyone was off the ship and had been told no, but still he had given the order to fire again on the disabled ship. The American seamen in the first lifeboat watched this action in horror. Most U-boats had at least one crewman who could speak English, and he usually asked if all hands were off of a targeted ship before the submarine crew tried to sink it with another torpedo or with gunfire. Whether the German officer had misunderstood the sailors in the lifeboat or had decided to sink the vessel without waiting for the rest of the crew to abandon ship will never be known. But general policy among German submarine captains was to inquire and wait for the ship they were attacking to be evacuated.[20]

On May 10, 1942, a medium-sized American ship in the Gulf was struck by three torpedoes and then riddled by machine-gun fire. After the torpedo hits, the crew evacuated the ship to one lifeboat and two rafts. Several of the men were wounded by shrapnel; one died. The ship did not

18. Morison, *Battle of the Atlantic*, 129; Corkern "U-Boats in the Gulf of Mexico, World War II," 33.

19. New Orleans *Times-Picayune*, May 24, 1942, Sec. 1, p. 1.

20. *Ibid.*, May 31, Sec. 1, p. 1. For examples of communication with German U-Boat crewmen, see scattered articles in New Orleans *Times-Picayune*, May and June, 1942, and Morison, *Battle of the Atlantic*, 130.

sink, despite the gunning it received. Later, after it had been towed into a Gulf port, a full-grown porpoise was found on its bridge, blown there by the torpedoes.[21]

Although the merchant ships carried guns and naval gun crews for protection, the submarines struck at night from beneath the surface, leaving the gunners little or no time to retaliate or defend their ship. Such a crew did save the *Eastern Sun,* a tanker that dodged three torpedoes fired at it off the Mississippi Passes. The U-boat finally gave up the chase when the ship's naval gunners began returning fire. On May 13, however, the *Gulf Penn* was sunk in the same vicinity while being escorted by a patrol bomber. Before midnight a second ship, the *David McKelvey,* was sunk in this area west of Southwest Pass. The latter sinking brought personal tragedy to the family of Oliver's old friend Captain Albro Michell: his twenty-six year old nephew, Bernard Michell III, third mate on the *David McKelvey,* was one of the crew who died when the ship was torpedoed. His brother Albro (named for his uncle) was aboard another ship nearby when the torpedoing occurred, and he saw the fatal explosion of the *McKelvey* without knowing that it was Bernard's ship.[22] Survival or destruction seemed to be a matter of pure chance.

One of the worst losses near the Mississippi River Passes occurred on May 12, 1942, the day before the sinking of the *McKelvey.* The oil tanker *Virginia* was waiting a mile and a half off the Passes for a bar pilot to take it into the river. Before he could reach the ship, it was torpedoed and broke in half, sending up a great tongue of fire. Hit by three torpedoes, the *Virginia* was a complete loss; twenty-five men burned to death that night, and another died later.[23] Earlier that day, a U-boat had attacked a destroyer getting ready to enter Southwest Pass. The torpedo missed and hit the jetties instead, blowing debris all over. The blast shook the slender fingers of land at the river's mouth, terrifying the few inhabitants still living at Burrwood. One employee at the Southwest Pass lighthouse had a heart attack as a result of the explosion.[24]

Persons at Burrwood and Port Eads had a front-row seat for the drama in the Gulf. Sometimes they actually saw submarines rise and dive back

---

21. New Orleans *Times-Picayune,* May 15, 1942, Sec. 1, p. 1.

22. Morison, *Battle of the Atlantic,* 138; Corkern, "U-Boats in the Gulf of Mexico, World War II," 38; New Orleans *Times-Picayune,* May 20, 1942, Sec. 1, pp. 1–2; Statement of Captain Jacques Michell concerning his uncle's death aboard the *McKelvey* to the author on September 1, 1989, Jefferson, La.

23. New Orleans *Times-Picayune,* May 16, 1942, Sec. 1, pp. 1–2, May 19, 1942, Sec. 1, p. 23.

24. Goodwin *et al., Evaluation of the National Register Eligibility of Burrwood,* 186–87.

into the waters offshore. At night when a hit caused fire and destruction to a vessel out in the Gulf, they watched it burn miles away, just as Oliver had watched the lights of ships many years earlier from the bar pilots' *Underwriter*.[25] One Burrwood resident, Eric Guidry, had an eerie experience. He was asked one day to go from Southwest Pass to South Pass to pick up a man who had injured his hand badly cutting cane and to take him to a doctor. While crossing the eighteen miles of water, Guidry kept his eyes mainly on his compass. Suddenly he glanced up and saw what looked like a mop handle sticking up out of the water dead ahead. When he got within three hundred feet of it, the "mop handle" stirred itself, "bubbled up and down," and disappeared. He was shaken by the realization that "it had to be a submarine!"[26]

Shortly before the United States entered the war, the navy began building a base on the lower portion of the Burrwood reservation. Only a barbed-wire fence separated the base from the civilian housing section of Burrwood. Among the numerous buildings constructed for the modest base were the administration building, a barracks, officers' quarters, a mess hall, a storehouse, and a heating plant. The base also had a 100,000-gallon water tank with an observation tower and signaling platform, four fuel-storage buildings, and a fire pump stored in another building. Five buildings were constructed to hold ammunition and explosives. Two of them were large bunkers—one of which was a high-explosives magazine. This latter group of structures was located on the lower edge of the base as far from the Burrwood population as possible. A sentry box was placed at the lower end of the Navy post, and a gun battery was installed near the mouth of Southwest Pass with a wide range of fire.[27]

This station was supposed to help in antisubmarine warfare, but it never had the fast, powerful boats or the aerial backup necessary to make this objective a reality. Nor were the gun battery at Southwest Pass and a similar one placed at the mouth of South Pass of much practical value in fighting the terrible submarine menace in the Gulf in 1942.[28]

Early that same year the navy had organized the Gulf Sea Frontier, with headquarters at Key West. The commandant of the Seventh Naval District, Captain Russell S. Crenshaw, directed defense operations against enemy vessels. The area included in this "frontier" consisted of the entire Gulf of Mexico, the Yucatán Channel, the Florida Straits, the Bahamas, and a portion of the waters around Cuba. The vessels and planes available to Crenshaw for searching out submarines were totally inadequate at first.

25. *Ibid.*, 174, 186.
26. *Ibid.*, 174.
27. *Ibid.*, 30–43, 113–15.
28. *Ibid.*, 74–75, 115.

In April the Gulf Sea Frontier forces were increased by the acquisition of two converted yachts, six cutters, two destroyers, and additional air support. The May onslaught of submarine attacks in the Gulf shipping lanes brought further enlargement of the defensive fleet, but it also proved to the navy how precarious was the Key West base as the headquarters for the Gulf Sea Frontier. Its remote location was linked to the mainland only by a bridge, causeway, and public telephones. In June, 1942, the headquarters was moved to Miami, and a crack submarine fighter who had been stationed in Iceland and had beat back the submarine threat in the North Atlantic was appointed to head the Gulf Sea Frontier. He was Rear Admiral James L. Kauffman.[29]

As German submarines continued their attacks, convoys were organized by the Gulf Sea Frontier fleet to escort ships. All vessels were advised to travel without lights, to zigzag, and to stay close to shore whenever possible.[30] A call went out for the dimming of onshore lights, which could be seen miles out at sea and provided a background against which ships' dark profiles made excellent targets. In New Orleans the dimout called for turning off neon advertising signs above the first floor of buildings and for cutting out some of the lighting on the neutral ground in the center of Canal Street. Citizens were asked to use blackout curtains in their homes, but this precaution was not widely followed.[31]

During the terrible month of May, 1942, Mexico entered the war against the Axis after one of its ships was torpedoed despite its neutrality and the display of the Mexican flag on the side of the ship. One Mexican captain found himself in an ironic situation. Several months earlier he had rescued a lifeboat of American seamen whose ship had been torpedoed. In gratitude, they presented him with their lifeboat, which he added to those already aboard his vessel. After Mexico declared war on Germany, his ship was one of the first Mexican vessels to be torpedoed in the Gulf. When the captain abandoned his ship, he took refuge in the same lifeboat that had been given to him by the Americans. Once again it saved lives: eventually, the captain and some of his crew were picked up and brought to New Orleans.[32]

29. Morison, *Battle of the Atlantic*, 142; Corkern, "U-Boats in the Gulf of Mexico, World War II," 35–36; New Orleans *Times-Picayune*, May 31, 1942, Sec. 1, p. 1; Cronenberg, "U-Boats in the Gulf: The Undersea War in 1942," 172.

30. Corkern, "U-Boats in the Gulf of Mexico, World War II," 36.

31. New Orleans *Times-Picayune*, June 5, 1942, Sec. 1, p. 3, June 13, 1942, Sec. 1, p. 1, October 17, 1942, Sec. 1, pp. 1–2, November 4, 1942, Sec. 1, p. 8, November 10, 1942, Sec. 1, p. 34.

32. Morison, *Battle of the Atlantic*, 139; Cronenberg, "U-Boats in the Gulf: The Undersea War in 1942," 171; New Orleans *Times-Picayune*, May 25, 1942, Sec. 1, p. 13.

Sometimes civilians unwisely traveled on ships in the Gulf. One American family returning to the United States from Central America booked passage on an American ship that was torpedoed by two submarines simultaneously, from opposite sides. The Raymond Downs family—father, mother, eleven-year-old Betty Lucille, and eight-year-old Raymond, Jr.— were separated as they scrambled to abandon ship. All survived and were reunited after rescue, but Betty Lucille recalled clinging to a hatch cover while sharks swam nearby and "tickled her feet." Her mother spent fifteen hours in the water holding on to a plank and fighting off pilot fish from a school of sharks. The loss of life was high in this sinking, with thirty-six deaths reported by the navy.[33]

Harrowing stories of being blown out of their shoes or clothing, of being burned badly by fires aboard ship, and of close brushes with sharks while waiting for rescue were told by survivors of such sinkings and appeared almost daily in the newspapers. Pilots like Oliver heard similar stories from officers aboard the fortunate ships that got through to the Mississippi River. Often these men had already survived at least one torpedoing and had returned to sea as soon as they could.

The pilots in all American ports were finally drawn into the war effort in the last two months of 1942, when the United States Coast Guard enrolled all state-commissioned pilots on a temporary basis in the Coast Guard Reserve. This move covered 581 pilots in thirty-five state pilot associations. The men were to receive no remuneration except the regular fees they earned through piloting. They were issued regulation uniforms, shoes, hats, and overcoats. A navy announcement in regard to this enrollment, issued on November 27, 1942, stated that "by being in uniform, pilots would be subject to military discipline." The announcement further explained that "the object is to assure that the pilot arrives without delay aboard the vessel to be piloted, that he is professionally, physically, and morally qualified for a job, that he is militarily responsible for the vital war information daily entrusted to him, and finally that the fee for his service is reasonable."[34]

The three Mississippi River pilot associations (the Associated Branch Pilots, the Crescent River Port Pilots Association, and the New Orleans–Baton Rouge Steamship Pilots Association) entered the Coast Guard Reserve by the end of the year. Oliver was sworn into the reserve as a lieutenant commander on December 30, 1942. Two months before the pilots were mustered into the reserve, the bar pilot boat *Underwriter* was

---

33. New Orleans *Times-Picayune*, May 25, 1942, Sec. 1, p. 13.
34. *Ibid.*, November 28, 1942, Sec. 1, p. 7.

also put under government supervision, just as it had been in the Spanish-American War and World War I.[35]

By that time the number of incoming ships had been dramatically curtailed by sinkings in the Atlantic and the Gulf. The month of May, 1942, had set a record for tonnage sunk in the Gulf and the Caribbean. More ships were lost in that area in May than in any other war zone during a single month throughout the entire war. The New Orleans–Baton Rouge pilots had experienced a steady reduction of their income since the early months of 1942. In December, 1942, there were only five pilots still actively working with the association; four were on leave and working elsewhere. For the first half of the month, the collections for ships totaled enough to pay each pilot a modest salary. But in the last two weeks, only two ships paid the association. No new ships arrived in port to seek their services. Their salary for the last two weeks in December, 1942, was probably the lowest this group of pilots ever received: Oliver and his colleagues each took home a check for $3.19! Oliver went first on turn on December 9, 1942, and remained in that slot until twenty-three days later—January 1, 1943—when he finally got a ship to take upriver.[36] One to two days was usually the longest a pilot remained first on turn. Now the New Orleans–Baton Rouge pilots were experiencing hard times of crisis proportions.

Oliver remained with the association for the first two months of 1943, but on March 25 he took a temporary position working for Coyle Company in the harbor and, occasionally, on their run to Texas through the Intracoastal Canal. In an ironic twist, the German submarines had forced Oliver to leave his job just at the very moment when he was getting the charter for his association.[37]

The situation at Coyle's was exactly opposite that of the upriver pilots. The towing company was overwhelmed with work. As the U-boats made the Gulf of Mexico a graveyard for ships, refineries and war industries in

35. Disenrollment, Temporary Member, United States Coast Guard Reserve, Office of District Coast Guard Officer, Eighth Naval District, November 30, 1945. This disenrollment form gives both the date of enrollment and disenrollment. It is in Oliver D. Jackson Papers. Reference to the *Underwriter* appears in the New Orleans *Times-Picayune*, September 24, 1942, Sec. 1, pp. 1, 3.

36. On record number of ships sunk in a single month in one area during the war, see Morison, *Battle of the Atlantic*, 142. Information on the upper-river pilots' decline in work load is in Ledger Listing Ships Handled by New Orleans-Baton Rouge Steamship Pilots, 1939–1943, pp. 108–109.

37. New Orleans *Times-Picayune*, September 26, 1942, Sec. 1, p. 5; State Commission presented to Oliver D. Jackson to pilot ships between New Orleans and Baton Rouge, signed by Governor Sam Jones, September 21, 1942, in Oliver D. Jackson Papers.

Texas and Louisiana turned to inland waterways, pipelines, and rail travel to move fuel, cargo, and other needed war materials. The creation of the Federal Barge Line during World War I, which had revived barge traffic and encouraged canal building, and the extension of the Intracoastal Canal system in the 1920s and 1930s, now put the United States inland-waterways traffic in a much better position than it had been in 1916 to cope with a world war. The Intracoastal Canal between New Orleans and Texas had been extended twice since Oliver had made trips to Houston in 1934. In 1940 the waterway expanded from Galveston to Freeport (with Coyle's *Clara* leading the opening-day parade of boats). In 1942 the canal moved another 160 miles along the Texas coast to Corpus Christi.[38]

As with all other maritime companies after the United States got into the war, Coyle's tugs were taken over by the federal government and purchased by the United States Defense Plant Corporation. The tugs, however, were still operated by Coyle's, which received compensation from the government. Two types of services were offered to the New Orleans port by Coyle tugs during the war period. Some were used in harbor work to aid ships carrying war materials to the East Coast or the war zones. The larger canal towboats, such as the *Clara*, and tugboats that handled wooden barges leased by Coyle's from the Defense Plant Corporation traveled back and forth between Louisiana and Texas, and from Texas eastward along the Intracoastal Canal, carrying oil to Carrabelle, Florida. From that point, it was piped to the Atlantic coast. This inland route protected the oil from the submarines in the Gulf.[39]

Elsewhere fuel and other war materials were moving cross-country by rail, by pipeline, and by barge up the Mississippi and its tributaries. Trains made up of tank cars were given top priority on the nation's tracks and traveled at express speeds. Standard Oil's affiliated companies alone increased their use of tank cars by July, 1942, to over five times what it had been in December, 1941. Pipelines for fuel products were also increased in size and capacity. Mergers were sometimes arranged to improve efficiency. The pipelines of Standard Oil of Louisiana and of the Oklahoma Pipe Line Company were consolidated into the Interstate Oil Pipe Company. This move by two Standard Oil affiliates facilitated the movement of oil north and northwest.[40] But like the increased railroad carriage of fuel, it decreased the coastwise tanker traffic up and down the Mississippi River.

38. Dufour, *Story of Coyle Lines*, 12.
39. *Ibid.*, 14.
40. Larson, Knowlton, and Popple, *New Horizons*, 532–37.

Between 1941 and 1944, barge deliveries by Standard Oil–affiliated companies in the United States increased about 50 percent.[41] Some made the trip from Baton Rouge up the entire Mississippi Valley waterways system via the Mississippi and Ohio rivers. The "Big Mama" of the Esso river fleet, the *Sprague,* was used along with the company's regular-sized towboats to move oil and gas barges upriver.

Corps of Engineers statistics for traffic on the Mississippi River during World War II reflect the increase in inland traffic and the decrease in coastwise and foreign traffic brought on by the war. In 1941, the year the United States entered the war, internal traffic on the river amounted to 22,821,000 tons, coastwise traffic between points on the Mississippi and other domestic ports was 7,927,000 tons, and foreign traffic with Mississippi River ports amounted to 5,606,000 tons. During 1942, the year of the German submarine terror, inland tonnage increased by about 23 percent on the Mississippi River to 28,040,000 tons. But coastwise trade dropped by a little over 61 percent, to 3,106,000 tons. Foreign traffic fell by about 9 percent to 5,097,000 tons. In 1943, the inland traffic continued to rise, reaching 30,817,000 tons, almost an 11-percent increase over 1942. But the coastwise traffic plunged downward to 1,814,000 tons, approximately 41 percent below the 1942 figure. Foreign traffic rallied slightly in 1943 to 5,211,000 tons, around a 2-percent increase, probably aided by the lessening of the submarine menace in the second half of the year. By 1944, inland, coastwise, and foreign traffic were all on an upward trend.[42] Radar equipment had been perfected for ships and planes, which used it to search out German submarines and destroy them. By mid-1943 commerce was reverting to normal for Gulf of Mexico ports. Oliver returned to work with the pilots' association in August, 1943.[43]

A host of wartime shortages and the introduction of rationing of scarce items went into effect between late 1942 and mid-1943. Food prices rose sharply. Rationed items included coffee, sugar, butter, canned goods, meat, shoes, gasoline, and tires. White margarine with a packet of yellow food coloring to be mixed into it became easier to secure than real butter. In the Jackson household, it was Joy's job to mix the margarine with the coloring. Neda found shopping for meat and poultry frustrating and disappointing at times. One day she witnessed a fight between two housewives in a market over the last live chicken in the market's coops.[44] The

41. *Ibid.,* 532.

42. William H. Baughn, *The Impact of World War II on the New Orleans Port–Mississippi River Transportation System,* Louisiana Business Bulletin, XII (Baton Rouge, 1950), 25.

43. Jackson Notebook, No. 8, p. 1.

44. Personal recollection of the author.

coffee and chicory the Jacksons brewed strong also became scarce. Cereal drinks—substitutes for coffee—were used when the real thing was not available. They did not taste the same.

The shortage that worried the Jacksons the most was the shortage of automobile tires. Even when Neda had a certificate to purchase a tire, she could not find a store or service station in New Orleans that had one to sell. Since she drove Oliver to his ships, some as far away as St. Rose or Destrehan, and often had to return home alone in the middle of the night, she needed four good tires. One tire on the Jackson automobile was almost threadbare and might give out at any time. It had been patched but was marginal at best. Just when Neda was about to give up hope of ever getting a replacement, the owner of the service station where she bought gasoline offered her a new tire he had just received. Although he had a waiting list on which the Jackson name was only one of many, he explained that he had decided to sell it to them because their situation was the most critical. Neda was overwhelmed with gratitude. She quickly gave him the certificate, which she kept in her purse "just in case," paid for the tire, and had it put on the car. The old patched tire became the spare.[45]

In 1944, when Oliver was settling back into the routine of ship handling on a regular basis, the Jacksons had a burglary that pointed up the nature of the wartime shortages. Their washing machine had been repaired and returned to the Jackson residence by the repair firm. Two days later Oliver came into the kitchen for breakfast, looked out the back door, and asked his wife, "Did you leave the car out of the garage last night?" It was sitting in the driveway with the garage doors open. Neda knew intuitively what had happened. She cried out, "Oh, my washing machine! Is it there?" They hurried out to the garage. The washer was gone. The thieves had pried open the garage doors and pushed the car out of the way to get at it. Although the Jacksons reported the theft to the police, the machine was never recovered. The police told them that the theft of appliances was a common occurrence now that such items could hardly be purchased new. The Jackson washing machine was probably sold somewhere in the city on the black market.[46]

Although the Jacksons had a difficult time financially in 1942 with the drop-off in ships, New Orleans as a community prospered during the war. Shipbuilding was a booming industry in the city, supplying jobs for over 47,000 workers during the war years.[47] Andrew Higgins, the boat-designer

45. Ibid.
46. Ibid.
47. The estimate for total workers in the shipyards of New Orleans during World War II is taken from two sources: Raymond J. Martinez, *The Story of the River Front at New Orleans*

genius, had six plants operating in the Crescent City during the 1940s. Five were engaged in shipbuilding or marine-engine construction, and the Michoud Plant was the site for aircraft construction.[48]

Oliver's friend Harry Koch was also busy building various deep-sea and river craft for the government at Avondale Marine Ways, above New Orleans on the west bank, one of four shipyards in the greater New Orleans area under the direction of the Gulf Coast Region of the United States Maritime Commission. Captain Koch had chosen the Avondale location for his shipyard while he was still piloting. It was the abandoned site of the former train ferry that had carried railroad cars across the Mississippi before the advent of the Huey P. Long Bridge. The train tracks were still in place, and Koch wisely realized that this would be an advantage for his enterprise. The other three shipyards were Pendleton Shipyards and Delta Shipbuilding—both located on the Industrial Canal—and Canulette Shipbuilding, in Slidell. These yards worked as swiftly as possible to turn out Liberty ships to replace the sunken vessels of the nation's merchant marine. Delta Shipbuilding even worked on Thanksgiving Day to launch one of its ships. These four shipyards built more than 250 ships and other craft during the war years. In addition to the yards located in or near New Orleans, the United States Maritime Commission directed the work of ten others in the Gulf Coast area. The director of the commission's Gulf Coast office was Leigh R. Sanford, a master shipbuilder in his own right.[49]

The last two years of World War II saw a steady rise in the number of ships coming upriver to the refineries, grain elevators, and bauxite plants. The intense submarine warfare of 1942 had slackened off in the Gulf of Mexico by October of that year, although it continued in the Atlantic. The total number of ships attacked and sunk in the Gulf from May through September, 1942, was fifty-eight, of which twenty-eight were tankers. Two submarines were sunk in the Gulf, one by a direct hit from a Coast Guard plane.[50] The effect of the ship sinkings in 1942, both in the Gulf and the Atlantic, was keenly felt through the spring of 1943. But by the summer of that year, shipping was rebounding as the shipyards turned out new vessels and submarines began to be contained in the At-

---

(New Orleans, 1955), 133 (using lowest figure given of 25,000 for Avondale, Delta, Pendleton, and Canulette), and Lucille B. Schwab, "Andrew Jackson Higgins, Boatbuilder," *Southeastern Louisiana Historical Association Papers*, VII (1980), 62, where the estimate for workers at Higgins' shipyards is 22,500.

48. Schwab, "Andrew Jackson Higgins," 60–62.

49. Martinez, *Story of the River Front at New Orleans*, 132–36; New Orleans *Times-Picayune*, November 27, 1942, Sec. 2, p. 22.

50. Corkern, "U-Boats in the Gulf of Mexico, World War II," 41–42; Cronenberg, "U-Boats in the Gulf: The Undersea War in 1942," pp. 163, 172–73.

lantic. In 1944 foreign ship commerce reached 6,915,000 tons, 23 percent above the tonnage for 1941. Coastwise traffic returned to 3,048,000 tons, about what it had been in 1942 but a leap of 68 percent from the level for 1943, the worst of the war years for the coastwide trade. Inland traffic was still climbing and reached 34,708,000 tons.[51]

The total of ships handled by Oliver as a New Orleans–Baton Rouge pilot reflects how he, personally, was affected by the war. In 1941 he handled 113 ships. In 1942 he had only 70. But in the last year of the war, 1945, the business of the upper-river pilots had begun to boom, and Oliver handled 176 ships.[52]

The Jacksons' return to a modest prosperity was overshadowed by the death of Oliver's father on January 17, 1944.[53] Oliver had not seen Monroe for fifteen years when one day in 1939 the doorbell rang at the house on St. Claude Avenue. Oliver answered it and came face to face with his father—thin, bent-over with age, and wearing thick glasses that greatly magnified his light blue eyes.

Monroe was carrying a battered suitcase. "I've come to stay with you'ens," he said with the Kentucky accent he had learned from his father, Captain Andy.

"Come on in, Dad," Oliver answered matter-of-factly, as if the long years since their last meeting had been only a few days.[54]

That afternoon, Oliver took Monroe to get a haircut and some new clothes. Neda arranged the extra bedroom upstairs for him. For about a year Monroe lived unobtrusively with his son's family. He had chronic bronchitis and a hacking cough, and felt cold all the time. As a rule he stayed in the kitchen near the gas stove, where warmth from the oven comforted him. Sometimes he felt spry enough to reminisce about old times on the river. He told Joy stories about his early life and the building of the jetties on South Pass.

When Oliver's sister Viola Barrios, her husband Robert, and their children moved to New Orleans in the early 1940s, Monroe went to live with them. He had a deep love for his youngest daughter and her family. Unfortunately, he grew steadily sicker. Finally Oliver and Eric (who now lived in Algiers) decided to find a good nursing home where their father could get professional care. They settled on the Bethany Home, a Pres-

51. Baughn, *Impact of World War II on the New Orleans Port–Mississippi River Transportation System,* 25.

52. Jackson Notebook, No. 8, pp. 1–2.

53. New Orleans *Times-Picayune,* January 18, 1944, Sec. 1, p. 2.

54. The following paragraphs about Monroe Jackson's life in New Orleans prior to his death are from the personal recollections of the author.

byterian establishment that was operated like a boarding house. A lovely old residence on Claiborne Avenue, it had a parlor where residents could entertain visitors, a large dining room in which they ate their meals around a long table, and nicely furnished individual rooms for each resident. Monroe liked to sit on the large front gallery in one of the rocking chairs. He could carry on conversations with some of the other residents and watch the constantly changing parade of pedestrians and vehicles going by on busy Claiborne Avenue. At that time, Claiborne was still one of the most beautiful streets in downtown New Orleans, with a wide neutral ground down its center covered with grass and shaded by majestic oaks. Neighborhood children and families held picnics or played softball on the neutral ground on weekends, giving the Bethany residents a great deal of pleasure watching their activities.

Oliver visited his father two or three times a month, bringing him little gifts of candy or clothes. Monroe seemed happy at Bethany, although he sometimes missed the mouth of the river. Like his father before him, he had loved the isolation of the Passes, the fresh breeze from the Gulf, going out early in the morning to tend oyster beds, and listening to the surf beating against the shore. Not many of his relatives were left living on South Pass or Southwest Pass. One by one they had died or come up to New Orleans. Monroe had been one of the last to give up his beloved but spartan way of life.

When Monroe died, from bronchial complications, Oliver felt a deep sadness. He knew that a whole way of life had died with the old man. Although Monroe had lived in New Orleans twice—once when he operated the oyster shop in Algiers and later when he engaged in the barroom business with his brother John—he was not comfortable living there. He was a shy, reticent man who had spent all of his life in a remote outpost on the lower river either self-employed as a fisherman or working as an oarsman for the Customs Service. When he came up to the city he found himself handicapped by his illiteracy. As long as he had someone literate to help him, as his wife had done in the early 1900s and his brother had done later, he could survive in the city. But during the dark days of 1914 when Oliver languished in the Charity Hospital and the only job Monroe could secure was longshore work on the docks, he had yearned for Port Eads and oyster fishing. At one point he began courting a New Orleans woman, whom he finally asked to marry him and move down the river. She replied that she would marry him only if he stayed in New Orleans. Monroe chose returning to Port Eads over marriage and life in the city. That was how strong his preference was for his childhood home.

Monroe never understood why Oliver wanted to leave the Passes and work upriver. Oliver never understood how his father could stay in the remote community at the river's end. They could reach across the great gulf of their differences with love, but true appreciation and empathy for their conflicting life-styles eluded them. Monroe was buried in St. Vincent de Paul Cemetery in New Orleans.

When the end of the war came with V-J Day, August 14, 1945, the Jacksons were preparing to give a party for Joy's high-school girl friends. The girls were supposed to go to a public swimming pool and return to the Jackson home for wieners and Cokes. But by midday the Japanese surrender was announced over the radio and in extra editions of city newspapers. The teenaged guests began calling to cancel their participation in the party. They explained that they were going to go to Canal Street, or out to Lake Pontchartrain with their families, or just to shoot off fireworks in their backyards. Joy's party collapsed, but in the great excitement and gladness of the moment, that hardly mattered. Oliver, Neda, and Joy decided to join the general celebrating by driving out to the Lakefront. Along Elysian Fields Avenue they saw crowds of people milling casually up and down the neutral ground waving American flags and signs reading Peace, or Victory. Occasionally someone touched off fireworks in front of a house. People were waving and calling out to one another from the sidewalks and their front porches. Celebrants in automobiles jammed the avenue, heading out to the lake to picnic on the sea wall. Oliver stopped at a corner where someone was selling an extra edition of the New Orleans *States*. He bought a copy as a memento of the day. It had PEACE blazoned across the top of the front page in nine-inch letters.[55]

All over the city that afternoon, bells were ringing and automobile horns were blowing. On Canal Street, masses of people gathered, creating a carnival atmosphere. It was like Mardi Gras in August. While most people laughed and danced in the streets or stepped into a bar to toast peace with a drink, some crowded into churches to give thanks more quietly. Streetcars and buses were largely deserted as passengers left them to walk along streets and join in the celebration.[56]

Hearing the raucous din of whistles, horns, and human voices, Oliver and Neda remembered the same type of frenzy when World War I ended on November 11, 1918. Oliver felt grateful that he and his family had been spared the ravages of this war. The economic hardships of 1942 seemed trivial compared to the losses of others in the war zones or of those

55. New Orleans *States* Extra, August 14, 1945.

56. New Orleans *Times-Picayune*, August 15, 1945, Sec. 1, pp. 1, 6, 7, 14, August 16, 1945, Sec. 1, p. 5.

in America who had lost young men in the service. Oliver's own sister Retta Nicholson was a Gold Star mother. One of her twin sons, Oliver, named for his uncle, had died in action in the Pacific in 1942. He was only twenty-two years old.

With the ordeal of the war over, Oliver and his fellow pilots were promoted to the rank of commander in mid-November, then on November 30 finally disenrolled from the Coast Guard Reserve.[57] Shipping on the Mississippi was picking up steadily by the beginning of 1946. Trade with Europe resumed on a full-time basis through the port of New Orleans, and aid to European nations to rebuild after the war added to that trade. A new mayoral administration in the Crescent City that year headed by deLesseps S. Morrison also encouraged more trade between Louisiana and South America. All of this brought expansion and prosperity to the lower Mississippi River's maritime and commercial complex. Oliver and his association were destined to share in that bright and busy future.

57. Memorandum from E. B. Briggs to New Orleans–Baton Rouge Steamship Pilots Association, concerning promotion of pilots to rank of commander in the Coast Guard Reserve to take effect date of memo, November 16, 1945; Disenrollment, Temporary Member, United States Coast Guard Reserve, Office of District Coast Guard Officer, Eighth Naval District, November 30, 1945. Both documents are in Oliver D. Jackson Papers.

14

CHALLENGES AND CHANGES AT MID-CENTURY
The Association in the Postwar Boom

In the last half of the 1940s, Oliver was busier than ever before as traffic on the Mississippi recovered from its slump during the early years of the war. This was the beginning of a hectic growth period in which new petrochemical plants, grain elevators, and general cargo docks sprang up along the river from New Orleans to Baton Rouge in rapid succession. The 1950s brought more work and prosperity to Oliver and the other New Orleans–Baton Rouge pilots, but it brought problems as well—such as a constant struggle to expand their membership and services to meet the insatiable demand for upriver pilots, problems with transportation to ships, the setting up and operation of an office, new hazards of increased traffic on the river, and controversy concerning their jurisdiction in the port of New Orleans. Oliver took an active part in his association's growth in the late forties and fifties, serving as president in 1948, 1950, 1951, and from 1955 though 1957.[1]

In many ways the decade from 1946 to 1956, was the most fulfilling in Oliver's life. He had reached the top of his profession, which he loved, and he and Neda bought a new brick house on Pauger and Sere streets. His daughter Joy completed her education and after graduating from college became a newspaper reporter. With their daughter grown, Oliver and Neda had reached a midpoint in their lives. As it is for many, it was a time when their mortality was brought home to them by the loss of close family members. Oliver's brother Eric died in 1950 of cancer. When Neda told him after he returned home from a trip, he sat down and cried. Eric had been closer to him than any other sibling, or even his parents. It was difficult to accept that his "little" brother had died. In 1951, Neda lost her father, and in 1953, her mother.[2]

Just as changes occurred in Oliver's family circle, the growth of his

1. Jackson Notebook, No. 2, p. 21.
2. Obituary for Eric Jackson, New Orleans *Times-Picayune*, November 6, 1950, Sec. 1, p. 2; Obituary for John Joseph Drouant, New Orleans *Times-Picayune*, August 29, 1951, Sec. 1, p. 2, and New Orleans *States*, August 29, 1951, Sec. 1, p. 4; Obituary for Josephine Drouant, New Orleans *Times-Picayune*, December 13, 1953, Sec. 1, p. 18.

business brought about considerable personnel changes in his association. Its membership began changing the year after the charter was adopted. By the end of 1944, the upper-river pilots were ready to add a new member. There were only eight of them actively employed—Captain Koch had actually retired in 1940, although he had kept his name on their roster and given his support in getting the charter. The man chosen as the new pilot was a native of Algiers, Siegfried Sprada, whose father owned a bar and restaurant that was a landmark on Algiers Point. Rivermen and seamen frequently came into the place, and through contact with them the young Sprada had developed a desire to follow a river profession. He first went to sea at fourteen, traveling to Puerto Rico and New York out of New Orleans. After that first summer job, each spring when school was out at Rugby Academy, which he attended, he recalled "I would go on up to Lykes Brothers and get a job . . . as a wiper on deck, ordinary seaman, or fireman in the engine room." Through a towboat captain who was a friend of his father's, Sprada was invited to take a trip up to St. Louis on a Federal Barge Line towboat. He did light tasks aboard the boat. This was probably a tryout opportunity for him, since the towboat was in need of another crew member. Young Sprada must have impressed the captain enough for him to contact his headquarters with a good report. By the time the boat reached Vicksburg, the captain showed him a telegram from the home office offering him the job. He accepted and stayed with the company as a crew member and later one of their captains until he became a New Orleans–Baton Rouge pilot.[3]

Captain Sprada came to work for the pilots in late December, 1944, as a cub. He was made a full member on April 11, 1945.[4] Since he was not yet thirty-five, the minimum age to be named a lieutenant commander in the Coast Guard, he was commissioned a lieutenant. Sprada found his new job satisfying and enjoyable. He loved piloting the large ships after years on towboats, although he had to admit that it took a little while to learn to judge distances looking from the bridge of a tanker, which was much higher than the wheelhouse of a towboat.

In the 1970s, Captain Sprada wrote an essay on the pilots and their work, which was published by them in booklet form. It contains this description of apprentice training:

> As an apprentice pilot during the term of his apprenticeship, the applicant is taught ship handling, docking and undocking, the use of the anchor, and the ship's equipment, to be calm and patient and to exercise good judgment

3. Interview with Captain Siegfried Sprada and Captain Frank Furr, by Joy Jackson, January 8, 1990, Metairie, Louisiana, 2. Hereinafter cited as Sprada-Furr Interview.

4. Sprada-Furr Interview, 2; *NOBR Charter and Roster*, 2.

during periods of stress and emergency. He is afforded experience in the judgment of distance, ship's weight and momentum and familiarizes himself with the entire pilotage route. At the end of the apprenticeship period he appears before the Board of Commissioners of the New Orleans Baton Rouge Ship Pilots for examination, which may be either written or oral. If the applicant successfully completes his training or examination he is recommended to the Governor of the State of Louisiana for appointment as a pilot. The Governor, after considering the qualifications of the applicant and the recommendation of the commissioners, may in his discretion, issue a commission to the applicant as a pilot of the New Orleans Baton Rouge Steamship [Pilots] Association.[5]

Sprada quickly caught on to the routine of piloting and came to be regarded as an excellent pilot and an intelligent leader; he was entrusted with elective offices numerous times during his long tenure in the association.

In 1946, the beginning of the postwar era, tonnage leaving and coming into Baton Rouge by river hit 8,367,965, the largest total since 1926, when it had reached 8,944,589. With American armed forces setting up long-term peacetime bases overseas and with economic aid to Europe in the form of foodstuffs, fuel, and other materials spewing out of American ports, river trade through Baton Rouge continued to expand in the late 1940s and into the 1950s. The New Orleans–Baton Rouge pilots had to add a second new pilot to their roster in 1946 to help with their hectic schedule. He was Captain Pierre "Pete" Trudell, Jr., a riverman who had worked on tugs and towboats.[6]

At the other end of the pilot spectrum, the association's oldest member—and the oldest active river pilot in the United States—Captain Charles Jackson, retired at eighty-three in December, 1947. He had piloted steamboats and then ships on the river for sixty-two years. His boyhood had been spent at Rising Sun, Indiana, on the Ohio River, in a setting very much like that which Mark Twain had depicted in *Tom Sawyer*. Now, as the Mississippi River traffic between New Orleans and Baton Rouge was growing dramatically, "Old Man" Jackson was retiring. He had a little book in which he kept a log of the vessels he handled. "I don't guess anybody's been writing a book as long as I have," he told a reporter who interviewed him, as he fingered the faded, ragged logbook. Referring to his last trip, which had yet to be made and recorded, he said with a catch in his voice, "It'll be the hardest to write."[7]

5. Siegfried Sprada, *Men, Ships, and the River: The New Orleans Baton Rouge Pilots Story* (New Orleans, n.d.), 3–6.

6. On tonnage at Baton Rouge, see Pat Wilson, "Ships to the Sea and from It," Baton Rouge *Morning Advocate*, August 1, 1948, magazine section, 6; and on Trudell, see *NOBR Charter and Roster*, 2.

7. Clipping from the New Orleans *Item*, December 22, 1947, Sec. 1, p. 8, in scrapbook, Oliver D. Jackson Papers.

As their business increased and their membership grew, the upriver pilots faced the problems of securing more reliable transportation to ships and more professional attention to the administrative details of their business. Transportation was particularly an issue as more and more ships called at docks between New Orleans and Baton Rouge. One reason Captain Charles Jackson had decided to retire (in addition to his age) was his difficulty in getting to and from ships. He could not drive and had no family to take him. Captain Sprada had volunteered to drive the elderly pilot to ships occasionally, and sometimes changed turns with him when Jackson asked to be given a Baton Rouge trip instead of a short turn. Buses no longer traveled on River Road as they had once done; now they left their passengers off on Airline Highway, far from the river. It was up to a pilot to get from Airline to the River Road and out to his ship if he had no automobile transportation. Sometimes the company sent a car or truck. Other times, local cabdrivers picked up pilots and took them to the river. In getting back to New Orleans from St. Rose, if Neda was unable to pick him up, Oliver often got a ride with one of the huge trucks that carried petroleum products in large drums from the plant.[8]

Adequate reimbursement for transportation had to be secured if the pilots were to get to ships on time and get home again from one of the refineries at St. Rose, Destrehan, Good Hope, or Norco. As these trips increased sharply in number, the pilots requested a raise in their transportation allowance from the New Orleans Steamship Association in 1947. They also requested more in transportation money for trips to and from Baton Rouge by cab and bus.[9] The requests were granted, and the pilots used the funds to engage a professional driver.

By the end of the 1940s, a dispute with the lower-river pilots had forced the association out of the office the two groups long had shared. They acquired their own office and hired Julius Prinz's son Robert as their full-time office manager in 1947. He was to become invaluable to them and remain manager for over four decades (in later years his brother Carl A. Prinz and his son Kurt V. Prinz also came to work for the pilots). In 1948 Oliver, as president of the association, urged his fellow pilots to go back to the Louisiana Legislature—this time to raise their rates by fifty cents per foot (of a ship's draft) and to secure various fringe benefits. Inflation was the companion of prosperity in the late 1940s, and the pilots found themselves working harder yet having difficulty keeping up with the cost of living. They also had the lowest rates in the country and one of the

8. Sprada-Furr Interview, 11–12; Jackson Transcripts, No. 11, p. 25.
9. H. W. Roberts to John Flettrich, secretary, New Orleans Steamship Association, January 6, 1947 [regarding requests made by New Orleans–Baton Rouge Steamship Pilots for additional transportation reimbursement], in Oliver D. Jackson Papers.

longest routes. They were successful in their bid for the modest raise. Several other times during the fifties, as inflation kept climbing, the association requested and received rate hikes from the legislature. [10]

National prosperity and the revival of world trade after the war stirred both of the major ports on the lower Mississippi, New Orleans and Baton Rouge, to upgrade their facilities, encourage more ships to call at their docks, and attract new industry to locate along the river. The pilots found their business increasing rapidly as a result of this activity.

When deLesseps S. Morrison became mayor of New Orleans in 1946, one of his prime objectives was to increase trade between New Orleans and the major markets in the world, especially Latin America. In 1926 a Permanent International Trade Exhibition had been set up on Poland and Dauphine streets, featuring products from at least twenty countries in its opening exhibit. Designed to act as a clearinghouse between Mississippi Valley and foreign businesses, it operated until 1931. But the depression caused its demise, and not until the 1940s did the idea of such a permanent trade organization based in New Orleans take shape again. [11]

While the Crescent City port was going through some of its darkest days due to German submarine warfare, two advertising executives, Lawrence H. Stevens and Harlet B. Howcott, came up with a plan for a trade club and center that would bring foreign businessmen together with local entrepreneurs to exchange information and promote commerce. Others werebrought into the planning of the center, and in December of 1943 it was officially incorporated as International House. In June, 1945, its headquarters opened to local and foreign visitors. The operation was an unqualified success. Before the end of the year, a second organization was established emphasizing trade exhibitions and merchandising facilities. Out of this initiative developed the International Trade Mart, opened in 1948. [12]

Besides these two organizations with their influence in drawing foreign commerce to New Orleans, the mayor set up within city government a Department of International Relations to assist foreign businessmen. Morrison himself made several goodwill tours of Latin American countries to

10. "History and Scope of Operations of the New Orleans–Baton Rouge Steamship Pilots Association" (typescript in Oliver D. Jackson Papers). This brief history was probably written in 1956 to acquaint legislators with the background of the pilots, who were requesting a raise in rates.

11. Gary Arnold Bolding, "Efforts to Develop New Orleans as a World Trade Center, 1910–1960" (M.A. thesis, Louisiana State University, 1966), 45–60.

12. *Ibid.*, 60–75; Edward F. Haas, *DeLesseps S. Morrison and the Image of Reform: New Orleans Politics, 1946–1961* (Baton Rouge, 1974), 63–65.

promote trade with the Crescent City. On the river, the city's official yacht, the *Good Neighbor*, took prominent visitors on tours of the harbor to show off its assets.[13]

The Dock Board also reached out to encourage foreign trade. Through a grant from the United States Department of Commerce, the board set up Foreign Trade Zone No. 2 in the public commodity warehouse in 1947. This facility allowed long-term storage of foreign goods not subject to customs while they remained in the zone. There were also considerable improvements to wharves and storage sheds, to the public cotton warehouse, and to public grain elevators within the harbor.[14]

The port of Baton Rouge also enjoyed a period of rapid development in the late 1940s and 1950s. During the war, a form of synthetic rubber, Buna-N, was perfected in a plant set up by the Chemical Products Division of Standard Oil in the Baton Rouge refinery.[15] Because of the vital need for rubber for military purposes, the government took over the plant and operated it until 1950. Standard Oil sold it that year to Uniroyal. Other rubber-allied chemical plants grew up nearby and were sold and resold as the rubber industry expanded. Soon Baton Rouge was a major center for making synthetic rubber.[16]

Another industry that came to the capital as a result of wartime needs was the aluminum industry. The Aluminum Company of America, known as Alcoa, cooperated with the Defense Plant Corporation to build an alumina plant at Baton Rouge in 1942 (alumina, or aluminum oxide, is a powdery substance intermediate to making of the familiar metal aluminum). In 1949 Permanente Metals, later Kaiser Aluminum, purchased this plant from the government and Alcoa. Henry Kaiser added to his aluminum complex on the Mississippi with a reducing plant (for converting alumina to metallic aluminum) in 1951 at Chalmette and a second alumina refinery and chemical plant at Gramercy in 1959. By that year, Kaiser's plants along the river from Chalmette to Baton Rouge were employing 4,250 workers. At Burnside, another alumina refinery was opened by Ormet in 1958. The raw material for all these aluminum-industry

13. Haas, *Delesseps S. Morrison*, 65; "A Yacht That Sells a Port," *New Orleans Port Record*, X (September, 1951), 8, 9, 37.

14. Baughman, "Gateway to the Americas," in *The Past as Prelude*, ed. Carter, 277; Bolding, "Efforts to Develop New Orleans as a World Trade Center," 88; "Economy Zone," *New Orleans Port Record*, XIII (November, 1954), 13–15.

15. *Fifty Years*, 18; Raymond E. Shanafelt, "The Baton Rouge–New Orleans Petrochemical Industrial Region: A Functional Region Study" (2 vols.; Ph.D. dissertation, Louisiana State University, 1977), I, 248–53, and II, 457–58.

16. Shanafelt, "Baton Rouge-New Orleans Petrochemical Industrial Region," II, 457–58.

plants, bauxite, came mainly from mines in Surinam in the 1940s; later, Jamaican bauxite dominated. Whatever the source of the ore, the bauxite ships in their growing numbers were piloted upriver to Baton Rouge by Oliver's association.[17]

Other industrial growth along the Mississippi between Baton Rouge and New Orleans in the 1950s included the opening of the Trans/Match plant at St. Rose in 1952, and on the west bank of the river, the inauguration of operations in 1953 of American Cyanamid at Waggaman and Lion Oil (Monsanto) at Luling. These three were the first of ten ammonia-producing plants to be located in the area. Upstream from these plants on the east bank, Shell Chemical constructed its Norco plant, which began operation in 1955. The Wyandotte Chemical plant opened its first units in 1958 using process chemicals from such oil refineries as Standard Oil and Shell. On the west bank near Plaquemine, a steel-barrel plant began operations in 1954 and the large, sprawling Dow Chemical plant began production in 1958. Dow Chemical was the pacesetter on the west bank ten miles below Baton Rouge. This was mainly sugarcane country, rural and green when this corporation purchased Union Plantation in 1956 and started constructing their facilities to manufacture "Clorothene" solvents and ethanolamines. But other industries would follow them to the west bank in the next decades.[18] Between 1945 and 1961 in the area along the river from Baton Rouge to Port Sulphur below New Orleans, 150 new industrial plants came into existence.[19]

The port of Baton Rouge itself was completely restructured in the forties and fifties. In 1940, recognizing the importance to military defense of the barge and ship traffic on the Mississippi, the United States Senate approved a $4,200,000 dredging project to deepen the channel of the river from Baton Rouge to the Gulf. At Baton Rouge the channel would be 35 feet deep and 500 feet wide. Five years later a second act authorized dredging in the channel from Baton Rouge southward to a depth of 40 feet.

17. *Ibid.*, 458–60; "Kaiser Aluminum in Louisiana" [statistical chart], *Kaiser Aluminum News* (July–August, 1959), 16; "Aluminum Ore Shipment from New Operation," *New Orleans Port Record*, XI (March, 1953), 15; "New Orleans and Aluminum," *New Orleans Port Record*, XII (February, 1954), 14–18; "Kaiser Aluminum to Build La. Plant," *New Orleans Port Record*, XIV (January, 1956), 24; "Mathieson's Louisiana Chemical Investment Grows," *New Orleans Port Record*, XV (July, 1957), 26–27.

18. Mark T. Carleton, *River Capital: An Illustrated History of Baton Rouge* (Woodland Hills, Calif., 1981), 154–55; Shanafelt, "Baton Rouge–New Orleans Petrochemical Industrial Region," II, 460; "Lion Oil Dedicates $30 Million Plant," *New Orleans Port Record*, XIII (November, 1954), 20; "Announce Plans for Geismar Plant," *New Orleans Port Record*, XV (November, 1956), 33.

19. William A. Garnett, "Baton Rouge to the Gulf," *Fortune* (January, 1961), 105–13.

This assured Baton Rouge the title of the farthest inland deep seaport in the United States. It also assured that 600-foot-long tankers servicing Baton Rouge refineries and those downstream would have a deep enough channel for safe passage. [20]

The Baton Rouge Port Development Association was organized in 1944 to promote the growth of the city's river commerce. Two projects that this body proposed were studied by the Corps of Engineers and authorized in the River and Harbor Act of July 24, 1946: the building of the Devil's Swamp barge canal within the city limits to give barges from upriver a safe place to load and unload away from the wakes of passing ships, and the Port Allen–Indian Village link to the Intracoastal Canal, which would shorten the towboat-barge route to Morgan City—and thence to Texas— by about 160 miles. [21] Although neither the Port Allen offshoot nor the first section of the Devil's Swamp canal was completed and opened for use until the early 1960s, the association did play a strong role in keeping these two projects before the public and Congress.

The most crucial step toward improving the Baton Rouge harbor was the realization on the part of businessmen and politicians that the industrial complex of Baton Rouge was larger than the city boundaries. The Baton Rouge City Council created a city port authority in 1949. It restored to service the municipal dock long out of use. But modernizing the port required much more attention and money than the council could offer. Like the New Orleans port, which embraced river frontage in adjacent parishes, the port of Baton Rouge could be defined as a three-parish area—East Baton Rouge, West Baton Rouge, and Iberville parishes. After a study of the harbor by an independent firm of engineers, the city council along with other political and commercial groups in the area, decided that state organization was needed. In March of 1952, the Greater Baton Rouge Port Association drafted plans for a state port authority that would cover the three parishes. [22] Using their plan as a model, the 1952 state legislature approved a constitutional amendment creating the port authority. Later in the year, it was passed into law by Louisiana voters. [23]

20. Baton Rouge *Morning Advocate*, August 1, 1948, magazine section, 6; Corps of Engineers, U.S. Army, *The Ports of Baton Rouge and Lake Charles, Louisiana*, Port Series, No. 21 (1979; rev. ed. Washington, D.C., 1982), 1–4.

21. Clipping from Baton Rouge *Morning Advocate*, March 6, 1949, in Vertical File on Baton Rouge Harbor, State Library of Louisiana, Baton Rouge.

22. Clipping from Baton Rouge *State Times*, March 29, 1952, *ibid.*

23. Clippings from Baton Rouge *State Times*, April 28, 1952, and New Orleans *Times-Picayune*, January 25, 1953, *ibid.*; "Modern Public Port Facilities to Boost Baton Rouge Trade and Industry," *Construction News Monthly*, June 8, 1955, pp. 20–21.

At the time the Greater Baton Rouge Port Authority came into existence, the only docks in the Baton Rouge harbor suitable for oceangoing vessels were privately operated by Standard Oil, the Solvay Process Plant, and Kaiser Aluminum on the east bank. The one municipal dock in operation was only accessible during high water. Silting was common along this dock, hindering ships drawing more than eighteen feet from taking on cargo there.[24]

One of the first actions, therefore, of the Board of Commissioners of the Greater Baton Rouge Port, was the acquisition of a 350-acre tract on the west bank across from downtown Baton Rouge. The tract offered six thousand feet of deep-water river frontage and lay along the right-of-way for the future Port Allen lock. Another tract of land, approximately 395 acres with five thousand feet of river frontage, was purchased below Baton Rouge. The commission also leased the municipal dock on the east bank from the city council for general cargo use.[25]

Initially, the port commission had received $200,000 from the 1952 legislature. The same constitutional amendment that established the commission authorized the issuance of revenue bonds, and a special session of the legislature in 1953 awarded the commission another $100,000. These actions covered the purchase of the land and allowed for the beginning of construction of a grain elevator, a molasses terminal, and a general cargo wharf on the west bank in 1954.[26]

The opening of the grain elevator in the summer of 1955 marked a new era for greater Baton Rouge. The elevator was leased to Cargill, Inc., the world's largest grain contractors. Grain-handling equipment at the elevator was capable of loading and unloading 30,000 bushels per hour.[27] The first oceangoing vessel to take on grain at the elevator was the *Trans-Arctic*, flying the Honduran flag and taken away from the dock and downriver by a New Orleans–Baton Rouge pilot.[28] In the next decade, other grain elevators were constructed on the Mississippi between Baton Rouge and New Orleans as grain shipping overseas developed into a mammoth industry in the Mississippi Valley. In March, 1956, the molasses terminal at the new west bank docks went into operation. It was followed in July,

24. Clippings from Baton Rouge *Morning Advocate*, March 6, 1949, and Baton Rouge *State Times*, May 3, 1951, in Vertical File on Baton Rouge Harbor, State Library of Louisiana.

25. "Modern Public Port Facilities to Boost Baton Rouge Trade and Industry," 21.

26. Clipping from Baton Rouge *Morning Advocate*, July 25, 1955, in Vertical File, State Library of Louisiana.

27. *Ibid.*

28. Clipping from Baton Rouge *State Times*, September 25, 1955, *ibid.*

1956, by the opening of the general cargo dock. The first ship to call at this dock was the *Clarissa*, from Yugoslavia, which unloaded a cargo of lead and cement.[29]

The Greater Baton Rouge Port Authority also moved downriver in 1954, purchasing a new bulk marine terminal from Olin Mathieson Chemical Corporation at Burnside. This facility was the only one of its kind at that time on the deep-water section of the Mississippi to accommodate the rapid handling of ores (such as bauxite) and other dry bulk materials.[30]

By 1957, the first full year of operation for all of the public port facilities of the Greater Baton Rouge Port, 55 vessels called at the General Cargo Docks to load and unload 300,000 tons of foreign commerce, while 100 vessels loaded wheat, soybeans, corn, and oats from the grain elevator. The port commission had also attracted a fourth parish, Ascension, into the Greater Baton Rouge Port.[31]

Work on both the Devil's Swamp project and the Port Allen lock and Intracoastal Canal connection was in progress by 1958. The first two and a half miles of the Devil's Swamp canal was completed in April, 1959. It was called the Baton Rouge Barge Canal and later the Baton Rouge Harbor Channel. The Greater Baton Rouge Port Commission shared with the federal government in the costs of building the canal. The commission also constructed a four-hundred-foot steel-and-concrete public terminal on the canal, with truck and rail connections.[32]

The Port Allen lock and Intracoastal Canal extension opened on July 14, 1961. An impressive list of state dignitaries turned out to participate in the dedication and opening of the lock, along with hundreds of curious citizens. The honor of leading the parade of boats through the lock was accorded to Chotin Towing Corporation, owned by Captain Joseph Chotin, whose two brothers were members of the New Orleans–Baton Rouge Steamship Pilots Association. Captain Chotin had been aboard the second boat to go through the Plaquemine Lock when it opened in 1906. Now he was host to Governor Jimmie Davis and Senators Russell Long

29. Baton Rouge *Morning Advocate*, August 18, 1957.

30. *Deep Water, Port of Baton Rouge* [a publication of the Greater Baton Rouge Port Commission], I (October, 1957), n.p. (pages unnumbered); "Port Development and Greater Baton Rouge," *World Ports* ["Published for the Waterfront Terminal Industry and Its Shippers and Carriers"], (October, 1957), clipping in Vertical File on Baton Rouge Harbor, State Library of Louisiana.

31. "Port Tonnages Up for 1957," *Deep Water*, II (January, 1958), n.p. (pages unnumbered); Corps of Engineers, U.S. Army, *Ports of Baton Rouge and Lake Charles*, 1.

32. Baton Rouge *State Times*, April 3, 1959, Sec. A, p. 1, Sec. C, p. 6, June 10, 1959, Sec. A, p. 1, Sec. C, p. 10, March 24, 1960, Sec. A, pp. 1, 8; Baton Rouge *Morning Advocate*, June 10, 1959, Sec. A, pp. 1, 16.

and Allen Ellender aboard his towboat, *Irene Chotin,* as it was the first vessel to pass through the lock; it had three barges in tow. Two Chotin captains, J. B. Kleinpeter and R. E. Peavy, were on special assignment to take the towboat through the lock. This lock was 84 feet wide and 1,200 feet long, at the time the largest lock on the Intracoastal system between Florida and the Mexican border. The new outlet from Port Allen connected at Morgan City with the original Intracoastal via a sixty-five-mile canal 12 feet deep and 125 feet wide along its entire length.[33] The opening of this extension and the harbor barge canal sharply increased barge traffic through Baton Rouge, making it a major barge terminal on the lower Mississippi.

All of this expansion forced the New Orleans–Baton Rouge pilots to enlist new members. A total of eighteen pilots were taken into the association in the 1950s—twice the entire membership at the time the charter was adopted. After Captain Charles Jackson's retirement, Joseph Scott was elected a pilot in 1949. In 1951 the association elected Walter S. Wright, who had been a tugboat captain at Coyle Company. The next year Carlton F. Trosclair and William P. King were added to the roster: In 1954 Charles P. Henley, another tugboatman from Coyle's joined, followed in 1955 by Joseph A. Lennox, Jr., Worday P. Bordelon, and Ruel H. Reichert, Jr. In 1956, five men were added to the membership. They were Thomas D. Doyle, Peter L. Fitzgerald, Charles H. Hough, James M. Seaman, and Oliver R. Trowbridge. The last year of the fifties, 1959, six men became upper-river pilots: Frank T. Furr, Joseph M. Kenny, Tilman J. Pizani, Sr., John W. Sarbeck, Canton P. Seitz, Jr., and Robert B. Streckfus. In 1963, the year before Oliver retired, five more pilots joined: Arthur Bezette, Aubrey O. Dowell, Henry K. Durham, Gayle B. Holt, and William O. Watson, Jr.[34] The professional backgrounds of these men varied from tugboat and towboat experience to service on oceangoing vessels.

As traffic in the form of ships, tugs, towboats, and barges became heavier between New Orleans and Baton Rouge, small diesel-powered boats presented a special problem to river pilots. In the 1940s and 1950s, the operation of diesel boats did not require a pilot's license. Thus a man at the wheel of a diesel boat might not be fully familiar with the ship channel or with the rules of the road. Accidents resulted from this ignorance.

Oliver was involved in one of them in 1945 about twenty miles south

---

33. Clippings from *Baton Rouge* [publication of the Baton Rouge Chamber of Commerce], IX (February, 1958) and X (May, 1959), n.p. (pages unnumbered); Baton Rouge *Morning Advocate,* July 13, 1961, Sec. E, p. 5, July 14, 1961, Sec. A, pp. 1, 8, July 15, 1961, Sec. A, pp. 1, 8.

34. NOBR *Charter and Roster,* 2–4.

of Baton Rouge and a half mile below Virginia Light.[35] He was proceeding upriver to the Standard Oil docks in Baton Rouge aboard the ship *William Crompton* a little after 4 A.M. when a tugboat, the *John H. McCullough*, coming downriver with one barge, blew two whistles, signaling that the tug wanted to pass starboard side to starboard side.

Oliver explained what happened in his report to the Coast Guard:

> Tug blew two whistles, when about a half mile off . . . at the same time using search light from side to side, but showing port red light, and was a little off port bow. I put left wheel on ship and was about to answer his two whistles, when he flashed one light with his search light, which is a custom used sometimes instead of whistles on the river when passing at night. He pulled to right and then immediately pulled back to his left heading right down on the ship's bow, showing his port light all the time. At no time did I see his starboard green light on the barge. I at once put my ship at full astern, which was 4:30 A.M. About a half minute later the barge struck the ship on the bow. Barge immediately blew up and caught fire. I kept backing away from fire. Seeing men in the water, I threw a ring buoy, with light attached from bridge, which two men caught. The tug and barge sank immediately.
>
> I then stopped my ship, which was at 4:30 A.M., as the ship was clear of fire and danger. We then dropped anchor, at the same time lowering lifeboat which picked up five men, returning them to ship at 5:30 A.M. Lifeboat made a second trip and searched area for the rest of the tug's crew, without any success. Boat returned at 6:30 A.M. We then proceeded to Baton Rouge at 7:03 A.M., arriving at Baton Rouge at 11 A.M.[36]

Three of the tug's crewmen drowned. The confusing whistle and light signals and the smaller boat's crisscrossing movements caused the collision. Oliver had only twenty to thirty seconds to give the order to put the ship in reverse. There was no time left even to blow a danger signal before the fatal crash. He had taken the only action he could to avoid the accident by backing away, but the large ship could not move swiftly enough to elude the tug and barge, which were traveling with the current downstream.

Although Oliver was not responsible for the accident, he became especially concerned with safety measures on the river after this tragedy. He advocated regulations and stricter control over diesel boats and served for a number of years on the Safety Control Committee of the New Orleans Propeller Club.

Another danger of the crowded river was the damage the wake of a ship could do to ships and barges tied up to landings. A heavy wake could cause

---

35. New Orleans *Times-Picayune*, June 19, 1945, Sec. 1, p. 1.

36. Lt. Commander O. D. Jackson to U.S. Coast Guard Hearing Board, June 18, 1945, copy in Oliver D. Jackson Papers.

lines to break between a ship and the dock, damage or pull loose pipelines or hoses supplying chemicals or fuel to vessels, and even sink some smaller craft. As the river commerce increased, the New Orleans–Baton Rouge pilots had to slow down ships they piloted when passing dock facilities or moored barges.[37]

They also encountered problems in docking and undocking ships at the Baton Rouge private industrial docks. For years the upper-river pilots had docked and undocked ships at the Standard Oil docks without the aid of tugs and without charging extra for this service. By the mid-1950s, however, the maneuver of turning for a descending passage down the river from the Esso dock had become quite hazardous. The activity in the harbor greatly increased the risk of hitting a passing vessel, and the outgrowth of facilities and equipment on the banks reduced the space for maneuvering. In 1956 Oliver wrote a letter complaining of this situation to Captain A. C. Steinmuller, the port captain at Esso. He concluded, "I must go on record that as the harbor activity at Baton Rouge increases, there will be a time in the near future when my members will not want to dock or undock where conditions are hazardous without the assistance of a tugboat." Although Esso officials at first opposed hiring outside tugs to aid the pilots, they eventually agreed to such a course. Tugs began to be used at private industrial docks and at the public docks of the Greater Baton Rouge Port by the end of the 1950s.[38]

The upper-river pilots set up their own pilots' station in Baton Rouge in January, 1956, in a suite in the Heidelberg Hotel.[39] As their business became more and more diversified and included other companies in addition to Standard Oil, they felt they could no longer occupy the pilots' quarters on the Esso plant grounds. The station was moved later from the hotel to another location, and finally, after Oliver had left the association, the pilots decided to keep only a shift pilot in Baton Rouge. All other pilots now travel back to New Orleans and return only when needed to take a ship downriver.[40]

The fifties saw a proliferation of much longer ships with greater cargo

37. Jackson Transcripts, No. 11, pp. 10–11; Captain V. G. Niebergall, U.S. Coast Guard, to New Orleans Baton Rouge Steamship Pilots, August 3, 1961, copy in Oliver D. Jackson Papers.

38. Captain O. D. Jackson to Captain A. C. Steinmuller, May 10, 1956, copy in Oliver D. Jackson Papers; Jackson Transcripts, No. 11, pp. 14–15; Sprada-Furr Interview, 7–8.

39. Statement of Robert Prinz to Joy Jackson, September 18, 1988, Kenner, Louisiana; Sprada-Furr Interview, 10.

40. Sprada-Furr Interview, 10.

capacity. But their increased size had serious drawbacks. Captain Frank Furr, who joined the pilots in 1959 after service with the navy and a career of working on Corps of Engineers towboats, pointed out that the shipbuilders "were taking those ships which they had built during World War II and extending them, just making them a whole lot bigger. But they were not putting in any bigger engines or bigger rudders."[41] This short-sightedness created genuine problems in steering these vessels—for example, in going around bends during the high-water season. Handling large ships required experience and a subtle sense of observation. Captain Furr explained that a pilot had to pay attention to movements of a vessel: "A ship will tell you a lot of things. . . . If it's in deep water, it'll rattle all over, and if it gets into shallow water, it gets quiet."[42]

Through all of their difficulties, the upper-river pilots persevered. They increased their membership to meet the demand for pilots, adjusted their speed to suit the heavy traffic on the river, got the tugboat help they needed in docking and undocking, set up their own pilot station, and began to break away from the dominance of Standard Oil as their business broadened.

The greatest conflict they faced in this period, however, concerned their jurisdiction in the harbor of New Orleans. It began as a bitter struggle in which Oliver and his fellow upper-river pilots were in sharp disagreement with the lower-river pilots and the steamship companies. It ended with the upper-river pilots winning the last battle but losing the war.

41. Ibid., 7.
42. Ibid., 4–5.

15

TROUBLED WATERS
Final Years as a Pilot, 1956–1966

Serving as president of his association for five years out of ten during the 1950s, Oliver was deeply involved, emotionally as well as intellectually, in all of the many conflicts on the river during that decade. He always faced up to a problem—never backing down or taking a hands-off attitude. He still had a fighter's instincts and the passionate urge to stand up to intimidation—character traits that had gotten him in trouble as a child in the orphanage. At sixty years of age in 1956, he was straight as an arrow and skillful in climbing the rope ladders to the ships he piloted. Always a neat and stylish dresser, he wore a suit, starched shirt, and tie to board a ship. The hats he had favored in the 1940s were now replaced by English driving caps, which gave him a casual, country-gentleman appearance. He had become a father figure to some of the younger pilots, who affectionately called him "Pops."

At a stage when he should have been leading a routine, easygoing life, taking time off to relax, Oliver was plunged into the most traumatic conflict he had ever faced as a pilot. It was a long-drawn-out controversy over the jurisdiction of the New Orleans–Baton Rouge Pilots in regard to the New Orleans harbor. The tradition that they should board and leave ships at the lower end of the city went back to the early twentieth century, when independent pilots first took ships up to Baton Rouge. But the established territories of older organizations of pilots had their roots in colonial times. The determination of who would pilot ships across the Mississippi River bars to points upriver had changed as the governments of Louisiana changed.

In the French and Spanish periods, colonial officals had control over pilots who operated between the Passes and New Orleans. In the early American period, private contractors controlled the right of pilotage and hired a variety of good and bad pilots. Later, more regulation of individual pilots was enacted into state law, but each man acted virtually on his own to board ships and get the right to take them into the river. There was vigorous competition to row out to a ship and gain the right to board it.

Occasionally, small groups of pilots who had received individual state licenses might band together in an informal association. But the first post–Civil War group to get a state charter that spelled out specific territory in which its members had exclusive rights was the Associated Branch Pilots, chartered in 1879. They took vessels from the Gulf into the Passes and up to Pilottown on the main river.

In 1908, when the Crescent River Port Pilots Assocation received a charter to pilot ships between Pilottown and New Orleans, the charter simply designated those two points on the river without stating exactly what the assocation's rights of pilotage were in the New Orleans harbor. Traditionally, the group handled all ships within the harbor. But in the era of World War I, when seafaring vessels began coming up the river and seeking pilots to take them on to Baton Rouge, the lower-river pilots allowed a few men, who were hired to do such piloting, to board these ships at Quarantine Anchorage—the Point—on the west bank at the lower end of the city and of Orleans Parish (the two were contiguous). This place was probably chosen because it was a safe, straight portion of the river where ships already were boarded by quarantine officers and sometimes detained at anchorage. There was also a commercial port ship service with a launch below the Quarantine Anchorage on the east bank at Goodyear's Landing. The launch took sailors off vessels lying at anchor who wanted to visit New Orleans. It also ferried pilots back and forth to ships.

The lower-river pilots had no desire to extend their route from Pilottown all the way to Baton Rouge. Because only a small number of ships made the run anyway, they allowed a few independent pilots to handle the work. Sometimes a ship might come to New Orleans and unload and load cargo and then go up the river to St. Rose, Destrehan, Norco, Good Hope, or all the way to Baton Rouge. When this happened, the lower-river pilots again allowed the pilots who worked above New Orleans to take such ships away from the docks within the city and head upriver. Likewise, an upper-river pilot might bring a ship down from Baton Rouge and tie up at a dock or get off at the Point. A lower-river pilot then took the ship downriver to Pilottown, where he turned it over to a bar pilot.

Because 80 or 90 percent of the ships that traveled above New Orleans from 1916 through 1950 were headed for the Standard Oil docks in Baton Rouge, the upper-river pilots became known as "Standard Oil pilots." During that period their membership never went over nine. They were a small group dependent upon the giant corporation for most of their business. But the securing of their charter, the growth of other industries on the upper river after the war, and the building of the Greater Baton Rouge

Port facilities in the 1950s began to broaden their business and allow them to move away from domination by Standard Oil.

In the late 1940s and 1950s, as recounted earlier, the upper-river pilots won higher rates through legislative action (sometimes opposed by Standard Oil), set up their independent pilot station in Baton Rouge, and gained the help of tugs in docking and undocking ships at Baton Rouge. One other objective they tried to achieve during the 1950s was to change the place where they boarded and disembarked from ships in the New Orleans harbor. They wished to make the pilot exchange at the upper end of the city, at Southport, instead of at the Point, at the lower end of the city. This intention was vehemently opposed by Standard Oil and other shipping and industrial interests, as well as by the lower-river pilots. The shippers opposed it for monetary reasons: it would raise pilotage costs for them. The lower-river pilots opposed it because it would add an hour onto their run from Pilottown and because they viewed the suggested point of exchange at Southport as dangerous.

The question of jurisdictional rights first came up between the lower- and upper-river pilots in 1942 when Act 291 gave the New Orleans–Baton Rouge pilots state sanction and authorized them to draft their charter. The lower-river pilots requested that Oliver, as president of his association, sign a letter stating that his group would not handle ships strictly within the harbor of New Orleans (Act 291 somewhat ambiguously gave them the right to pilot ships "from Port of New Orleans to and including Baton Rouge and intermediate ports and return"). Oliver complied with the lower-river pilots' request and tried to reassure them that his group had never intended to take shift work away from them within the New Orleans harbor.

The Crescent River Port pilots' concern stemmed from the fact that Act 54 of 1908, which had made them state pilots, did not spell out their jurisdiction within the harbor. It simply stated that they were "to pilot seagoing vessels from the head of the Passes opposite Pilottown to the Port of New Orleans and return."[1] To clarify matters, the Crescent River Port pilots also introduced a bill into the state legislature in 1942; Oliver helped them to get it passed along with Act 291. It seemingly settled the issue by stating that it was their duty "to pilot seagoing vessels from Pilot-

1. Original Brief on the merits on behalf of Defendants and Appellants, New Orleans and Baton Rouge Steamship Pilots Association, *Esso Standard Oil Company* v. *Crescent River Port Pilots Association and New Orleans and Baton Rouge Steamship Pilots Association*, et al., Supreme Court of Louisiana (1957), 6, hereinafter cited as Original Brief, *Esso* v. *Pilots*; *Acts Passed by the Legislature of the State of Louisiana*, Regular Session, 1908, Act No. 54, pp. 57–60.

town to Southport and return and within the Port of New Orleans."[2] Since Southport was at the upper end of New Orleans, this language gave them exclusive rights to all foreign ships whose destination was New Orleans, and to the shifting of such ships within the New Orleans harbor.

Recognizing that the New Orleans–Baton Rouge pilots boarded upriver-bound ships at the lower end of the city and sometimes at docks within the city, Act 134 (1942) provided for this by stating that "the said River Port Pilots shall be entitled to the exclusive right to pilot vessels within the Port of New Orleans between Southport and Mereauville, Louisiana . . . ; provided, however, nothing herein contained shall prevent an exchange of pilots at what is known as 'Algiers Point,' between the pilots herein named and the pilots engaged in the piloting of vessels beyond Southport, nor shall anything herein provided prevent pilots engaged in piloting vessels above Southport from ending or beginning the pilotage from any wharf or point of anchorage in the harbor of New Orleans."[3]

In 1952 the lower-river pilots changed the description of the point of exchange in their Act 177, Section 6 of which substituted "Quarantine Anchorage or the point of general anchorage" for "Algiers Point."[4] This was done to make the description more exact and correct, for although river pilots always referred to this place as the Point, it was actually below Algiers Point, which itself was far too dangerous to serve as a point of exchange.

The first request by the New Orleans–Baton Rouge pilots to exchange pilots in the vicinity of Southport or Oak Street in uptown New Orleans was submitted to the Crescent River Port pilots in a 1947 letter written by the upper-river pilots' secretary-treasurer, Captain Sprada. At that time, the two associations shared the same office in New Orleans.

Crescent River Port pilots turned down the request for the Southport exchange in a letter dated August 26, 1947. They gave two reasons for the negative response. First, they claimed that "conditions prevailing at Oak Street and the river" made an exchange impractical. Second, they pointed out that "it is to the advantage of the steamship interests that the exchange should be made as it has been for a great many years."[5] They claimed costs to shippers would go up. Since their fees were higher than those of the upper-river pilots, this assertion was basically correct. But it

2. Original Brief, *Esso* v. *Pilots*, 6; *Acts Passed by the Legislature of the State of Louisiana*, Regular Session, 1942, Act. No. 134, p. 429.

3. Original Brief, *Esso* v. *Pilots*, 6–7; *Acts Passed by the Legislature of the State of Louisiana*, Regular Session, 1942, Act No. 134, p. 430.

4. Original Brief, *Esso* v. *Pilots*, 8.

5. *Ibid.*, 12–13, 45–47.

addressed the problem in terms of the economic interests of the shippers, rather than the legal jurisdiction of the upper-river pilots.

In consequence of the strained relations between the two pilot groups over the exchange issue, the Crescent River Port pilots in this letter also asked the New Orleans–Baton Rouge pilots to move out of their shared office by November 1. Captain Sprada had the difficult task of finding a suitable office and a full-time office manager. As already noted, Robert Prinz filled this position.[6] With this opposition from the lower-river pilots, the upper-river association decided to drop the question of the exchange site at that time.

This was the second challenge to their charter the Crescent River Port pilots had to face in 1947. That may have been one of the reasons they reacted in such a testy fashion. The other had been a court case brought by a group of independent pilots who did some piloting of United States registered ships in the New Orleans harbor and who were seeking the right to be given state commissions to pilot foreign ships within the harbor, even though they had not been elected members of the Crescent River Port Pilots. That case was settled in 1947 with the United States Supreme Court denying their petition and upholding the legislature's right to grant exclusive rights to a group such as the Crescent River Port Pilots Association. This was a landmark case that protected the charters of all three piloting associations.[7]

The exchange at Southport came up again in 1950 when the New Orleans–Baton Rouge pilots tried to persuade both the Crescent River Port pilots and the shipping companies to accept it. Immediately, House Bill 913 of 1950 was introduced into the legislature with the purpose of repealing the charter of the New Orleans–Baton Rouge Steamship Pilots Association. Although no one openly admitted responsibility for this bill, the upper-river pilots realized that it had been instigated by opponents of the Southport exchange. Before the bill came up for consideration, they decided to meet with the opposition and compromise. They arranged several meetings with the Crescent River Port pilots and representatives of shipping interests. Oliver was serving as president of his association at that time. The meetings concluded with the New Orleans–Baton Rouge pilots agreeing to continue the exchange of pilots at Quarantine Anchorage.[8] At this point the attorney for the New Orleans Steamship Association

6. *Ibid.*, 47; Sprada-Furr Interview, 14–15.

7. New Orleans *Times-Picayune*, April 1, 1947. The case was *Marion B. Kotch, John L. Richards, Adolph Clark and others* v. *Board of River Port Pilot Commissioners for the Port of New Orleans.*

8. Original Brief, *Esso* v. *Pilots*, 48.

also tried to get the upper-river pilots to sign a statement admitting their legal obligation to use the Quarantine Anchorage location. This suggestion was rejected. Instead, in a letter of June 29, 1950, the upper-river pilots stated that they would continue the exchange at Quarantine Anchorage, but declared that this was by voluntary agreement only. That same day the bill threatening their charter was withdrawn.[9]

For the next six years, the jurisdiction quarrel lay dormant. Then, at the end of 1956, as river traffic grew heavier and construction began on the Greater Mississippi River Bridge, which would have at least one pier out in the New Orleans harbor, the dispute erupted again. The upper-river pilots decided to seek legal advice on what they could do to assert their jurisdictional rights. The task fell to Oliver as president and to Captain Joseph "Joe" Lennox, an energetic, hardworking young man who, although he had only joined the association in 1955, was already its secretary-treasurer. The two took the matter first to a lawyer and then, on his advice, to the state attorney general's office for clarification.[10]

This was not merely a legalistic fight. Guiding ships through the harbor of New Orleans when a pilot might not be legally obligated to do so involved a number of problems. In addition to the obvious hazards of navigating a busy harbor crowded with tugs, tows, barges, dredges, and the new bridge pier (which was to be built out in the river against the advice of the upper-river pilots), several other difficulties might arise. Oliver carefully wrote down some of these problems as he saw them.[11]

First, a ship coming upriver that was to make quarantine sent a message for an upper-river pilot to be there when it arrived. Before he was allowed to board, however, he might have to wait five or six hours while a doctor inspected two or three other ships. After this long wait, the ship might take eleven to thirteen hours to reach Baton Rouge. Although the shipping company paid for the detention time, the pilot could be involved for as much as nineteen hours. This tiring stint could be greatly shortened if he got on at Southport.

A second difficulty arose when a ship coming downriver wanted to anchor at the Point to take on stores before heading down to the Gulf. If the Quarantine Anchorage area was filled with ships, the pilot would have to take his ship below the anchorage and turn around before anchoring. This maneuver added one to two hours to an ordinary run.

9. *Ibid.*, 47–49.
10. Captain Joseph A. Lennox, Jr. to Honorable Jack P. F. Gremillion, Attorney General, February 21, 1957, copy in Oliver D. Jackson Papers.
11. The objections discussed in the next few paragraphs are raised in "Reasons for Changing at Carrollton Avenue" (typescript, undated, in Oliver D. Jackson Papers).

Another problem was negotiating the New Orleans harbor as fog set in. It was rarely advisable to do so; in most cases, an upper-river pilot would turn around and anchor at the upper limit of the harbor, rather than risk an accident. (Even anchoring in such a situation was dangerous: the anchor might strike a cable crossing the riverbed.) If the point of exchange were Southport, decisions about running in fog and the task of doing so would fall to those who knew the harbor best, the Crescent River Port pilots.

Coming down on Algiers Point in high water presented yet another dilemma. The upper-river pilot never knew whether he had the red or green light. If pilots changed at Southport, the lower-river man could call the traffic light tower before boarding the ship and request the right of way (this, of course, was before pilots began routinely using two-way radios on the river).

Finally, a major concern to Oliver was the liability of himself and his associates if an accident occurred within the New Orleans harbor when one of their members was piloting a foreign ship. Since their territory, according to their charter, could be interpreted to end at Southport, how would this affect them in litigation?

For all of these reasons, but mainly because the upper-river pilots felt that their charter plainly named Southport as the lower limit of their territory, Captain Lennox requested an opinion from the attorney general's office. His letter, dated February 21, 1957, was answered on March 4 by Carroll Buck, special assistant to Attorney General Jack Gremillion, who had requested that Buck handle this matter.[12]

The attorney general's answer was startling. It cited legal precedents for the opinion that "under the present law there is no duty of the Baton Rouge Pilots to pilot vessels into the Port of New Orleans." Buck also pointed out that the board of commissioners of the New Orleans–Baton Rouge pilots had no jurisdiction over the harbor of New Orleans, whereas the board of commissioners of the Crescent River Port pilots did have such jurisdiction, but it did not include the Baton Rouge pilots passing through the harbor. He concluded with the recommendation that "until such time as the legislature may change or clarify the law dealing with this situation, it is our opinion that the Baton Rouge Pilots should not pilot vessels below Southport or into the harbor of New Orleans."[13]

After receiving this authoritative opinion, Oliver and Lennox wrote to

12. Lennox to Gremillion, February 21, 1957, Jack P. F. Gremillion, Attorney General, to Captain Joseph A. Lennox, Jr., March 4, 1957, prepared by Carroll Buck, copies of both in Oliver D. Jackson Papers.

13. Gremillion to Lennox, March 4, 1957.

the Crescent River Port Pilots Association informing them of Buck's assessment and requesting that a meeting be arranged between representatives of the two associations to work out the details of changing the place of pilot exchange.[14] The lower-river pilots' response was a refusal to meet or discuss the matter. A second letter was sent to Captain Harry Post, president of the Crescent River Port pilots, requesting that his association reconsider meeting with the upper-river pilots. The letter informed him that the Baton Rouge pilots had set April 4, 1957, as the date after which they would no longer pilot ships below Southport. The letter also stated that the upper-river pilots were "arranging for facilities and a boat to be available to both associations at Carrollton Avenue, which said boat will transport pilots of both associations and any other interested parties to and from the point off Southport where pilots will be exchanged."[15]

With the threat of the April 4 deadline, the Crescent River Port pilots finally agreed to a meeting, which took place on March 28. Pilots from both associations—about twenty altogether—met with representatives of the attorney general's office in Baton Rouge. No agreement was reached concerning the Southport exchange.[16] In order to allow for negotiation, the upper-river pilots dropped the April 4 deadline, but announced their intentions of pursuing the transfer point at Southport.

During April the New Orleans Steamship Association and the Crescent River Port pilots voiced their fears that the Southport exchange point would be dangerous to traffic on the river, and rejected it on that ground. To counter this argument, the New Orleans–Baton Rouge pilots arranged for an inspection tour of Southport and the river at that point aboard the *Good Neighbor*. The tour was set for May 3, and invitations were sent to those individuals who had personally criticized Southport as hazardous as well as to all shipping interests or other groups concerned, including the Crescent River Port pilots.[17]

The inspection tour attracted representatives of the Corps of Engineers, the Dock Board, the Coast Guard, the Greater Baton Rouge Port Commission, the American Waterways Operators, and the Sewerage and Water Board of New Orleans. The Crescent River Port pilots and the New Orleans Steamship Association were conspicuous by their absence.

14. Captain Oliver D. Jackson and Captain Joseph A. Lennox, Jr., to Captain Harry Post, March 13, 1957, copy in Oliver D. Jackson Papers.

15. Captain Oliver D. Jackson and Captain Joseph A. Lennox, Jr., to Captain Harry Post, March 20, 1957, copy in Oliver D. Jackson Papers.

16. New Orleans *Times-Picayune*, March 30, 1957, Sec. 2, p. 14.

17. Captain Oliver D. Jackson to New Orleans Steamship Association, April 28, 1957, copy in Oliver D. Jackson Papers.

The trip covered the river from Quarantine Anchorage through the harbor to Southport. Captain Lennox served as narrator, giving a running commentary through the *Good Neighbor*'s loudspeaker. He told the audience aboard the yacht that "conditions at Southport were not only less hazardous than claimed by the Crescent City [pilots] group, but that it was actually easier to change pilots at Southport." He noted that the river was about the same width at both Quarantine Anchorage and Southport, approximately 2,300 feet, but "fewer tugs . . . get in the way at Southport since two canal entrances are located near Quarantine Point." When the *Good Neighbor* reached the vicinity of Southport, two sets of upper-river pilots switched in a pilot boat to and from the Panamanian oreship *Andros Heights,* headed from Jamaica to Baton Rouge with a load of bauxite. The exchange took four and a half minutes. Captain Lennox pointed out to the observers that there were "comparatively few shore installations in the vicinity," with a clear stretch of river for about two miles. The exchange of pilots to and from the Panamanian vessel went smoothly. Both Oliver and Joe Lennox considered it a success.[18]

With this demonstration in mind as a refutation of the charge that Southport was a hazardous exchange point, Oliver sent telegrams on May 4 to the major shipping interests whose vessels his association handled, advising them that as of midnight, May 10, 1957, members of his association would no longer accept vessels tendered for pilotage below Southport.[19]

As the deadline approached and the Crescent River Port pilots still had not agreed to move the point of exchange, Oliver notified shippers that his pilots would be willing to take ships below the Southport landing for a grace period of five days if the Crescent River Port pilots did not show up there on May 10. After that, he stated, "we will accept for pilotage a vessel bound from a point above Southport to a point below only with the understanding and on the condition that the vessel will be met by a pilot of the Crescent River Port Pilots Association in the vicinity of Southport and pilots exchanged there."[20]

The threat of river traffic being disrupted by the difference of opinion between the pilot organizations caused Esso to file a declaratory-judgment action in civil district court in New Orleans against the two pilot groups

18. New Orleans *Times-Picayune*, May 4, 1957, Sec. 1, p. 11.

19. A copy of the telegram sent by New Orleans–Baton Rouge Steamship Pilots Association to all its members, to shippers, and to others informing them of May 10 deadline is in Oliver D. Jackson Papers.

20. Form letter of Captain Oliver D. Jackson sent to each of the shippers who employed the pilots, May 8, 1957, copy in Oliver D. Jackson Papers.

on May 13. Judge Frank J. Stitch granted a temporary restraining order to prohibit the exchange of pilots at Southport. He ordered the two associations to keep exchanging pilots as they had done in the past under their mutually accepted agreements.[21] Later the civil district court issued a preliminary injunction to be in effect until a trial could determine a permanent solution.[22] During the three days between May 10 and May 13 before the temporary restraining order was issued, the Crescent River Port pilots had ignored the Southport exchange and pilots from both associations had continued to switch at the Point. Exchanges at Southport, in fact, never did take place.

The tension between the two pilot groups kept Oliver and Joe on edge. Harry Post had been Oliver's friend since his tugboat days. Although the jurisdictional controversy was not a personal one, Oliver did not like having to oppose him now. Another friend and highly respected colleague of the Baton Rouge pilots was Captain George S. Vinson, a Crescent River Port pilot who wrote a letter to the *Times-Picayune* explaining his association's side of the controversy. His letter also addressed and rejected a compromise that the New Orleans–Baton Rouge pilots offered their lower-river counterparts:

> The New Orleans and Baton Rouge Steamship Pilots Association having demanded a change of pilots at Southport instead of at Quarantine in the neighborhood of the "general anchorage," as has been the custom for some 40 or 50 years, having met with opposition from all interested parties, offers a "compromise" whereby the Crescent River Port Pilots Association would bring inbound vessels to Southport, and the New Orleans–Baton Rouge Association bring outbound vessels to the general anchorage. Under such "compromise" the controversy remains in original status. The Crescent River Association, never having made any demands, find themselves giving all, receiving nothing.
>
> Certain anchorage locations in the Mississippi are designated by the U. S. Engineers. "General Anchorage" is below the Industrial Canal on the right descending bank. The reach in the vicinity of the "old Engineer fleet" [Southport] is not an anchorage; has never been . . . for a number of reasons— mattress works on the bottom of the river, cable crossings, poor holding ground, water intakes, inconsistent currents. The law states that only in emergencies can ships be anchored other than in designated anchorages.
>
> The recent demonstration by up-the-river pilots could not prove anything. It was done on a calm day in broad daylight. . . .[23]

---

21. Petition for a declaratory judgment, *Esso v. River Port Pilots and Baton Rouge Pilots,* Louisiana Civil District Court (1957), 1–9; New Orleans *Times-Picayune,* May 15, 1957, Sec. 1, p. 1.

22. Original Brief, *Esso v. Pilots,* 15.

23. New Orleans *Times-Picayune,* May 27, 1957, Sec. 1, p. 12.

When the case of the Esso versus the two pilots' associations went to trial in civil district court, the court found in favor of Esso, stating that both pilot associations had the legal obligation of piloting within the port of New Orleans between Quarantine Anchorage and Southport. The Crescent River Port pilots had the exclusive right to pilot in the port between these two points and the New Orleans–Baton Rouge Pilots had a limited right—but, nevertheless, a right and duty they were expected to exercise.[24] The judgment of the court in this case was based mainly on custom, rather than state laws.

The New Orleans–Baton Rouge Pilots appealed to the state supreme court, where the lower court's ruling was overturned. Justice Amos Ponder explained the majority decision:

> It would seem to us that the provision of the statute making it the duty of the New Orleans Pilots to pilot vessels between Pilottown and New Orleans and return is no more inclusive or exclusive than the provisions in the Baton Rouge Pilots act which provides for pilotage from New Orleans north and return. In either instance at what point did the legislature intend for their jurisdiction to end? The Port of New Orleans is 13 miles long and this Court cannot designate under these statutes at what point the exchange of pilots should be made. To do so would be usurping a legislative function.
>
> Since the intention of the legislature in fixing duty of these two groups of pilots does not impose upon either of them the duty to exchange pilots at any given point, we are not warranted in giving a declaratory judgment and this Court is powerless to settle this dispute. We cannot legislate.
>
> For the reasons assigned, the judgment of the lower court is overruled. The injunction issued herein is recalled and set aside.[25]

The decision was not a justification of the New Orleans–Baton Rouge pilots' position, but at least it set aside the injunction and declared the upper-river pilots' desire to change at Southport to be as legally valid as that of the Crescent River Port pilots to change at the lower end of the city. If this was a moral victory, however, that was all: just when Oliver felt some small measure of satisfaction and was trying to find a new way to persuade the opposition to accept Southport, Standard Oil's lawyers announced that the great corporation would appeal the case all the way to the United States Supreme Court. This was a blow. When Oliver called a meeting of his association to tell them of the costly litigation that lay ahead, they voted to give up their quest for the Southport exchange.[26]

24. Original Brief, *Esso v. Pilots,* 15.

25. Majority decision, Justice Amos Ponder, *Esso v. Pilots,* Supreme Court of Louisiana (1957), 5.

26. Personal recollections of author. Up to the 1990s, the Point remains the exchange place for the two sets of pilots in the New Orleans harbor.

The cost of a lawsuit that might last for years was a routine matter for Standard Oil, but for the upper-river pilots, who had about sixteen members at the time, it was too much of a burden to sustain. Oliver understood their feelings and accepted the common sense of their decision. But he felt a bitter sadness at the forced abandonment of their cause, which he considered had been almost won. The Point would remain the exchange place for the two pilot associations.

By the end of 1957, Oliver was feeling his age. The battle of Southport had taken a great deal of his energy and optimism. He was just going through the motions of working. Early in 1958 he contracted a cold that seemed to linger, further draining him. Then, one long night on the bridge of a ship headed for Baton Rouge, he got drenched in a cold, blustery rain. By the time he reached the city and went to the hotel to rest, he was burning up with fever.

He slept poorly and woke feeling weakness, pain, and tightness in his chest. He felt so bad that he took a cab to the emergency room of a Baton Rouge hospital. After a careful examination and X-rays, the doctor advised him that he had pneumonia in both lungs and was a very sick man. The physician wanted to hospitalize him immediately, but Oliver insisted on calling Neda to come to Baton Rouge to get him. The drive took about an hour and a half each way, so between three and four hours passed before she could get him to a New Orleans hospital. He remained there for over a week. When he was released, his family physician warned him to stay home and rest for a month to six weeks. He had undergone a severe illness, and he needed time to recuperate. Moreover, it was February, when the worst weather of the year usually comes to New Orleans.

The day after Oliver got home, it snowed—the rarest of occurrences in the Crescent City. He sat in a chair looking out the picture window in the front room, watching the snow falling and children running and playing in it. He did not do much else to heed the doctor's warnings, however. Within two weeks he claimed he was well enough to return to work, and he did. It was a mistake. A few weeks later, he woke up one night gasping for breath, with severe pain in his chest. Neda thought he was having a heart attack and called an ambulance and his doctor, who met them at the hospital. The problem turned out to be asthma. It was difficult for the doctors who examined him to believe he could acquire this allergic condition so late in life. He was sixty-two and had never shown any sign of asthma. They concluded that the severity of the pneumonia had weakened his bronchial tubes and lungs, and adversely affected his immune system.

For the next five years, Oliver fought asthma—taking medicine, using inhalers, going into the emergency room for shots, and sometimes enduring a short stay in the hospital under an oxygen tent when the attacks were the most severe. He made a valiant effort to keep working, but work became an ordeal instead of the privilege and pleasure it had always been to him. Grain ships were particularly difficult for him to handle. The grain dust affected his bronchial tubes immediately. A long night's traveling up or down the river on a slow ship could be agonizing. As the pilot, he was the only one aboard who knew the channel. Even if he began to be short of breath, he could not give way to his illness.[27]

Once the captain aboard a Greek ship Oliver was piloting fell ill between New Orleans and Baton Rouge; he said he was going to lie down awhile and rest. A few minutes later one of the ship's officers came to the bridge and told Oliver and the helmsman that the captain was dead, apparently of a heart attack. Oliver immediately called by ship-to-shore telephone to the ship's agent in New Orleans and asked if the company wanted him to continue upriver to Baton Rouge or to stop at the next landing to have the body removed. The agent told him to go on to Baton Rouge; there the captain's body was taken off. This crisis made Oliver realize how isolated and helpless one is when illness strikes aboard a ship.

For five years he mustered every ounce of will power he possessed to keep working despite the asthma. In 1963, however, he decided to retire at the end of the year, which would mark twenty-five years in the pilot association for him. When December of 1963 rolled around, he spoke to the board of commissioners about retirement. Since he appeared to be in good health at that time, they persuaded him to stay on a little longer.[28] Barely a month later, on January 28, 1964, he got a call to go to Destrehan to take a grain ship down to the Point. The association's driver took him up to Destrehan. Early in the evening Oliver went aboard the ship, which had not finished loading, and waited for it to be ready to depart. Within a short time he began to wheeze terribly from the grain dust. He was too sick to function properly and knew that he would never make it down to the Point without passing out. He instructed the captain to call for a substitute pilot. He went ashore, called his driver back, and told him to take him home as fast as possible. As he drove away from Destrehan, he knew this was the end. His career as a pilot had begun with happy fireworks over New Orleans harbor on New Year's Eve, and it was ending painfully in a cloud of grain dust at Destrehan. Captain Ruel Reichert, a young pilot who was a close friend of Oliver's, was sent to handle the grain

27. Jackson Transcripts, No. 11, pp. 20–21.

28. *Ibid.*, 42–43, 46; Captain Oliver D. Jackson to Captain Siegfried Sprada, May 12, 1963 (copy) in Oliver D. Jackson Papers; "Pilots Notice 63-9," May 16, 1963 (newsletter of the New Orleans–Baton Rouge Pilots), in Oliver D. Jackson Papers.

ship. Loading continued for another six to seven hours, and Captain Reichert did not get away from Destrehan until after midnight.[29]

The next day Oliver wrote a short letter of resignation to Captain Sprada, the president of the association in 1964. He set the date of his retirement as January 31, 1964. Captain Sprada wrote a letter of acceptance in which he said, "Your pilotage service and friendship will be sorely missed by the shipping industry and our members, but you have earned your days of leisure, so enjoy them as much as you enjoyed the days of service as a pilot on 'ole' man river."[30]

During the next two years, Oliver was simply too ill battling asthma to wish he were back on the river. On those days when he did feel relatively well, he might go to the pilots' office to visit with Bob Prinz and the office staff, then take a turn around town to the pilots' favorite bar and meeting place, the Acme, on Iberville Street. Frequented by river pilots, lawyers, judges, bank executives, and businessmen, this establishment could be counted on for someone he knew and some story about the river that he had not heard yet—or that he told himself. But when the smog closed in on New Orleans and the humidity was heavy, he suffered immensely and yearned to move to some cleaner, dryer environment.

In 1964 when Oliver retired, Joy, who had gone back to school to get two advanced degrees, was living in Thibodaux, Louisiana, where she was an assistant professor of history at Nicholls State College. Oliver and Neda made occasional trips to visit Joy in the new home she had purchased. But Thibodaux, farther south even than New Orleans and in the heart of Louisiana's bayous, did not agree with Oliver. He always became sick there. Then, in 1966, Joy accepted a position at Southeastern Louisiana College in Hammond, in the Florida parishes in pine tree country. Thinking that the climate might improve her father's condition, Joy invited her parents to come live with her. There would be plenty of room for them in the house she planned to build. Oliver and Neda accepted the invitation. In the summer of 1966, Joy sold her home in Thibodaux and built a new one in Hammond.

Oliver and Neda also sold their home. It was located on Robert E. Lee Boulevard. They had lived in it since 1957. The act of sale took place after they moved to Hammond. It was on October 17, 1966, their forty-

29. Jackson Transcripts, No. 11, pp. 44–45.

30. Captain Oliver D. Jackson to Captain Siegfried Sprada, January 29, 1964 (copy), Captain Siegfried Sprada to Captain Oliver D. Jackson, January 31, 1964, both in Oliver D. Jackson Papers. News stories on Oliver's retirement appear in New Orleans *Times-Picayune*, March 25, 1964, Sec. 1, p. 9, and "River Pilot Retires," *Waterways Journal*, April 4, 1964, p. 16.

third wedding anniversary. They drove over to New Orleans for the closing. Afterward, they stopped by their old house one last time to pick up some items that had been left there. They promised to mail the extra house key they had kept to the new owners. As they locked the door, Oliver looked at his watch and asked Neda, "Do you know what time it is?" She answered no and asked what difference it made. He replied, "It's seven o'clock—the time we got married forty-three years ago. That night we moved into our first home together. Now we are leaving the last house we will ever own together at the same time." Both of them were filled with emotion. Oliver took Neda by the arm as he had done more than four decades earlier, and they walked away together.

EPILOGUE
Last of the Big Nine

When Oliver moved to Hammond, some of his closest friends in New Orleans believed that he would not live long in retirement. During his first two years after leaving the pilots' association he had become thinner and noticeably short of breath, with little energy. It was not unusual for him to be in the hospital two or three times a year. Once he was carried there unconscious from a reaction to an antiasthma drug and given the last rites of the Catholic church before recovering. Summer and the autumnal months of October and November were the hardest on him. Halloween was always more of a trick than a treat for Oliver.

But his friends did not take into account his capacity for fighting back and his wonderful optimism and zest for the small pleasures in life. Ultimately, it was these traits that got him through nine more years of asthma attacks and hospital confinements until he found an allergist who worked out a serum that stopped the violent reactions. He never again experienced much trouble from asthma as long as he got regular shots.

Neda and Joy had worried about how Oliver would get along in Hammond when he had spent all of his life on or near the Mississippi River. He did miss the river and his job, but he did not complain or vegetate in a rocking chair. Instead, he found a rather surprising hobby in gardening—especially the growing of roses, one of the most difficult plants to cultivate in the hot, humid climate of Hammond. At one time he had eighty-five rosebushes of every variety and description blooming in the backyard. He read books on their care and joined the New Orleans Rose Society. Although he could attend the meetings only infrequently, he read every one of the society's newsletters and followed the new suggestions these contained to the last detail.

He also developed the habit of writing to relatives with whom he had not kept up in his younger days, such as his sisters and nieces. They responded enthusiastically. He enjoyed the correspondence and looked forward to the arrival of the mail. He also fulfilled a lifelong ambition when he was seventy-five by making a trip to Minnesota to visit Lake Itasca, the headwaters of the Mississippi River. Having been born at the mouth of the river, he had always wanted to see the place where it began its long journey to the Gulf of Mexico. Neda and Joy made the trip with him and took pictures of him standing on a footbridge that straddled the tiny trickle of a stream as it left the lake.

Occasionally Neda and Oliver drove into New Orleans to visit relatives or shop; Oliver sometimes stopped by his old office. But these trips became less and less frequent as time passed. One by one the relatives, friends, and associates who had been close to him died. He would clip out the obituaries and paste them into a book he kept for that purpose. By the time he had reached his eighties, the book was nearly filled. In the last few years of his life, he did feel a sense of isolation and melancholy when he realized that he was the "last of the Big Nine," referring to the nine pilots who had been in the New Orleans–Baton Rouge Pilots Association when it won its charter. All of them were dead but him. He was also the last of nine brothers and sisters in his family. Even in his eighties, although he cut back on the rose garden, he still worked in it for three to four hours a day.

His health began to decline rapidly, however, after his eyesight was almost completely lost by the time he reached eighty-six. Glaucoma and hardening of the arteries, which affected his optic nerves, blurred his vision and constricted it until he could not read or write anymore. All he could see were shapes and blobs of darkness and light. The asthma and his age also finally took a toll on his heart, and he suffered from angina, as well as severe circulatory problems. All of this left him depressed and low in spirit.

In 1984, Joy took him to visit the World's Fair on the New Orleans riverfront. He was still strong enough to walk the entire length of the fairgrounds, and he enjoyed listening to jazz music and eating at a German restaurant. But when Joy asked him if he wished to be led out to the river's edge, he replied sadly, "No, I can't see it, but I can smell its freshwater scent. That's enough." Later, he confided that when he was sitting quietly in his reclining chair at home, the one scene he liked to envision in his mind's eye was the Algiers Ferry crossing the river. Somehow, this seemed logical: he had waited for it so many times in the lean years of the 1930s that it was now one of his fondest memories.

Oliver became ill for the last time in February, 1985. After three weeks of hospitalization, he died on March 3, 1985, at 6 A.M., in Seventh Ward General Hospital outside of Hammond, at the age of eighty-eight. He had slowly slipped away during the last week and had lost consciousness for a day before he died. His funeral was held in New Orleans, and he was buried in St. John's Cemetery on Canal Street. Neda, to whom he had been married sixty-two years at the time of his death, survived him by five years. She died at ninety-two on April 30, 1990. She, too, is buried in St. John's Cemetery, alongside her husband.

One of the younger pilots who had joined Oliver's association after he retired commented at Oliver's wake that his death was the end of an era. To this younger generation of pilots, Oliver was already a legend before he died. He was the last of the charter members. Within his own family, Oliver was also respected as the last of his generation. He had followed the family tradition of choosing work connected to the river and had out-lived others who had done the same, including his grandfather, Captain Andy; his father, Monroe; his uncle John; and his brother Eric. Each of these men saw events and people and even communities come and go on the river.

In Oliver's case, he had outlived many things that he might have thought would never change. The little idyllic outpost of Port Eads had been a small but thriving community when he was a boy. By 1985, it was a ghost town, with most of its buildings gone and only about one or two residents, who ran a fishing camp, remaining. Only the lighthouse and a few oleanders growing along the riverside survived as reminders of the early twentieth century. Burrwood was another casualty of time, left with-out a population and sinking fast into the mud by 1985. In New Orleans, the St. Joseph orphanage with its rigid way of life that had seemed in-destructible to young Oliver had been torn down in the 1940s to make way for a housing project. St. Mary's Assumption Catholic Church fared better. After being closed for repairs, it was finally reopened in the 1980s in a beautifully restored condition. W. G. Coyle Company, which had straddled the levee at the foot of Eliza Street in Algiers for over a century, was sold and its office, yard, and boat fleet completely broken up in 1975. The steamer *President,* which every riverman had viewed as an institution on the river, sailed upstream to begin a new life as a floating gambling casino, and the grand old lady, "Big Mama," the *Sprague,* was given to the city of Vicksburg by Standard Oil. It was allowed to suffer from fire and decay until it disintegrated completely.

Oliver had seen growth, too. His own association burgeoned from six-teen men when he retired to over seventy by 1985. The piloting profession prospered as many more industrial facilities sprang up along the "Chemical Corridor" between Baton Rouge and New Orleans. Working conditions also improved vastly over what Oliver and his colleagues had known. As president of the association in the 1960s, Captain Sprada pioneered the practice of pilots' carrying two-way radios onto ships in order to be able to communicate quickly and directly with one another, rather than losing time and risking misunderstanding by working through a ship's radio-man. The 141-mile trip from Quarantine Anchorage to the industrial docks of north Baton Rouge—the long turn that had sparked the attempt to change at Southport—was finally alleviated. With more resources and men at their disposal, the Baton Rouge pilots broke the trip into two parts. A relief pilot boards a ship halfway up or down the route; no pilot has to take a fifteen-hour turn anymore.

Environmental pollution, unfortunately, accompanied industrial development on the Mississippi River, contaminating land, air, and water along the Chemical Corridor. The new Mississippi River Gulf Outlet, used by the bar pilots and the lower-river pilots as an alternate to the longer river route, was opened the year before Oliver retired. Although it cuts forty miles off the river route, it has steadily eaten away at its banks and caused saltwater intrusion into the marshes of St. Bernard Parish, heavily damaging both the marshlands and their wildlife.

Oliver was the last of his family to work on the river. His brother Monroe had died young, leaving one son who moved to Texas. His brother Eric's sons both worked on the river but retired about the same time as Oliver; neither one had children to follow in his footsteps. The story of Oliver's family had been that of plain people who lived along the great river and often took their livelihood from it, affected by both its prosperity and its rampaging destruction—handing down to each new generation a share of the legacy. Oliver was fortunate to live in the twentieth century, when the stretch of the Mississippi River below Baton Rouge was being transformed and the river was enjoying a renaissance of activity after the decline of the steamboat. His own life was a testament to these rapid changes. He had started out guiding a simple sailboat across South Pass. Next he ventured out into the Gulf to pull a yawl boat for the bar pilots. Later he piloted the *Underwriter* on Southwest Pass and served as captain of the *Corona* at New Orleans and the *Donie* on the Intracoastal Canal. He left Coyle's to work at Standard Oil on the largest tug on the Mississippi, the *Istrouma,* and ended his career as a pilot taking supertankers to and from Baton Rouge refineries and other industrial plants along the way. Always he had followed the course of the ship channel. Although the Mississippi is endlessly changing and shifting in subtle ways, it has a timeless constancy that rivermen respect and love. Oliver was part of its life cycle in the twentieth century and was privileged to pilot vessels along its course for most of his lifetime.

APPENDIX A
CHART OF THE ANDREW JACKSON FAMILY

Andrew Jackson
    b. 1825
    d. 1902

1. First Wife: Amelia Cosse
    b. 1835
    d. 1858
2. Second Wife: Sarah Celeste Buras
    b. 1844
    d. 1914

Children:

Name	Spouse	No. of Children
1a) Amelia Adeline b. 1855 d. 1941	John Labash	6
1b) Euphanie Virginie b. 1858 d. unknown	Jean "John" Breny	8
2a) Andrew b. 1860 d. 1935	Mary Loar	7
2b) Monroe b. 1862 d. 1944	Eliza Jane Loar	9
2c) Thomas Randolph b. 1864 d. 1955	Mary Loomis	8
2d) Joseph Penrose b. 1867 d. 1936	Irene Buras	7

2e) Isabella "Ella"   (1) George Garrett Vogt   4
    b. 1869   (2) Anthony Roig
    d. 1936
2f) Mary Elizabeth
    b. 1870
    d. unknown, but died in childhood
2g) Mary
    b. 1872
    d. unknown, but died in childhood
2h) Angeline "Nan"   William Lawrence   1
    b. 1874
    d. 1933
2i) Agnes   Louis Castell   5
    b. 1875
    d. 1936
2j) John Walter   (1) Marie "Mary" Buras   2 (d. as infants)
    b. 1882   (2) Annie Goff
    d. 1932
2k) Pearl Mary   John Burth Ronquillo   6
    b. 1885
    d. 1949

APPENDIX B
CHART OF THE MONROE JACKSON FAMILY

Monroe Jackson   Wife: Eliza Jane Loar
    b. 1862   b. 1868
    d. 1944   d. 1904

Children:

Name	Spouse	No. of Children
1) Rosaline	Hugh Kelley	8
b. 1884		
d. 1913		
2) Lillian	William Franko	4
b. 1886		
d. 1963		
3) Alvaretta	Thomas Nicholson	7
b. 1888		
d. 1978		
4) Monroe, Jr.	Louise Pratt	1
b. 1890		
d. 1911		
5) Sarah	Michael Budenich	4
b. 1892		
d. 1943		
6) Oliver Daniel	Oneida Drouant	1
b. 1896		
d. 1985		
7) Eric John	Dora Williams	4
b. 1898		
d. 1950		

8) Viola   Robert Barrios   8
   b. 1901
   d. 1964
9) Charles Vincent
   b. 1903
   d. 1903

APPENDIX C

ROSTER OF NEW ORLEANS – BATON ROUGE STEAMSHIP PILOTS ASSOCIATION, 1911–1963

Early Pilots

(The pilots are listed here as they were recorded in Jackson Notebook No. 6. Oliver placed them in the order of their entry into the group as best he could determine this. Asterisks indicate those men who were charter members in 1943.)

Bill Neihiesel
Trim Wadlinton
Pat Morrison
W. Arbo
Bill Wrigley
Bill Martin
Seth Simpson (later joined Crescent River Port pilots)
A. B. Critton
Charles M. Jackson*
William L. Heuer
Harvey Brown
Sam McNeely (later joined Crescent River Port pilots)
P. A. Chotin*
James Guy Mallory
Lemuel L. Bailey
J. P. T. Roberts*
Harry G. Koch*
R. B. Chotin*
Charles J. Lauterbach*
Oliver D. Jackson*
Eugene F. Higbee*
Adolph P. Schwalb*

Pilots Elected Under the Charter, 1945–1963

1945
  Siegfried K. Sprada
1946
  Pierre Trudell, Jr.
1949
  Joseph Scott
1951
  Walter S. Wright
  Carlton F. Trosclair
  William P. King
1954
  Charles P. Henley
1955
  Joseph A. Lennox, Jr.
  Worday P. Bordelon
  Ruel H. Reichert, Jr.
1956
  Thomas D. Doyle
  Peter L. Fitzgerald
  Charles H. Hough
  James M. Seaman
  Oliver R. Trowbridge
1959
  Frank T. Furr
  Joseph M. Kenny
  Tilman J. Pizani, Sr.
  John W. Sarbeck
  Canton P. Seitz, Jr.
  Robert B. Streckfus
1963
  Arthur J. Bezette
  Aubrey O. Dowell
  Henry K. Durham
  Gayle B. Holt
  William O. Watson, Jr.

BIBLIOGRAPHY

PRIMARY SOURCES

Manuscripts and Public Papers

Biloxi Public Library, Biloxi, Mississippi
Interment Ledger of the Biloxi Cemetery for 1900–1904 (microfilm).
Division of State Lands, Baton Rouge, Louisiana
Federal Land Grants, Southeast District, Tract Books 41a, 45a, and 54.
Historic New Orleans Collection, New Orleans
Vieux Carré Historic Survey.
Howard-Tilton Memorial Library, Tulane University
Louisiana Collection
Louisiana Historical Center, Louisiana State Museum, New Orleans, Louisiana
French Superior Council Records, 1748–1763.
New Orleans Public Library, Main Branch, Louisiana Collection
Vital Statistics of New Orleans, Marriage Records, 1894–1909 (microfilm);
obituary records in card file.
Plaquemines Parish Courthouse, Pointe a la Hache, Louisiana
Conveyances, 1790–1900; Inventories, Wills, and Successions, 1800–1860;
Marriages, 1859.

Private Papers

Buras-Brown Family Bible, copy of pages with marriage and death records. Copy
in possession of James J. Jacobsen, Poplarville, Mississippi.
New Orleans–Baton Rouge Steamship Pilots Association, Kenner, Louisiana
An Agreement made this 26th day of September 1920, by and between the
New Orleans–Baton Rouge Steamship Pilots . . . and Julius Prinz.
New Orleans–Baton Rouge Steamship Pilots Association Charter Book.
Oliver D. Jackson Papers, in possession of the author
Personal and business papers, letters, baptismal and marriage certificates; state
pilot commission; appointment to Board of Commissioners of New Or-
leans–Baton Rouge Steamship Pilots Association; original charter of New
Orleans–Baton Rouge Steamship Pilots Association; Jackson Notebooks
pertaining to piloting; disenrollment from the Coast Guard; manuscript on
pilot history; ledger of ships piloted by New Orleans–Baton Rouge pilots,

1939–1941; notarized statement on a ship fire; and conveyance records of property bought and sold.

Church Records

Immaculate Conception Cathedral Archives, Mobile, Alabama
Marriage records, 1727–1737; baptismal records, 1728–1736; interment records, 1736.
Little Red Church records of St. John the Baptist Parish, in Louisiana Historical Center, Louisiana State Museum, New Orleans.
Mount Calvary Lutheran Church, New Orleans
Marriage records, 1923.
Our Lady of Good Harbor Catholic Church, Buras, Louisiana
Baptismal records, 1868–1884.
St. Louis Cathedral Archives, Archdiocese of New Orleans Archives, New Orleans
Marriage records, 1726–1796; baptismal records, 1740–1806.
St. Mary's Assumption Catholic Church, New Orleans
Baptismal and confirmation records, 1909–1910.
St. Thomas the Apostle Catholic Church, Point a la Hache, Louisiana
Marriage records, 1847; baptismal records, 1844.

Interviews with and Statements to Author

Buras, Richard, September 26, 1987
Furr, Frank, and Siegfried Sprada, January 8, 1990.
Jackson, Oliver Daniel, tapes 1 and 2, June 20, 1980; tapes 3 and 4, July 2, 1980; tapes 5 and 6, August 7, 1981; tape 7, August 9, 1981; tape 8, June 6, 1982; tapes 9 and 10, June 7, 1982; tape 11, August 10, 1982; tape 12, August 18, 1982; tape 13, February 20, 1978. Thirteen interviews on tape and in transcripts.
Jackson, Oneida Drouant, June 23, 1987.
Manson, Gilbert, Jr., June 30, 1984.
Michell, Jacques, September 1, 1989.
Prinz, Robert, September 18, 1988.

Newspapers

Baton Rouge *Morning Advocate*, 1948–1961.
Baton Rouge *State Times*, 1909–1910, 1951–1960.
New Orleans *Daily Picayune*, 1902, 1909–1910, 1914.
New Orleans *Item*, 1927, 1930, 1942–1945, 1947, 1948, 1959.
New Orleans *Morning Star*, 1905.
New Orleans *States*, 1927, 1934, 1942–1945, 1948, 1958.
New Orleans *Times-Picayune*, 1914–1916, 1920–1928, 1930–1964, 1985.

City Guides and Directories

New Orleans City Guide. Written and compiled by the Federal Writers Project of the Works Progress Administration for the City of New Orleans. 1938; rpr. St. Claire Shores, Michigan, 1974.

Norman, Benjamin Moore. *Norman's New Orleans and Environs*. Edited by Matthew J. Schott. 1845; rpr. Baton Rouge, 1976.

Soards' *New Orleans City Directory* for the years 1902, 1907, 1914, 1920, and 1933. New Orleans, 1902, 1907, 1914, 1920, 1933.

STATE DOCUMENTS

Acts Passed by the Legislature of the State of Louisiana, Regular Session, 1908. Baton Rouge, 1908.

Acts Passed by the Legislature of the State of Louisiana, Regular Session, 1942. Baton Rouge, 1942.

Board of Commissioners of the Port of New Orleans. *Fortieth Report of the Board of Commissioners of the Port of New Orleans*. New Orleans, 1936.

———. *A Long-Range Program for the Development of the Port of New Orleans*. New Orleans, 1978.

FEDERAL DOCUMENTS

Alperin, Lynn M. *History of the Gulf Intracoastal Waterway*. National Waterways Study, Corps of Engineers, U.S. Army. Washington, D.C., 1938.

American State Papers: Documents, Legislative and Executive, of the Congress of the United States, Public Lands. Gales and Seaton edition. Serial Nos. 28–35, Class 8, 8 vols. Washington, D.C., 1832–1861. On microfilm in Linus A. Sims Memorial Library, Southestern Louisiana University, Hammond, and in the Louisiana State Archives, Baton Rouge.

Department of Commerce and Labor, Bureau of Navigation. *Forty-Second Annual List of Vessels of the U.S.: Lists of Vessels Belonging to the U.S. Government for the Year Ending June 30, 1910*. Washington, D.C., 1910.

Department of Interior, U.S. Census Bureau. Population Schedules for Plaquemines Parish, United States Census records from *Fifth Census* through *Thirteenth Census*, covering the years: 1830, 1840, 1850, 1860, 1870, 1880, 1890, 1900, and 1910. On microfilm in Linus A. Sims Memorial Library, Southeastern Louisiana University, Hammond, and State Library of Louisiana, Baton Rouge.

Department of Transportation, U.S. Coast Guard. *Lighthouses and Lightships of the Northern Gulf of Mexico*. Washington, D.C., n.d.

Department of the Treasury, U.S. Coast Guard. *Rules of the Road, International-Inland*. Washington, D.C., 1959.

Department of War, Corps of Engineers, U.S. Army. *Annual Report of the Chief of Engineers, U.S. Army*, for the years, 1904, 1910, 1911, 1915, 1916, 1921, 1936, and 1939. Washington, D.C., 1904, 1910, 1911, 1915, 1916, 1921, 1936, 1939.

Department of War, Corps of Engineers, U.S. Army, United States Maritime Commission. Port Series No. 5. *The Port of New Orleans, Louisiana*. Prepared by Board of Engineers for Rivers and Harbors, Corps of Engineers, U.S. Army. Washington, D.C., 1939.

The War of the Rebellion: A Compilation of the Official Records of the Union and Confederate Armies. Vol. VI, Ser. 1, of 128 vols. 1882; rpr. Ann Arbor, 1985.

Work Projects Administration. *Ships Registers and Enrollments of New Orleans, Louisiana.* Prepared by the Survey of Federal Archives in Louisiana, Service Division, Work Projects Administration. Baton Rouge, 1942.

LEGAL DOCUMENTS

Majority Decision, Justice Amos Ponder. *Esso Standard Oil Company* v. *Crescent River Port Pilots Association and New Orleans and Baton Rouge Steamship Pilots Association,* et al. Supreme Court of Louisiana (1957).

Original Brief on the merits on behalf of Defendants and Appellants, New Orleans and Baton Rouge Steamship Pilots Association. *Esso Standard Oil Company* v. *Crescent River Port Pilots Association and New Orleans and Baton Rouge Steamship Pilots Association,* et al. Supreme Court of Louisiana (1957).

Petition for a declaratory judgment. *Esso Standard Oil Company* v. *Crescent River Port Pilots Association and New Orleans and Baton Rouge Steamship Pilots Association,* et al. U.S. Civil District Court (1957).

MISCELLANEOUS PRINTED DOCUMENTS

Armstrong, Gladys Stovall, ed. and comp. *Plaquemines Parish Obituary Notices, 1865–1898.* Buras, La., 1983.

Conrad, Glenn, ed. and comp. *First Families of Louisiana.* 2 vols. Baton Rouge, 1972.

———, ed. and comp. *Sainte-Jean-Baptiste des Allemands: Abstracts of Civil Records of St. John the Baptiste Parish with Genealogy and Index, 1753–1803.* Lafayette, La., 1972.

DeVille, Winston, ed. and comp. *Gulf Coast Colonials.* Baltimore, 1968.

Maduell, Charles R., Jr., ed. and comp. *The Census Tables for the French Colony of Louisiana, from 1699 Through 1732.* Baltimore, 1972.

Murray, Nicholas Russell, ed. and comp. *Computer Indexed Marriage Records, Orleans Parish, Louisiana, 1830–1900, Gust B to Juzan.* Hammond, Louisiana, n.d.

New Orleans Baton Rouge Steamship Pilots, Louisiana State Charter and Roster of State Commissioned Pilots and Members. New Orleans, 1980.

"Records of the Superior Council of Louisiana: Adjudication to Terrière of the lease of a house and lot belonging to the Milhet minors, November 5, 1764, and Release by Joseph Burat to Widow Turangin concerning rendition of account of her tutorship of the Milhet minors, April 6, 1764." Translation in *Louisiana Historical Quarterly,* XXV (April, 1942), 537–88.

"Records of the Superior Council of Louisiana: Murder Case against Baraca, a negro slave of the King, February 9, 1748." Translation in *Louisiana Historical Quarterly,* IXX (April, 1936), 467–509.

Robichaux, Albert J., Jr., ed. and comp. *Louisiana Census and Militia Lists, 1770–1789.* Vol. I of 2 vols. New Orleans, 1977.

Rowland, Dunbar, and Albert Godfrey Sanders, eds. *Mississippi Provincial Archives.* Vol. III of 3 vols. Jackson, Miss. 1929.

Voorhies, Jacqueline K., comp. and trans. *Some Late Eighteenth Century Louisianians: Census Records of the Colony, 1753–1796.* Lafayette, La., 1973.

SECONDARY SOURCES

Books

Advisory Information on Normal Sailing Route for Ships on Mississippi River Between Baton Rouge Harbor and Huey Long Bridge. Published by the American Waterways Operators, Inc. Washington, D.C., n.d.

Baughn, William H. *The Impact of World War II on the New Orleans Port–Mississippi River Transportation System.* Louisiana Business Bulletin, Louisiana State University. XII, No. 3. Baton Rouge, 1950.

Bradbury, R. W. *Water-Borne Commerce of New Orleans.* Louisiana Business Bulletin, Louisiana State University. I, No. 2, Baton Rouge, 1937.

Baughman, James P. "Gateway to the Americas." In *The Past as Prelude: New Orleans, 1718–1968,* edited by Hodding Carter. New Orleans, 1968.

Calhoun, James, ed. *Louisiana Almanac, 1984–85.* Gretna, La., 1984.

Carleton, Mark T. *River Capital: An Illustrated History of Baton Rouge.* Woodland Hills, Calif., 1981.

Chotin: Of Men and Water and the Movement of Cargo. New Orleans, n.d.

Daniel, Pete. *Deep'n as It Come: The 1927 Mississippi River Flood.* New York, 1977.

Davis, Edwin Adams. *Louisiana: A Narrative History.* Baton Rouge, 1965.

Deiler, J. Hanno. *The Settlement of the German Coast of Louisiana and the Creoles of German Descent.* Baltimore, 1969.

Dimitry, John. *Confederate Military History: Louisiana.* New York, 1962. Vol. X of Clement A. Evans, ed., *Confederate Military History.* 12 vols.

Duffy, John, ed. *The Rudolph Matas History of Medicine in Louisiana.* Vol. II of 2 vols. Baton Rouge, 1962.

Dufour, Charles L. *The Night the War Was Lost.* Garden City, N.Y. 1960.

————. *The Story of Coyle Lines Incorporated.* New Orleans, 1965.

Fifty Years: Baton Rouge Refinery, 1909–1959. Baton Rouge, 1959.

Freund, Max, ed. and trans. *Gustav Dresel's Houston Journal: Adventures in North America and Texas, 1837–1841.* Austin, 1954.

Fritz, David L., and Sally K. Reeves. *Algiers Point: Historical Ambience and Property Analysis of Squares Ten, Thirteen, and Twenty, with a View Toward Their Archeological Potential.* New Orleans, 1983.

Gayarré, Charles E. A. *History of Louisiana.* 4 vols. 1854–1866; rpr. New Orleans, 1965.

Goodwin, R. Christopher, *et al. Evaluation of the National Register Eligibility of Burrwood, Plaquemines Parish, Louisiana.* New Orleans, 1985.

Haas, Edward F. *DeLesseps S. Morrison and the Image of Reform: New Orleans Politics, 1946–1961.* Baton Rouge, 1974.

Hansen, Harry, ed. *Louisiana: A Guide to the State.* 1941; rpr. New York, 1971.

Herring, H. S. *History of the New Orleans Board of Trade Limited, 1880–1930.* New Orleans, 1930.

History of W. G. Coyle and Co., Inc., and DeBardeleben Coal Corporation. New Orleans, n.d.

Jackson, Joy J. *New Orleans in the Gilded Age: Politics and Urban Progress, 1880–1896.* Baton Rouge, 1969.

Juhn, Daniel S. *Growth and Changing Composition of International Trade Through the Port of New Orleans, 1955–1964.* New Orleans, 1967.

Land, John E. *Pen Illustrations of New Orleans, 1881–82.* New Orleans, 1882.

Larson, Henrietta M., Evelyn H. Knowlton, and Charles S. Popple. *New Horizons: 1927–1950.* New York, 1971. Vol. III of N. S. B. Gras and Henrietta Larson, eds., *History of Standard Oil Company (New Jersey).* 3 vols.

Marionite Centennial Book. New Orleans, 1907.

Martinez, Raymond J. *The Story of the River Front at New Orleans.* New Orleans, 1955.

Morison, Samuel Eliot. *The Battle of the Atlantic, September 1939–May 1943.* Boston, 1961. Vol. I of Morison, *History of United States Naval Operations in World War II.* 15 vols.

Morison, Samuel Eliot, Henry Steele Commager, and William E. Leuchtenburg. *The Growth of the American Republic.* Vol. II of 2 vols. 6th ed. New York, 1969.

New Orleans Architecture. Text by Samuel Wilson, Jr., *et al.* Compiled and edited by Mary Louise Christovich *et al.* 7 vols. Vol. I, *The Lower Garden District,* edited and compiled by Mary Louise Christovich, Roulhac Toledano, and Betsy Swanson. 1971; 4th pr. Gretna, La., 1979. Vol. IV, *The Creole Faubourgs,* edited and compiled by Roulhac Toledano, Sally Kittredge Evans, and Mary Louise Christovich. 1974; 2d pr. Gretna, La., 1984.

Niehàus, Earl F. *The Irish in New Orleans, 1800–1860.* Baton Rouge, 1965.

One Hundred Years in New Orleans, Louisiana: A Centenary Souvenir, Redemptorist Fathers, 1843–1943 (celebration program). New Orleans, January 12, 13, 14, 1943.

Oneal, Marion S. *Garlic in My Shoes.* Philadelphia, 1969.

Reinders, Robert. *End of an Era: New Orleans, 1850–1860.* New Orleans, 1964.

Ricciuti, Italo William. *New Orleans and Its Environs: The Domestic Architecture, 1727–1870.* New York, 1938.

Rice, Otis K. *The Allegheny Frontier: West Virginia Beginnings, 1730–1830.* Lexington, Ky., 1970.

Riegel, Robert E. *Young America, 1830–1840.* Norman, Okla., 1949.

Roberts, Clayton, and David Roberts. *A History of England, 1688 to the Present.* Englewood Cliffs, 1985. Vol. I of Roberts and Roberts, *A History of England.* 2 vols.

St. Mary's Assumption Church. Pamphlet printed by the Redemptorist Order. New Orleans, n.d.

Samuel, Ray, Leonard V. Huber, and Warren C. Ogden. *Tales of the Mississippi.* New York, 1955.

Saxon, Lyle, Robert Tallant, and Edward Dreyer, comps. *Gumbo Ya-Ya: A Collection of Louisiana Folktales*. Boston, 1945.

Seymour, William H. *The Story of Algiers, 1718–1896*. Gretna, La., 1971.

Ships of the Esso Fleet in World War II. New Jersey, 1946.

Siegel, Martin, comp. and ed. *New Orleans: A Chronological and Documentary History, 1539–1970*. Dobbs Ferry, N.Y., 1975.

Sprada, Siegfried. *Men, Ships, and the River: The New Orleans Baton Rouge Pilots Story*. New Orleans, n.d.

Stringfield, William R. *Le Pays des Fleurs Oranges: A Genealogical Study of Eight Creole Families of Plaquemines Parish, Louisiana*. Baltimore, 1989.

Sydnor, Charles. *The Development of Southern Sectionalism, 1819–1848*. Baton Rouge, 1951. Vol. V of Wendell Holmes Stephenson and E. Merton Coulter, eds., *A History of the South*. 10 vols.

Weinstein, Richard. *Cultural Resources Survey of the Proposed South Pass Bulk Terminal, Plaquemines Parish, Louisiana*. Baton Rouge, 1984.

Wilson, Samuel, Jr. *The Vieux Carré, New Orleans: Its Plan, Its Growth, Its Architecture*. Vieux Carré Historic District Demonstration Study. New Orleans, 1968.

ARTICLES

Alliot, Paul. "Historical and Political Reflections on Louisiana." In *Louisiana Under the Rule of Spain, France, and the United States, 1785–1807*, edited by James A. Robertson. Vol. I of 2 vols. Cleveland, 1911.

"Aluminum Ore Shipment from New Operation." *New Orleans Port Record*, XI (March, 1953), 15.

"Announce Plans for Geismar Plant." *New Orleans Port Record*, XV (November, 1956), 33.

Armstrong, Gladys, comp. "Looking Back." *Deep Delta*, II (August, 1984), 208–209.

———. "Myrtle Wax." *Deep Delta*, II (May, 1984), 194.

Corkern, Carole F. "U-Boats in the Gulf of Mexico, World War II." *Southeast Louisiana Historical Association Papers*, V (1978), 31–43.

Cronenberg, Allen. "U-Boats in the Gulf: The Undersea War in 1942," *Gulf Coast Historical Review*, V (Spring, 1990), 163–78.

Cruzat, Heloise Hulse. "Sidelights of Louisiana History." *Louisiana Historical Quarterly*, I (January, 1918), 87–153.

"Economy Zone." *New Orleans Port Review*. XIII (November, 1954), 13–15.

Forsyth, Alice Daly. "Girault-Giraut-Giraud-Giro and Allied Families." *New Orleans Genesis*, XXIII (January, 1984), 111–13.

Forsyth, Hewitt L., comp. "Census, Parish of Plaquemines, Louisiana, August 1, 1850." *New Orleans Genesis*, XXII (October, 1983), 461–66; XXIII (January, 1984), 13–18.

Garnett, William A. "Baton Rouge to the Gulf." *Fortune* (January, 1961), 105–13.

"The *Istrouma*." *Waterways Journal*, April 11, 1925, p. 7.

Jackson, Joy J. "Prohibition in New Orleans: The Unlikeliest Crusade." *Louisiana History*, XIX (Summer, 1978), 261–84.

"Kaiser Aluminum in Louisiana." *Kaiser Aluminum News* (July-August, 1959), 16.

"Kaiser Aluminum to Build La. Plant." *New Orleans Port Record,* XIV (January, 1956), 24.

Lincoln, Rod. "The Balize, 1723–1888." *Deep Delta,* I (November, 1983), 331–38; II (February, 1984), 38–42; and (May, 1984), 124–26.

"Lion Oil Dedicates $30 Million Plant." *New Orleans Port Record,* XIII (November, 1954), 20.

Lipsey, T. E. L. "The Intracoastal Canal in Louisiana and Methods of Dredging." *Professional Memoirs,* VIII (May–June, 1916), 267–97.

Lowrey, Walter M. "The Engineers and the Mississippi." *Louisiana History,* V (Summer, 1964), 233–55.

"Mathieson's Louisiana Chemical Investment Grows." *New Orleans Port Record,* XV (July, 1957), 26–27.

"Modern Public Port Facilities to Boost Baton Rouge Trade and Industry." *Construction News Monthly,* June 8, 1955, pp. 20–21.

"New Bulk Terminal Downriver at Burnside." *Deep Water,* I (October, 1957), n.p.

"New Orleans and Aluminum." *New Orleans Port Record,* XII (February, 1954), 14–18.

O'Connor, Stella. "The Charity Hospital at New Orleans: An Administrative and Financial History." *Louisiana Historical Quarterly,* XXXI (January, 1948), 5–109.

"Port Development and Greater Baton Rouge." *World Ports.* Published for the Waterfront Terminal Industry and Its Shippers and Carriers (October, 1957). Clipping in Vertical File on Baton Rouge Harbor, State Library of Louisiana.

"Port of New Orleans." *Fortune,* IV (November, 1931), 42–49, 133.

"Port Tonnages Up for 1957." *Deep Water,* II (January, 1958), n.p.

"A Record Tow." *Waterways Journal,* March 27, 1926, p. 5.

"River Pilot Retires." *Waterways Journal,* April 4, 1964, p. 16.

Robichaux, Albert J., Jr., comp. "Census of the Fifth Isle Descending from the River." *New Orleans Genesis,* XXI (January, 1982), 35–47.

Salomone, Jerome. "Mississippi River Bar-Pilotage: The Development of an Occupation." *Louisiana Studies,* VI (Spring, 1967), 39–52.

Schwab, Lucille. "Andrew Jackson Higgins, Boatbuilder." *Southeast Louisiana Historical Association Papers,* VII (1980), 52–63.

"Seventy-Fifth Anniversary of Jersey Standard Oil Company, 1882–1957." *Lamp,* (1957), 1–80.

Smith, Joyce Hingle. "Census of Balize, 1860." *Deep Delta,* I, (November, 1983), 345–47, and (February, 1984), 45–50; II (May, 1984), 127–31.

Stringfield, W. Richard. "Jean Guillaume Burat (Buras) and Family Lines." *Deep Delta,* I (August, 1983), 193–202, and (November, 1983), 179–81.

"Towboat *Sprague*" and "Towboat *Sprague* Bought Thursday by Standard Oil Company," *Waterways Journal,* May 23, 1925. p. 9.

Viada, Sally Embry. "Buras Family Marriages, 1818–1850." *Deep Delta,* I (February, 1983), 37–38.

"A Yacht That Sells a Port." *New Orleans Port Record,* X (September, 1951), 8–9, 37.

"Young Wild West and the 'Salted Mine.'" *Wild West Weekly*, No. 91 (New York, July 25, 1904; rpr., Derby, Conn., 1965), 7–125.

MAPS

Baldwin, H. L., Jr. *Louisiana West Delta Sheet*. Compiled from surveys by U.S. Coast and Geodetic Survey, 1891.

Department of War, Corps of Engineers, U.S. Army. *Flood Control and Navigation Maps of the Mississippi River, Cairo, Illinois, to the Gulf of Mexico*. Prepared in the office of the president, Mississippi River Commission. Vicksburg, 1961. Maps 48 and 51.

Plaquemines Parish, La., in T. 21, 22, and 23; R. 31 and 32; S.E. District of La., West of Mississippi River. Drawn by George Guibault. New Orleans, 1927.

Sanborn Insurance Map of New Orleans, Louisiana for 1908 and 1909 (7 vols.) and 1937–49 (9 vols.). New York, 1908–1909, 1949.

Map of the State of Louisiana, Alluvial Lands in the State of Louisiana Flooded by High Water, 1927. Baton Rouge, 1927.

Survey of the Mississippi River. Made under the direction of the Mississippi River Commission, projected from a trigonometrical survey made by the U.S. Coast Survey in 1871. Julius Bien and Co., n.p., 1893. Chart No. 81.

Southwest Pass. U.S. Coast and Geodetic Survey Map, Register No. 4044, of Southwest Pass. Compiled from photographs by Naval Air Service. 1922.

THESES AND DISSERTATION

Bolding, Gary Arnold. "Efforts to Develop New Orleans as a World Trade Center, 1910–1960." M.A. thesis, Louisiana State University, 1966.

Parsons, Virginia. "A Study of the Activities of the Louisiana Board of Health from 1855 to 1898 in Reference to Quarantine." M.A. thesis, Tulane University, 1932.

Shanafelt, Raymond E. "The Baton Rouge–New Orleans Petrochemical Industrial Region: A Functional Region Study." 2 vols. Ph.D. dissertation, Louisiana State University, 1977.

INDEX